ROCKET
MANAGEMENT
HOW TO PROPEL YOUR BUSINESS
TO NEW HEIGHTS

With Focus on Six Key Functions to Uplift

Company Performance & Profitability

J.F. FORDHAM

Cover image by: Tracy Currer & John Fordham
Book design by: SWATT Books Ltd

Printed in the United Kingdom
First Printing, 2022

ISBN: 978-1-7396068-0-0 (Paperback)
ISBN: 978-1-7396068-1-7 (eBook)

John Fordham
Lymington. Hampshire

Contents

An Introduction

In business, key areas need to be well understood and focused upon to succeed. Performance and productivity can be dramatically improved when the proper knowledge about the basic techniques are acquired and implemented.

This book is intended for people in business and those who are studying for business. There are approximately 5.0 million companies in the UK of which around 90% are Small and Medium Size Enterprises (SMEs) generally with a management team. Every year there are about 350,000 University students studying Business Studies. In addition there are 100 business schools providing MBA (Masters of Business Administration) courses each year for some few thousands of participants who are generally older and already have business experience.

Interestingly, though available in the USA and Germany in the late 1800s, these business courses only became popular in the UK in the early 1960s. They are now the most in-demand course.

Rocketship Management is aimed primarily at informing and helping managing director owners (MDOs) and directors and managers of smaller companies. It will also provide valuable information to Business Studies and MBA students and graduates for their business career, and for those who later become directors and owners of companies. The practical advice, real-life examples and implementation of the Key Functions of Rocketship Management will boost productivity and guide future managers and entrepreneurs of start-ups on how to optimise their management of a business.

Why is that important? There is a significant lack of continuous improvement in productivity in the UK. In fact, for years, we have 'lagged behind' many other major countries. The following report shows the scale of the problem.

Causes Of UK Low Productivity

The Proudfoot Report is based on analyses of 1357 companies in 7 countries and a global poll of 2,700 chief executives, so it is very comprehensive. One paragraph stated, 'Three-quarters of British management would not even ask outsiders what they should do. I would be confident that it would be the reverse in America, where management is an academic discipline, and they have a more questioning view of what can be achieved.'

Another paragraph revealed that Britain scored worst for workforce and management skills. The countries surveyed were America, Britain, Australia, Austria, France, Germany, and South Africa and incredibly, only in management was Britain ahead of South Africa.

The report's findings on the percentage of causes for low productivity in Britain were as follows:

1. Insufficient Planning and control:- 43%
2. Inadequate Management:- 23%
3. Poor working morale:- 12%
4. IT related problems:- 8%
5. Ineffective communication:- 7%
6. Inappropriately qualified workforce:- 7%

Published in 2002, one would have expected that we would have seen improvements after the report's release. However, it appears that there is still a lot of work to be done! For example, in 2017, after further research, a report was issued by the UK Office for National Statistics (ONS) showing the trend over 15 years from 2002. The findings drew many similar conclusions, stating that UK productivity was now even lower when compared to other countries. The following is a brief synopsis:

ONS Report 2017: Eleven Reasons For Poor Productivity In The UK

According to the British Office for National Statistics (ONS), UK productivity has fallen to levels it held in 2007. Productivity in the UK has consistently lagged well behind Germany and France and has now been overtaken by many other countries. This is the key reason why wages, growth and competitive performance are all held back. Why is this, and what can be done about it?

The report concludes that the answer is **training, investment, innovation and finding smarter ways to do things. Above all, we need to improve the quality of management and leadership across the board.** The more detailed ONS report is included in Appendix 1 for reference and corroboration.

Sadly, there has been insufficient productivity improvement to catch up and then keep up with other countries over that period of 15 years.

Guide To Reading This Book

The six key functions are set out in separate chapters. Examples and experiences are not written in chronological order. The examples and memoir anecdotes are used to illustrate the importance of each function, irrespective of when the anecdote occurred in time.

The shaded sections inside boxes on some pages throughout the book denote a memoir experience as supporting evidence to a lesson learned. If the book is being used for reference after a first read, the boxed sections could be skipped.

For reference purposes, the companies worked for in chronological order are:

- Simms Motor and Electronics Corporation (a conglomerate)
- Crane Ltd (American company – industrial valves and fluid controls)
- Metal Box Ltd, (international packaging company)
- Autotype International (printing industry consumables)
- Geka Manufacturing (cosmetics packs)
- Consultancy, mainly to SMEs
- CVE Engineering (scientific equipment)
- Consultancy to SMEs.

Each chapter contains a useful 'how to'. For convenience and quick referencing when using the book, you will find the 'how to's in this order:

How to win more orders and increase sales .... Chapter 3

How using specific techniques will increase
productivity to improve profits .... Chapter 4

Chapter One

In The Beginning: Focusing On Key Functions And Methodologies

I have learned the value of 1% improvements throughout my career: this first chapter will share some of my initial managerial background and the big challenges I faced.

After securing my first managing director position, I soon discovered that making many seemingly small improvements soon made big differences. My 'new' job was to turn around a loss-making company and run the UK sales and manufacturing operation for a German-owned group. The company manufactured colour cosmetics packs, such as mascaras, eyeliners and lip gloss. The group was based in southern Germany and also had a factory in the USA and England. The basic manufacturing operations were injection moulding of plastics, extrusion blow moulding and injection blow moulding and printing of bottles, and mascara brush manufacturing. The various components were then assembled for shipment to the customers: colour cosmetics manufacturers.

For my first day, the arrangement was to go to London Heathrow Airport to meet Roswitha, the company's UK financial director, and the two of us were to fly to the Newcastle based factory for a management meeting.

Roswitha has been a huge part of my working life. Originally from Germany, she had married an Englishman and now lived in England (for 20 years). She is charming and always well-dressed. I had first met her during the recruitment stage before joining the company, so the flight up and general conversation were friendly and straightforward...it was the management meeting later that was the surprise.

The meeting was attended by the current UK managing director (who I was replacing), the two directors from Germany, the UK factory general manager, and the UK sales manager.

To say my first day on the job was an eye-opener would be a gross understatement. The sales manager gave an unclear and poor presentation of the sales and orders situation, and it did not sound very good. The factory situation and problems from the lack of investment worried me, as did the revelation that the outstanding order book was declining. On top of that, the accounts were not set out in a standard format that was comprehensible or useful to UK managers, so they were pretty meaningless.

When the management meeting had finished, and the usual small talk began, I chatted with Ian Stavert, the factory general manager. Ian is a Scotsman, quite a tough character, then about 50 years old, not too tall, stockily built and a rugby player who had played for the RAF when younger. Ian is the sort of person who 'tells it as he sees it' – which I find refreshing. On this occasion, he didn't hold back on his opinion of Fred, the Sales Manager. Ian said Fred's interpersonal skills were zero, he did not know the products very well, and he was not bringing in much business. Wow, I'm in at the deep end, I thought!

The next day I flew to Germany and spent the following two weeks on an induction programme, mainly learning about the products, meeting with senior managers, and meeting with office and production people to learn about the whole group operation.

During the meetings with the marketing and sales managers, no discussions were forthcoming about pricing, profitability, or even the best-selling products by volume of the different products and designs. Still, I was learning a lot about the product range and technical aspects of the products.

During this two-week induction, I wondered about the UK accounts and financial situation and when the joint managing directors would discuss this with me. It was not on the itinerary of meetings nor covered during casual meet-ups over the two weeks. It was muted once or twice that 'we will cover it before your return to England' – and that was it.

On the last Friday before leaving to fly back to England, we met up to review the two weeks, and I asked about the accounts and financial situation in more detail than I had seen in the accounts at the management meeting in England. After a bit of 'umming and aahing', the answer I received was, "You need to speak to Roswitha".

I thought that was a bit dismissive of such an important area. I also thought they should be informing me about their views and plans for the future of the UK operation. I continued the conversation. And asked, "So is there, for example, a job description? Or maybe an overall brief you want me to follow?" The group MD replied, "Just make the company profitable."

A pretty straightforward answer!

Well, I had learned that the company was unprofitable, so the job was basically to 'turn it around,' but I still had not been told what the full situation was…although I had a good idea about it from the management meeting in Newcastle.

I imagine they assumed I could discuss everything with Hans, the outgoing UK Managing Director, during the handover. However, I still thought it was a bit odd because surely if you are going to run a business, you need to look at the finances: what has happened, where it is going. I wanted to obtain the owners' views on such things as investment and timescales. My next question was, "There seems to be disquiet about the sales manager. Can I get rid of him if need be?" The answer was, "Yes. Do what you need to do". Good, I thought, I can get on with everything that needs to be done as I see it.

My query about the sales manager was not just as result of seeing him in action at the management meeting and the conversation with Ian but also an incident before I joined the company. Before I applied for the advertised job in the Sunday Times, I phoned the UK company and asked if they had some company and product literature they could send me. I was told they didn't have any but would enquire of the sales manager. I left my home phone number as requested. When I got home from work that day, my wife said she had received a phone call from a Mr Fred, and he wanted to come down and 'take our order'. No questions or anything. She had worked in Public Relations as an account manager and thought this was most odd! This was our home telephone number, and he kept saying he would like to come down and take our order. He didn't ask if he was calling a company or what products we made or might be interested in.

I said to my wife, "If I were applying for any other job than managing director at that company, I would not apply because if they employ a person like that, there's something wrong with the company. I'll carry on because as Managing Director, that is likely to be one of the first changes needing to be made." And so it happened.

Moving to the new company was an excellent opportunity to use the skills and experience I had gained up to that point. Also, the company had interesting products and markets. The job matched well with my knowledge of printing and plastics products and marketing and sales in the UK and export markets. So, with a lot of previous experience, I was not worried about getting stuck into the new company, and I was relishing the challenge this opportunity presented. I would gain a lot more expertise and, hopefully, enjoy it along the way.

Back In The UK: The First Few Days In My New Job!

The company's UK head office was on the first floor above an estate agency in Rickmansworth, Hertfordshire. The premises were rented and decidedly run down with old furniture and dirty white net curtains hanging from the leaky, draughty old sash windows. I intended that we should get out of those offices as soon as possible.

Hans, the departing UK MD, had been in the UK for three years. He had a reasonably sized office, and I shared it with him for a couple of months till he moved back to Germany. It enabled me to learn faster about the company, what he did, and what needed to be done.

Problems At Loss-making Geka. A Fairly Typical Situation At A Poor Company

On the first day starting at the office, I talked to everyone individually. I had a long chat with Roswitha, the FD. When I had flown with her to the meeting at the Newcastle factory, the conversations were more general. Now we got down to business.

Roswitha showed me the management accounts again, and once more, I was surprised and disappointed with their illogical format and the lack of flow in the financial information. This layout was how the German directors seemed to want it. I asked if there were any suggestions or changes from Germany for useful improvement to the format of the accounts, but there was not one. It was then that I also learned the company had run at a loss for the previous ten years and had been supported by the parent company. I was the third MD in ten years...and I was certainly in for a challenge!

I did not wish to be overly critical, so I did not ask many questions such as who had initially devised the format of the accounts. It did not matter; the objective was to improve the accounts layout and show meaningful information to understand the business performance.

Interestingly the problems with the layout of the accounts proved to be a foreshadowing of the future issues in the German parent company. After my conversation with Roswitha, I had separate chats with the financial accounts bookkeeper, office staff, and sales administrators. They were all keen to tell me about the sales manager, how rude and incompetent he was, and it turned out that he frequently left the office staff women in tears.

So on day one, there were already unhappy staff to sort out, which would obviously have affected customer service performance. I then had a chat with Hans about why Mr Fred was still in the company. Hans told me that Fred had been recruited by the Geka Germany MD and was sent over to the UK. Hans did not feel he could complain or go against the owners' choice of sales manager.

First Actions

On the second day, with Roswitha, I began reorganising the profit and loss accounts layout into a clearer, more traditional UK format that could be prepared monthly. The other information, such as order intake, debtors and creditors, and loan repayments that were intermingled in the existing so-called profit and loss account layout, needed to go onto a separate sheet. So that was good progress towards understanding the accounts. I was then finally able to see that there was a very low gross profit margin leading to the company's lack of profitability.

When looking at product and customer margins a bit later, I found very low margins on many products and that some products were losing huge amounts of money. For instance, one product costing £310 per thousand was being sold at £220 per thousand. Two products alone were losing £75,000 a year. So that was easy, raise the prices or drop the products and reduce losses by £75,000 a year almost immediately. I asked Roswitha why in general, the prices were so low. She replied that it was a question she had asked frequently, and the answer was always, "They are the market prices!"

Over the ensuing few weeks, I witnessed Hans have big arguments with Fred about his behaviour, his telephone manner with customers, and how he spoke to staff. Fred would tell me afterwards that Hans did not mean it, and I could see Fred did not seem capable of learning anything, further confirming my opinion he was not suitable for the sales position.

So the scenario was now set regarding sorting out some key areas; the sales manager situation and the need to fully clarify and understand the accounts. Then there was the need to understand what was happening in the two overall key areas:

1. Sales: regarding pricing, customers and orders.
2. Production performance.

Now, the turnaround had to get underway as fast as possible!

This introductory chapter has, I hope, set the scene for just some of the areas that had to be improved in Geka. I found similar situations when consulting for companies and later when owning an engineering company.

Therefore, throughout the book, I will recount experiences and examples acquired over the years and provide examples of the Six Key Functions requiring focus to succeed when managing a business. The examples are not set in chronological order and are not classroom theories. I use real-life examples as illustrations for each function, demonstrating the principles and methods to use.

The knowledge I have acquired from achieving major company improvements has led to Rocketship Management and its principles. The examples demonstrated will provide clear information for many managers and potential business owners about the key business functions, some important supporting departments, and actions that can be undertaken for improvements.

Each year, so many businesses fail. Figures vary year on year, but around 1000 to 2000 companies close down or cease trading in the UK a week. The key reasons companies fail are because of one or more of the following reasons:

- lack of sales (and at the right prices)
- lack of production efficiency and deliverance of product or service
- lack of gross profit management/lack of cash/too much borrowing
- lack of good IT information and clarity for management
- lack of management planning, organisation and control
- lack of focus on keeping overhead costs in check
- lack of leadership and motivating.

Note: I have placed 'lack of sales' first because it is an obvious cause.

In my experience, even a 1% improvement across various aspects can make big improvements. (This is similar in sports where nearly all the winners are only 1% or less better than the runner up!)

The Six Key Functions Of Rocketship Management And The Ensuing Principles Are:

- Sales (and customer service)
- Production, or product, or service, (and quality)
- Gross Profit management for control and profitability
- IT optimisation for efficiency
- Management and Percentages Management
- Leadership, Motivating and Training.

After describing my Rocketship Management concept in the next chapter, each of the Six Key Functions will be explored in detail throughout the book, with the intention that some of the valuable guidance will help save a few companies.

Chapter Two
The Rocketship Management Concept

What Is Rocketship Management?

While working at my previous employer Autotype International, we grew so excitingly fast that we considered we were 'Rocketing' along. Great teams and positive attitudes all helped. From understanding this success, and then later, when focusing on Geka's growth and profitability, the following concept emerged...

> There are two key functions in a company that are the foundations and are fundamentally important. All the other functions in a company support those two functions.

From time to time, I have asked business people, **What are those two functions?** I find it surprising that so many people in senior positions cannot quickly (or at all) name these two basic functions or drivers for company success. I have asked this question of a Unilever marketing manager looking after perfumes, a Siemens executive selling trains to the USA and even our auditor. They gave me answers like:

- Marketing and HR
- Production and Finance
- Sales and R&D
- Marketing and R&D

However, the basic answer lies in the fact that you have to have a product or service to sell, and you have to sell it to create a company and drive and grow the business successfully. So for Rocketship Management, there are two essential functions:

- Sales and Production, or;
- Sales and the Product or Service.

This applies whether a company is a micro-business or a multi-million-pound operation.

After asking my question, *"what are those two functions?"* and noting people's various suggestions and thoughts, I suggest they consider Sales and Production, or the product, with only momentary reflection, they invariably all agree!

Management and employees need to be clear that company success and their jobs depend on the sales function and customer service, combined with efficient product supply. All the other functions and departments in a business should be efficiently managed to support these two key functions.

At many companies, the sales function is weak (such as it was at Geka), or production is weak. Inadequate production means that it is inefficient and therefore too costly. Often, this translates to poor quality and failure to make timely deliveries. This was also the problem at Geka.

A weak sales function encompasses salespeople who have no sales training and, for example, MDs (managing directors) who dabble in sales part-time and also have no sales training.

This principle of the importance of the two functions can be applied to virtually every business. Let's use restaurants as an example. What if you get great food but poor and indifferent service? If the owner/chef does not know this is important, they may wonder why turnover is inadequate and the business is failing. Conversely, you might receive excellent, friendly service from the front-of-house staff and waiters, but the food is poor, so you don't want to go back. The same applies to banks. Friendly, efficient staff in the branch don't satisfy the customer if the bank services and 'production' are not good. Some IT system crashes in recent times have caused a couple of the big UK banks to lose many customers to competitors. If there is a weakness in any business in focusing on both the sales function and the product, service and production function, then customers can be lost.

I once worked with the MD of a plastics manufacturing company. He was an IT specialist and spent most of his time on the computer, not on sales work. His partner ran the production, but they lacked sales skills and generating sales. At the time, I helped them win new orders. However, I heard they sold out a couple of years later because of their lack of sales skills and customer servicing.

There is a need to recognise the importance of sales and production (or product or service) and ensure these are backed up by efficiency in other key processes, each supporting the six principle key functions.

One significant area that links the sales and production functions together is the INFORMATION AND DATA from sales administration and production via the IT systems. The important data, of course, provide information for each function to operate closely together. The information is also crucial to the finance function and the monthly reports for management. This can be illustrated in a simple graphic as a **Rocketship**.

FIG 1. *The Rocketship: The Six Key Functions (in bold).*

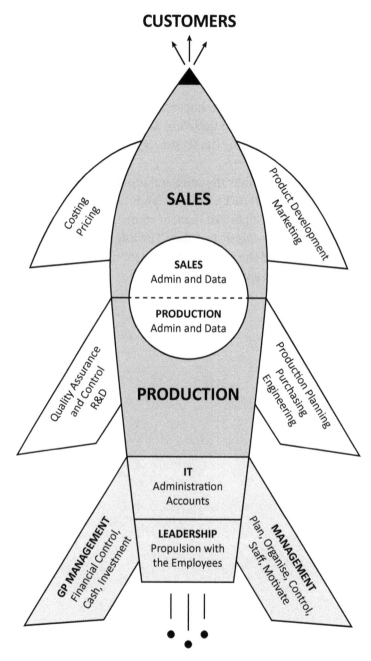

The **Rocketship Company** diagram shows the importance of the two main functions of sales and production, or products. These are central and linked to the critical IT and data systems. Next, many of the supporting functions to the two essential functions are shown. It is, of course, not comprehensive but is illustrative. The key functions in the Rocketship are at the centre, but it demonstrates that the whole rocket has to be *driven by management and the employees.*

There is much to add to this basic Rocketship concept to drive a company to success. But the main thing is that management and employees need to be aware of the drivers to success and how all the key functions and departments interrelate. Let's add a bit more light on the sales and production functions and how in combination, they drive success.

Fig 2. shows the key measurements used to arrive at the most crucial figure: gross profit. The chart shows that a company must drive sales at realistic and competitive prices. In combination, production and supply must get ever more efficient, and investment in continuous improvement is required. You can see an overview of the focus and the links between sales and production to arrive at the gross profit measurement. These sales, production and gross profit management functions will be discussed in detail in the following chapters.

FIG 2. *For Profitability, Production and Sales Focus*

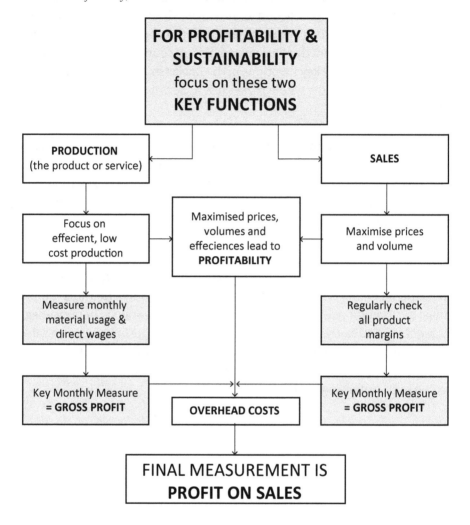

If good production efficiency is obtained, which supports sales, and the company sells at profitable prices to drive volume, the company can then be driven further upwards in growth and profitability. The performance improvement can allow prices to be decreased in future so the company can be driven further forward in growth and profitability by becoming increasingly more efficient and competitive.

The key boxes in **Fig 2.** show gross profit (GP) measurement. This is the most crucial measurement for monitoring and driving a company forward. Then following the GP measurement, the subsequent essential measurements are on overhead costs, followed by 'the bottom line' – net profit.

In the left and right-hand bottom boxes is the gross profit in money, i.e. £ or $ etc., which is the total sum of net money made by accumulating all the price margins of the products sold, and after deducting direct costs of materials and wages.

The gross profit revenue then has to cover all the overheads and make a profit. If prices are being reduced, then the increased volumes must maintain the gross profit revenue to cover the current overhead costs. Alternatively, the overhead costs must be trimmed down. You can be sure that careful planning to balance overhead costs with gross profit revenue ensured good results for companies like, for example, Ford Motor Company in the early days of its start up as volumes increased and prices were reduced.

Imagine if just a 1% improvement is made on the various parts of the two key functions; how much that could cumulatively improve performance. This will be demonstrated in the following chapters also.

If a company can maximise the production and sales performances, as shown in Fig 2., it can lead to a virtuous circle – what I have called **The PS Circle.** Production output leads to sales, then increased sales leads to efficiencies in productivity, which leads to more sales volumes, which leads to profitability (and investment), then success and security. When looking and working with various companies, it seemed to me that **The PS Circle** has four phases:

PRODUCTION	>>>	SALES Currently	>>	Stage 1
PRODUCTIVITY	>>>	SALES Additionally	>> Stability	Stage 2
PROFITABILITY	>>>	SUCCESS	>> Good Profits	Stage 3
PROSPERITY	>>>	SECURITY	>> Continuity	Stage 4

Sales volumes are almost needed first, and then the sales volumes link back to production (or product and service), and each function works hand in hand.

LESSON

If a company optimises sales performance and production efficiencies, that will create the virtuous circle, the P-S-P circle, for sales and production, production and sales, leading to profitability and success.

The focus on these functions, fully supported by the 'supporting functions' and departments, creates the route to profitability and future security. I mentioned Ford earlier: Henry Ford and many like him achieved this route to colossal success. The Virtuous Circle of P-S-P is illustrated in **Fig 3.**

FIG 3. P-S-P Focus

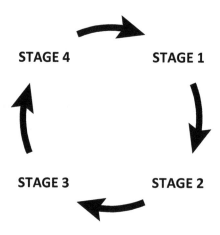

STAGE 4   STAGE 1

STAGE 3   STAGE 2

Showing PS1 at the beginning of the circle and the end shows that the organisation must still work on continuous improvement and investment even when successful. Interestingly, as a generalisation (and dependent on the size and problems of a company), it seems there is frequently a timescale for the cycles of P-S-P. My colleagues and I noticed that turning a company around can, as a broad generalisation, take a year for every two years it has been making a loss. However, as I demonstrate later in the book, sometimes a small company can be turned around in weeks or months. In other cases, it takes much longer. A broad time scale for the build-up of the

P-S-P scenario can be as follows, starting with the build-up from a current poor position.

PRODUCTION	>>> SALES Improvement	>> Stage 1	1-3 years
PRODUCTIVITY	>>> SALES VOLUME	>> Stability Stage 2	3-6 years
PROFITABILITY	>>> SUCCESS	>> Good Profits Stage 3	4-6 years
PROSPERITY	>>> SECURITY	>> Continuity Stage 4	6-11 years

The timescales depend not only on company size. They also depend on how much debt and loans have to be paid off and how much under-investment there is in everything, especially production equipment and infrastructure, and not forgetting people and IT systems. Companies, for example, with 15-year-old inefficient machines or old IT systems, need money and time to turn them around and are at the risk of losing customers.

In Stage 4, the Prosperity and Security phase, companies can get complacent; managers may have been changed, good people have moved on, and decline can start.

This concept of the PSP Circle can only apply to a certain degree. Even if a company is performing satisfactorily and profitably, it can be drastically and adversely affected in a very short time. There are three general classes for business disruption.

1. Political, Economic, Social and Technical reasons (PEST). You can see a detailed list in Appendix 3.
2. A 'step change' in business operations. This category could come under Technology reasons, but it is at a higher level than just automation. For instance, the recent step-changing innovations of AirBNB and Uber.
3. Superior competition. Other companies might be better than yours in all departments: management, sales, products, production and service. The latter point, excellent service, when combined with quality products, can soon knock out existing companies.

CHAPTER SUMMARY

1. Focus on the Rocketship Management concept of the key functions of Sales and Production, or Product or Service (which are then interlinked with the other four key functions).

2. Obtain the best performance from the Six Key Functions: such as costing and pricing.

3. Monitor the measurement and performance of GP (gross profit).

4. Understand and plan for the P-S-P stages and likely timescales for turning around or growing the business to help create a realistic strategy and forecasts for success.

This chapter has set the scene for Rocketship Management. Chapters on the 'Six Key Functions' now follow with a focus on the supporting functions and departments. Remember that adopting just minor changes, even as small as a theoretical 1%, can result in big improvements.

Chapter Three
The Sales Function

Key Function One: how to win more orders and increase sales. This chapter focuses on understanding the sales process is essential to the Rocketship concept. We then progress to pricing aspects, the sales focus, sales techniques, and the importance of customer service.

Without sales of products or services, you do not have a company. It seems obvious, doesn't it? Yet I am constantly surprised at how many business people are so carried away with 'daily stuff' that they do not pay enough attention to their customers and to growing the business.

While providing Business Advice for MDOs (Managing Director Owners) for many years, I have heard some fascinating comments. Here are just two noteworthy ones from a couple of small companies:

MDO 1. "I like working on the shop floor and try and do some selling on Friday mornings."

MDO 2. "I would like to increase my sales, and I have tried marketing. I put an 'ad' in the local directory, but it did not work." *When I enquired whether he or his staff had undertaken any sales training, the answer was" no."*

Fig 4 provides an overview using a sales funnel chart to understand the sales process better.

FIG 4. *The Sales Funnel*

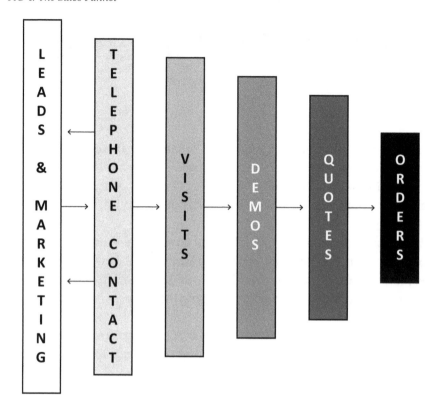

The chart shows *some* typical sales and marketing activities in the first two columns. Activities like direct mail, exhibitions and shows, and even virtual demonstrations by video or Zoom call could be added.

The left-hand side is the start of the funnel with the leads and enquiries to follow up on. The funnel then indicates that fewer visits or meetings may be established, then fewer quotes and, finally, fewer orders. In most sales situations, achieving orders is a numbers game. First, leads need to be generated and found.

The activities per column are clear but not to scale. Ideally, if there is a visit, it should include a presentation, demonstration or a show of examples, which leads to 'closing the order' or a quotation. At the end of the funnel, the company and salesperson should aim to obtain a high rate of order acceptance for the quotations.

When I asked about the conversion rate of quotes to sales of one company I know, I was told they get nearly 100% because they are in a specialist field with not much competition. Other companies generally obtain a much lower conversion rate. If too low a conversion percentage is being obtained, this book will hopefully provide you with some skills improvement that will enable an increase in the conversion rate. I used one of the techniques I share on a telecoms company I worked with; we simply clarified the quotation form and the sales team's words used for the product descriptions. This dramatically improved the orders by 30% (a very pleasant outcome for the managing director!).

The main problem I identified at that telecoms company was that the salespeople were selling to financial directors or personal assistants. However, those people would not generally understand (or need to know) telecoms terms or product codes. All they needed was the price of the main console or switchboard for a phone system; and the price of each extension. After that, the specific features and benefits were listed. Until then, the quotation listed items by product code...but what did that mean to most? Very little. But the new style of clear quotations mainly achieved a considerable 30% increase in orders.

Apart from a weakness in the skills and selling, one of the biggest common failures in SMEs (Small and Medium-sized Enterprises) is that they do not adequately establish the correct and complete cost of their products. Some MDOs and sales directors work out their pricing 'on the back of an envelope.' This leads to them offering low prices. Two leading companies I ran had previously lost money for years and were selling products at a loss. So too was the German parent company. Many SMEs I have visited were doing the same thing, selling products at a loss or with unprofitable margins.

The Importance Of Knowing The Costs Of Products

You can set a 'fallback' position on the lowest price you can accept if you really know your costs. Then when discussing products and prices with clients, you can still achieve a good basic profit margin. However, this 'fallback' price is one you must not go below. You have to say to yourself and the customer, 'no lower,' and you need to be prepared to walk away. As I will demonstrate later in the book, you can often win the business at this stage.

This is an essential aspect of selling, as are competitive pricing situations, and I cover both topics in more detail in Chapter Five: Costing and Pricing.

Methodology
How To Boost Performance

A salesperson, or the person doing the pricing, must know the product costs and set appropriate prices for sensible margins. Because, for example, a 1% improvement on the price can be an extra £10,000 in profit for a £1.0 million turnover company.

When this 1% margin improvement is added to other 1% improvements to be discussed in ensuing chapters, those small steps soon lead to big improvements in a company. Many SMEs might have set proper prices some years previously but have failed to increase prices as costs have risen. The customers' buyers do all they can to refuse price increases because it is their job to save money. I have encountered suppliers who have not raised prices for years.

So, Apart From Knowing Your Costs And Prices, How Do You Sell?

Selling is as much a technique and a skill as other job functions. Yet I am constantly surprised at how, despite the absolute necessity for companies to sell, so many people in a sales position have never attended a sales training course or had any training.

Fig 5 shows the key points involved in the sales function. Each has a particular focus to help identify areas for improvement. They are all linked to achieving optimum sales results.

Asking open questions and selling benefits, not features, are fundamental focus points.

FIG 5. *The Sales Focus*

THE SALES FOCUS

The key points to know at the start are the Features and the Benefits, the Open Questions, and the SPIN Sales Technique. These three key focus points need to be well developed for successful selling. The other focus points support those three, and some are the management team's responsibility, for example, providing incentive plans for enthusiasm and motivation.

Working with MDs and teams on benefits has shown that even when 'benefits' are described and discussed, people still just talk about 'features'. It seems it is not such a simple concept to grasp immediately. However, it is crucial to understand the differences and use them accordingly.

The SPIN sales technique is probably the primary skill to acquire in selling. This mainly covers the other Key Focus points that should be encompassed with SPIN in a sales meeting.

The SPIN acronym stands for:

S Situation questions
P Problem questions
I   Implication questions
N Needs and benefits

This format helps people who sell (MDOs, Salespeople, Technical people etc.), allowing them to follow a structure for identifying what a buyer wants or needs. Selling is not just about what you want to tell the prospect or immediately sell to them. Identify their needs first and then offer your products or service benefits. You start building the information about your prospect or customer's problems and needs by asking open questions. Moreover, and very importantly, **the quality of your questions will build personal credibility with the prospect.**

Fig 6 shows a guidance note on using the SPIN sales technique. The open questions for the Situation Questions are examples and will have to be changed depending on what you are selling. Of course, many sales training courses are available to help with more detail and skills development. People who are selling need only to learn and practice a few things to achieve a big difference in results for the company and themselves.

FIG 6. The SPIN Technique

S.P.I.N. SELLING AND EFFECTIVE QUESTIONING
SUMMARY OVERVIEW

The ability to ask effective questions is a fundamental skill required by successful sales people. During the sales process there are three distinct types of question that we need to ask our customers and our prospects.

1. Questions need to cover: the SPIN method:

    S. Situation questions- the present situation.
    P. Problem questions about difficulties and barriers.
    I.   Implication questions about improvements that changes will bring.
    N. Needs and benefits

2. Questions which seek facts and problems: the present situation

    - How is your company performing at the moment?
    - How are management decisions made in your organisation ?
    - What sort of KPI's do you use at the moment?
    - What are the problems you are experiencing in production?
    - Which are your poor performing products? Which are the best selling ones? What are the reasons for that? How long has this been going on for? What have you tried?
    - How are your other suppliers generally performing?

3. Questions which seek views on problems and implications

    - How will, or could an increase in sales affect your business?
    - What if you had a solution to that problem?
    - Why is .... of particular concern to you?
    - Why is .... of such importance?

4. Questions which seek a response to your proposals/ideas and clarify needs and benefits

    - How much do you think that ...... will answer your problem?
    - How does ...... sound to you?
    - What benefits do you think you will gain from ..... ?
    - What if..
    - Do you feel that we can move on to the next step now?

5. Presenting your Products or service:

    - Only after at least Situation questions and Problem questions should a presentation be made. Usually it will be better to present **after Implication** and **Needs** and **Benefits** questions.
    - A link sentence could then be something like, "let me now tell you about this product (or service), and how it could benefit you."

The ability to ask effective questions is a fundamental skill required by successful salespeople. We need to ask our customers and our prospects the initial three distinct types of questions during the sales process and then follow up with questions about Needs and Benefits for improvements in performance and ability.

When reading **Fig 6,** you might think, 'Yeah, yeah, I can do that!' However, look at **Fig 7**, and you will see there are many more specific skills to be developed for a salesperson to really succeed and achieve top results. MDOs need to know the skill sets needed when appointing a salesperson.

I once asked an MD to rate his salesman out of 10, and he gave a score of six. So on earnings of £60,000 a year, I pointed out that meant the MD was wasting £24,000 per year on him. Moreover, the salesman would be losing the company a lot of money by not winning enough profit-earning orders. That provided food for thought and something to take action on to improve his business.

FIG 7. *Sales Skills Checklist*

SALES SKILLS MEETING CHECKLIST

Name: Position: Organisation:

Completed by:

	SKILL AREA	RATING (1 - 10) 10 High	PRIORITY
1	Satisfactory icebreaker		
2	**Pertinent & effective introductory speech**		
3	**Using effective open questioning skills**		
4	**Using effective listening skills**		
5	**Not interrupting**		
6	**Not speaking over client or colleagues**		
7	**No unnecessary stories or examples**		
8	**Speaking with clarity and succinctness**		
9	**Selling benefits not features**		
10	**Good presentation, visual aids and samples**		
11	**No negative statements or any stories**		
12	Gaining and holding attention		
13	Building rapport		
14	Recognising **verbal buying/warning signals**		
15	**Understanding non-verbal buying/warning signals**		
16	Determining real buying needs and motive		
17	Developing solutions to satisfy the customer		
18	Handling objections		
19	Staying in control		
20	Creating desire/emotional commitment		
21	Closing the sale		
22	Exploring the possibilities of additional sales		
23	Persuasive communications		

The rating column is for scoring the sales visit skills out of 10. The scoring in the priority column is the priority for improvement. When visiting a customer with a particular MDO a few years ago, I marked him at 25% of ability on the whole checklist. That is, his score was 58 out of 230 points. I did not tell him that score, although he needed a few suggestions for immediate improvements. Apart from the need for sales skills, the following should be borne in mind:-

> *When selling, it is crucial to understand the position of buyers. At a base level, their job is to keep purchasing costs down.*

But buyers also have to ensure that their company's production and sales can be maintained and that performance is not impaired by poor quality or late deliveries from a supplier. If purchasing managers and buyers are to consider buying your product for the first time, you really must be able to sell the <u>benefits</u> **and** <u>features</u> of your product. What are the features of your product? How do they perhaps vary from competitors' features? When you have been clear on the features of your products or service, what then are the benefits? How important are they for your customer? Remember, the buyer will consider more than just price. Other considerations are:

- What is your product, and how good is it?
- What is the quality of your product?
- How reliable is your company?
- What are the lead times?

To provide credibility, buyers will also be interested in who else you supply. Samples or visual aids need to be shown to demonstrate company professionalism. Some of your competitors will put on a 'good show', so you have to match this to get the best chance of orders. Company and product literature are also needed as a 'leave behind'. Some companies might consider this an unnecessary expense as the relevant information can be found on their website. But when the salesperson leaves, is the prospect likely to look at the website once they become swamped in a busy week? Very unlikely, I would suggest! And anyway, is the website a good sales tool, or, as many are, just a general information site?

Excellent informative literature left on the prospect's desk can act as a reminder for what can sometimes be weeks, even months ahead. It might be passed on to a superior or peer, asking, "what do you think of this company?" Also, it is a good aide-mémoire to the prospect when you call back and refer to it. (I have included more guidance on leaving behind literature in Chapter Eight: The Marketing Function.

Of course, companies do need to have an excellent website providing comprehensive information about their products and services, and it must provide confidence. It should also generate enquiries. The website must include benefits. I point this out because when discussing benefits with many MDs and teams, I have found that although 'benefits' are described and discussed, people still just talk about features.

A good website must quickly state what is being offered. Many websites overlook this fundamental point. There should be clarity on the Home page or the Landing page on what the company offers and who it is for. The website can then include any other information the company wishes to share in other sections. A good website will differ slightly from company literature because of the necessity to optimise it for Search Engines.

Once the business has been won, the customers have to be well looked after, or you will lose them. The following sections focus on keeping customers.

Price, Quality And Service (and The Product Itself)

One of our large customers at Geka was the Rimmel/Coty Group cosmetics company.

I had an amusing welcome on one of my regular visits to the purchasing chief, Jonathan (JP). We had known each other for some years as we had stayed in the same hotel after he had just joined the company. When I sat down for our chat, Jonathan joked, "I should be wearing a t-shirt with "Faster, Better, Cheaper" on it. That was quite a punchy way of saying the key things buyers consider, and we progressed the conversation nicely. Needless to say, that was a good day's visit to Rimmel!

So at what stage was Geka at that time? Our turnover with Rimmel now exceeded £2 million a year. We were supplying around one million injection moulded or blow moulded components a week to them in a sole supplier situation. Our components went straight onto the production line, and we'd had no rejects or quality issues since the launch of the new Rimmel/Coty product ranges.

So price is not the only consideration. Quality and service must also be a top priority if the supplying MD wants his company to Rocket along. If you are a leading supplier, you must not fall into the trap of letting your margins drop. It is easy to give products away when tempted by the possibility of getting more volume. Generally, JP or his subordinates at Rimmel spoke to our sales manager or the sales office on a day to day basis whenever there was a need. Jonathan called me one day about upping the sales volume on one of their shorter run brands by using one of our standard mascara packs for another Rimmel/Coty brand. The conversation went approximately like this:

JP: "Hi John, I am at the airport to fly to Germany, so in a bit of a hurry. We want 'this' particular mascara pack of cap/rod/brush/bottle. Can you do it at this price of, (examples, not the real prices) £150 per 1000 for the whole pack. (Which seemed to be the same price as the main Rimmel brand.)

Me: " Sorry, the tools that make the pack are smaller, with fewer cavities, and the cap tool has far fewer cavities than the 16 impression tool for the main brands."

JP: "Can you do the cap/rod/ brush only without the bottle for £125 per 1000?" (A low price.)

Me: "I can do the cap/rod/brush for £144" (A lot higher price), which I remember (as this was years ago) was about 15-20 % more than he was asking for.

JP: "Well, OK then, at that price, can you do the bottle for £45?"

Me: "We can do the upper part –cap/rod/brush, but sorry, we just can't do the bottle at that price."

There was a bit of the usual groaning at this stage. I told JP that he was asking us to give the same prices as we supplied for high volumes that use large and efficient tooling. I added that he must be getting the lowest prices from anywhere at that high volume product, and we just could not match the main brand prices for the lower volumes on smaller, lower output tooling.

JP: "What if I give you the bottle and the upper part for '£200'.

He had raised the offer for the bottle to £56. The new price for the complete pack was then £200 compared to the £150 he first asked for. I had made it clear that I was prepared to walk away from the low bottle price. So we won the extra business at a sensible price for the smaller quantities.

METHODOLOGY
How To Boost Performance

1. Knowing your costs and your 'fallback' price position is imperative. With conviction from knowledge, you do not fall into the trap of agreeing to accept low prices just for the sake of volume.

2. When you have done your costing and used a formula to set a price, just add another 1%.

I put the phone down and went straight into our sales manager's office to inform Adrian that Jonathan had called me and that we had got some new mascara pack business. Adrian asked, "what is the price?" (Good question!) I replied, "about 30% more than JP originally wanted to pay". (Of course, that *could* have been JP's negotiating start position, but I didn't think so.)

In such circumstances as the one I've described, you have to be prepared to walk away if you could lose money. Many companies fall into this trap and don't walk away. There is a saying and variants on it: **volume is vanity, profit is prosperity, but cash is king.**

Provide Superior Customer Service To Win And Keep Business

The critical thing for repeat business is serving customers well and delivering quality products on time. In addition, regular visits build relationships which are beneficial to both parties. Sometimes special things have to be done, and there is a need to 'jump through hoops' to help your customers.

> I would always ensure I was available for customers (I still do), and I know people would respect that and not take advantage of it, always going through the sales manager or the sales department if they could. For example, we had a good relationship with one P&G (Proctor and Gamble) Purchasing Manager. I was in a board meeting when our secretary, Kate, popped her head around the door to say Roger was on the phone. I said to tell him I was in a board meeting, but if he needed to speak to me, I'd take his call. Kate came back a moment later and said, "That's OK. He'll wait till tomorrow and call you".

On another occasion, the same purchasing manager, Roger, called me at about 10 am. After the usual pleasantries, he said, "You know I don't usually call you for day-to-day things, but I have a big requirement for urgent production and delivery. The factory wants to produce mascaras next week, and I need 300,000 mascara packs. When I asked when he needed them, he replied, "Immediately." I promised to call him back and then made a quick call to Ian at the factory to ask him the question. He came back about an hour later and said, "We can put the tools on the machines in an hour or so and can ship 100,000 this evening to arrive tomorrow; then we'll ship 100,000 tomorrow for the next day and another 100,000 for the day after. In other words, we'll part ship the 300,000 each night over the next three days, starting tonight".

I asked which customer deliveries would be delayed, then agreed with the sales manager, Adrian, that he should call a few customers to see if they would agree to us delivering their products three days later than planned. Also, this was important because our *actual* delivery dates were measured against our quoted delivery dates and also against customers' required delivery dates. Most customers by this time were running 'Just-In-Time' with not a lot of stock in reserve; however, the majority kept about a week's supply or more...and knew we would help them in similar circumstances. I called Roger back within about 90 minutes and told him he could have 100,000 a day arriving tomorrow and over three days. Was that OK? He was delighted at the news!

I used to go up to the Yorkshire factory from time to time to visit Roger and discuss the business. At one of those meetings (after the urgent 300,000 mascara packs shipments), we discussed plans and volumes for the coming year. I was reviewing their forecast volumes with him so that we could plan our loadings and capacities for the coming year. I noticed we were the sole supplier on about 90%+ of their requirements. However, there was one product we did not have. I asked Roger, "What is the situation on that one?" Roger immediately replied, "Do you want it?" "Yes, I said". "OK," he said, "you can have it."

There was a short discussion on price, but once I had confirmed the details with the team back at the office, we got the business. Fantastic! And all because we provided excellent customer service and excellent products at a good price. Interestingly Roger said he had saved his company £7.5 million by reducing the factory stockholding.

I want to share one more example of good customer service. On taking over the running of Geka UK, the company, unfortunately, was delivering poor quality, poor on-time deliveries and poor sales service and representation. After a year, we were running much more efficiently. One of our key customers was Boots of Nottingham. We were (apparently) the third or fourth ranking supplier. It's no secret in business (or it shouldn't be) that if you want to increase business with a customer, you have to deliver quality products on time, with good service and representation. That credibility has to be worked on and built up. In those early days, and in other companies over the years, I found that if there are problems with service and quality, you just spend your time at customer meetings 'firefighting'. You do not have the opportunity to enquire about possible new business or more volumes against competitors because customers are not interested in increasing supplies from poor suppliers. Then back at the office, there is more 'firefighting' and time-wasting trying to find out what is going wrong.

By improving our performance, we increased our business with Boots. Therefore it was great news when Lynne, our sales manager in those early days, received a super letter from Boots:

FIG 8. Boots Letter. Supplier Performance

Re Supplier Performance

"Dear Lynne,

It always gives me great pleasure in writing to suppliers in order to thank them for their recent performance (a task that I unfortunately do less and less). I am very pleased that over a number of months there has been a consistent improvement in deliveries, all of them now on time. Communication is also very good.

However, as a company we are now entering into the realms of last minute Special Offers- specifically on cosmetics.

It is essential that if you wish to obtain a larger share of the business then your leadtime must come down to 4-6 weeks- as with your competitors.

Nevertheless, please thank everybody for such a concerted effort on delivery and quality performance.

It's nice to have a success story!

It is infrequent that you get something in writing from a major customer who says, essentially, *we want to give you more business, so bring your lead times down.* You can imagine the 'glow' around the company and the encouragement it gave everybody to continue with our plan to make improvements and changes. This letter arrived within a year after I arrived at the company, and we were well underway after the initial turnaround activities.

When we saw this letter, and after congratulating Lynne and everybody, it became the primary topic for a Management Meeting. How could we reduce our lead times down to four weeks? That would take some planning and investment. However, we *did* achieve the requested lead time target and accordingly, orders from Boots increased. Over time we moved from the third supplier to the number one supplier. Then when the brand redesign came, we won that and became the sole supplier. Some of the changes we made to achieve the reduced lead times are covered in Chapter Four: The Production (or Supply Function).

When talking to buyers and bidding for business, it must be emphasised yet again that it is essential to undertake detailed costing and estimating. Estimating should be done by trials, using the operators to test the estimates when necessary, not just a manager's or supervisor's estimates. If you get your costing wrong and the price is incorrect, it could eventually kill your business.

Pricing And Price Rises

Around 1990, Volkswagen hired a new Vice President of Purchasing from the USA, Mr Jose Ignacio Lopez, to be the purchasing chief for Volkswagen. One of Mr Lopez's key tasks was to cut VW's materials purchasing costs. He went about this ruthlessly. **Fig 9.** Shows a slightly redacted copy of his internal memo and a previous plan for 'use' at VW. You can see it is jaw-dropping in its content; Lopez's internal plan for his staff shows how he set about squeezing suppliers and frightening the life out of them. The Lopez Line sections 5 and 7 are fascinating.

FIG 9. VW: The Lopez Vice

PURCHASING VICE! 1.
STRATEGY

1. Immediate cost reduction.
2. Long term cost reduction.
3. Hold key suppliers.
4. Maintain supplier loyalty

PURCHASING VICE! 2.
TACTICS – OVERVIEW

1. Establish well qualified, well trained articulate purchasing "clones".
2. Plan the product by product and individual product campaign in detail.
3. Research each product across the world.
4. Establish short- and long-term price targets- go very low.
5. Know your potential winners inside out

PURCHASING VICE! 3.
TACTICS – UNDERLYING THEMES

1. Identify and parade the enemy
   - Japan not ■
2. Understand the balance of power
   - supplier / company
3. Offer (exaggerated) growth
   - the plateau, the vision, and gongs.
4. Start working with the potential 'winners' as early as possible on constructive activity

PURCHASING VICE 4.
TACTICS – THE DEAL

1. Establish long term contract as ultimate goal
2. Establish very early long-term contract rules but do not negotiate in detail
3. Establish that non - price factors like tools, r & d costs etc are not allowed
4. Resist all suggestions that some costs are controllable, and others are not (e.g. materials).
5. Focus all activity on reducing the immediate price dramatically.

PURCHASING VICE! 5.
TACTICS – HANDLING THE DEAL

1. Involve supplier top management totally.
2. Establish the supplier's friend to pass information (be prepared indirectly under pressure directly to lie) give "help".
3. High activity (de stabilise the supplier)
   - many meetings
   - many demands for information
   - always urgent
4. Set deadlines for suppliers to meet but increase anxiety by deferring decisions.

PURCHASING VICE! 6.
TACTICS – THE AGREEMENT

1. Tie up the short term price
   - keep nibbling even at the 13th hour (always appear to be in a desperate hurry but in reality take as much time as is needed).
2. Pull the long term deal out of the cupboard.
3. Sign (if supplier not too exhausted)
4. Intensify CIP (cost improvement programme) to squeeze some more

---

PURCHASING VICE 7.
The Results

1. ⅔ of ▇ Europe's 1990 profit generated by component cost reduction.
2. A shake up /shake out of ▇ component manufacturing.
3. Single source partnerships established at significantly lower prices that are baked into long term contracts e.g. Goetze lowered their ring prices between 18 and 30%
   - *and now they are busted!*

Note: *Lopez's plan was not kept within VW. You can understand that some people in the large purchasing department did not approve of some tactics – or of lying. It appears they showed the plan to relatives and friends, and consequently, it spread around a few other companies. My copy was obtained from a customer in Germany – it had become common knowledge quickly.*

Some large companies and buyers will take a hard approach with potential or existing suppliers. Moreover, it looks as if Goetze did not know the price point *below which they should not drop their prices.* I imagine they all said, "Whoopee, we've won the VW engines contract!" Little did they know at the time that it was going to kill the company.

So, to varying degrees, the Lopez type of approach is also used by some smaller companies.

It is interesting to see the VW Purchasing chief's hard-nosed approach to materials purchasing (at that time)...but he had left VW not long after.

> Soon after my colleague and I took over an engineering company, we were visited by the company's largest customer, which took about 30 per cent of the sales. The MD introduced his new purchasing manager to a few of us in our conference room. The purchasing manager then said he was a former motor industry buyer. It was not long into a general chat with us when he announced that he would be looking for 20% price cuts. This put disquiet among our colleagues. I decided to reassure them as soon as the customer had left. I said, "Don't be concerned about his aggressive statements about 20% price cuts. I've heard it before, and that's typical. If anything, we will probably need to be raising our prices".

Once we had settled in and checked the customers' costs and prices, we *did* raise prices as there were some terrible margins on loss-making products being supplied to them. The buyer who reported to the new purchasing manager revealed to me during a telephone conversation that some of the products and specials sold to them had not had price increases for the previous nine years!! It's no wonder the company had been loss-making.

Customers are obviously not going to readily tell you that your prices are low (and even lower than your competitors!). As usual, the customer resisted the price rises and complained. However, we negotiated increased prices, some of which were quite substantial. Of course, the customer's management team was unhappy, but they had not had an increase for years, and it had to be done. The increases brought the prices up to competitors' pricing. Again, this is another story about a company not correctly monitoring prices, costs and margins and not taking any actions for years, resulting in an annual loss-making situation.

Let me share an excellent example of customer pressure. One day in the office, Adrian, the Geka sales manager, told me he had just been on the phone with Boots, and they had told him that they had asked for 20% price cuts from their tier three suppliers, which were the raw material suppliers. Boots told Adrian that reductions had been achieved, and they would be looking at tier two next. This was our group of packaging suppliers.

So in due course, I had a call from Boots telling me that they were looking for 20% price cuts. I told the gentleman, "It's impossible. You already have very competitive prices, excellent quality and good service". I then added, "However, I suppose we could just about manage one per cent or one and a half per cent discount for more volume". That ended the conversation, and it was never mentioned again! What surprised me was to think of tier three suppliers possibly giving large price reductions. I wondered what happened to them subsequently? Did they survive any 20% price cuts?

The following internet tendering exercise is a further example of understanding costs, pricing and bidding for business. After running Geka, my next progression was as an Executive Associate Business Advisor of the Institute for Independent Business (IIB), working with MDs and senior team members. As a result of working with other Associates, I was sponsored by Enterprise Ireland to help an Irish company improve its export sales. I worked with a carton manufacturer based in Dublin to help them find new customers. I had arranged for a joint visit to Boots Head Office in Nottingham, where my client made an excellent presentation to the senior buying people. We had worked together on improving the visual aids and presentation, and at the end of the meeting, we received a positive response.

Following the presentation, the client was asked to participate in a Boots e-commerce tendering competition for carton business, with other suppliers all on the line at the same time. Toby, the Sales Director, did the tendering from Dublin, and I was on the phone with him from Buckinghamshire at the same time. Toby was prepared with his costings and knew below which price he would not go. He put in his first bid with other suppliers on the line; however, it was soon overtaken by lower bids from a couple of other carton manufacturers. Toby bid again. Then Toby told me that two companies had gone even lower. However, he quickly assessed that those prices were uneconomical, so I told him not to bid lower. I said, "I am sure Boots would not just accept the lowest price. Remember that your company is a big, reliable supplier of cartons to major pharmaceutical companies and others. It also provides excellent service and quality, so do not go lower than your last price bid".

Toby held his nerve, stuck to his best lowest but most profitable price...and proved to be correct. Boots chose to go with his company and then arranged to visit the factory in Dublin to work towards future supply.

I also arranged a visit to the purchasing chiefs at Proctor and Gamble, Europe, in Geneva with Toby and the MD. We were asked to quote for over £1.0million of business, and they won that business too!

Lesson

With good quality and service, and a positive track record, a good company does not have to have the absolute lowest prices and become a 'Busy Fool' – joining a death spiral to administration.

Of course, it can be tough dealing with customers and suppliers. But with knowledge and experience, difficult situations can be rationally and better managed for the good of both parties.

Geka used to supply Yardley Cosmetics. Inevitably with inflation on material costs, prices had to be raised. We went down to Yardley to see Eric, the buyer. After many discussions, he agreed to a price rise of 6% on our mascara packs and metal caps. Coincidentally, a week later, an old colleague of mine, David C. of CMB (Carnaud Metal Box,) phoned me to say he was on his way to see Eric at Yardley to discuss price rises. He asked if we had raised prices and would I mind telling him confidentially what we had achieved. I told him of the 6% price rise agreed.

When David had finished his meeting at Yardley, he gave me a call on the way back. He said, "Eric has agreed to 4%; Eric looked me in the eyes and said I was the only one to whom he was giving a price rise, and that already was a lot, and I should not tell anyone else!" David said he smiled to himself when he heard that but obviously could not say anything. There is much more to inform on Yardley, which

> I will cover later in Chapter Twelve: Management And Percentages
> Management.

I will share some further information on the importance of knowing your costs and pricing levels which concerned another client: Max Factor cosmetics. This is, again, about increasing prices from a silly low level up to competitive and acceptable levels.

On taking over Geka UK, detailed involvement was needed in preparing quotes for customers and prospects. We could pitch prices at sensible margins instead of the many previous minus margins by carefully looking at costs. We had a factory in the north of England near Newcastle that had lower labour costs than the south. Moreover, the factory was running on three shifts, so we were spreading the overheads compared to single shift operations, so I considered we should be able to be competitive in pricing with our competitors.

The products we were quoting at sensible new prices were winning business. So from this position of knowledge and success, we then reviewed our prices to existing important customers such as Max Factor. There were several brands in the Max Factor stable; one was the Max Factor brand, plus four or five other brands, including Mary Quant and Swedish Formula. When we reviewed our costs and prices to Max Factor, there were some big loss-makers.

Lynne, our sales manager, and I visited the buyer, Jerry W, in Poole, Dorset, to discuss price rises of 12%, 15%, 23% and 30 % on different products and brands. Of course, this appeared to be a bit of a shock to him. I explained these new prices were competitive, and Jerry was welcome to check them out elsewhere. I also said we were improving the quality, the service and on-time deliveries to compensate.

After some weeks of deliberations at Max Factor, we went back to a meeting with Jerry. He told us that the decision had gone up to the Chairman of Max Factor, and he had finally agreed to the price rises requested. Jerry then said to us that he knew we were right and that we were charging too low. He said he was the 'blue-eyed buyer' when he joined Max Factor and had saved the company £250,000 p.a. when he joined.

At the time of the price rise negotiations with Max Factor, we were doing about £85,000 of sales p.a. with them and continually improving our quality and service. By the end of the following year, our sales to them were £900,000, a more than a tenfold increase (although including the various price rises). We had the same experiences with other customers. Raising prices to sensible but competitive levels enables you to invest, achieve efficiencies, improve quality and service, give customers confidence, and grow profitably.

Raising prices does not kill the business as long as the new prices are still competitive, as the buyers will either know they are OK or will check. Also, you must then deliver quality and good service. Of course, the customer (the buyer) will resist all price rises, as that is his job. However, supplier companies cannot survive for long with loss-making products, and buyers know this.

Remember:

1. If prices are too low and unprofitable, a company cannot survive.
2. Industrial customers are (generally) unlikely to trust companies offering very low prices. Their view can be that it will be incompetent, give poor service, and perhaps the supplier won't survive anyway.
3. Suppliers must monitor costs and set profitable prices that will still win business. Cost increases in materials must be considered for price increases unless offset by production or volume efficiencies.

If a buyer can achieve low prices with a supplier and know the prices of other suppliers, they will generally keep with the low price supplier to save some money. But they will most certainly maintain supply from other suppliers at higher prices. This is demonstrated by the examples mentioned, such as the Max Factor cosmetics company.

With sensible margins, a company can invest in improving efficiencies, especially in manufacturing. For instance, after initially raising prices and some ongoing improvements and investments, we could be more competitive with our pricing and begin to quote lower prices for volumes after a year or two.

One further thought on Max Factor. Proctor and Gamble later took over the company, and our USA operation made mascara packs for Max Factor in the USA, while we remained manufacturing in the UK for P&G Europe. We were asked in the UK to quote for a redesign of the Max Factor brand mascara packs that Geka USA was making. I was not told of the reasons behind this at the time and did not find out till later that Max Factor was investigating a global strategy. They were looking at how the three groups of packs in the colour cosmetics range, lipsticks, compacts and mascaras, could be made as separate product groups in the three regions of the USA, Europe, and Japan.

I was concerned about quoting without knowing the exact prices of the Max Factor packs made by Geka in the USA. It is essential not to undercut your own business, even if products are manufactured elsewhere. We reviewed our existing products and prices with Max Factor, considered the USA production facilities, and that pricing could be similar to our UK prices. We then aimed at prices for the new packs a bit higher than we might typically quote to avoid undercutting the USA prices.

We then visited Max Factor with the quotations. After the initial pleasantries and some general business discussion, the moment came to present the written quotes for the pack redesign. After reviewing them for a bit, the lady buyer must have considered that we would not want to undercut the Geka USA prices, and she said to us, "I don't want any silly prices from you, or I won't trust you in the future! Go away and review those prices". That was a bit of a tough 'put you down.'

I checked with the director in Germany on the exact USA prices, and these looked to be sensible prices from the UK point of view. We rechecked our costings and added freight costs for shipping mascaras from the USA to the UK and Europe. Our new quotation was slightly higher than the USA prices allowing for exchange rates but marginally lower than our first submissions. The revised prices were then re-submitted: we heard nothing more for a long time.

Some months later, P&G/Max Factor had decided to redesign the packs for their Max Factor colour cosmetics brand, including mascaras. They had also been looking at restructuring the global supply side, and we were informed that the mascaras would be made in Europe. We had an important meeting with Max Factor in the UK, including the Geka Germany Managing Director and the Development Director.

The meeting outcome was that we later received a lovely letter from P&G awarding us the redesign mascara business. However, part of the awarding of the business was that Max Factor required the packs to be made in Germany, in line with their new worldwide manufacturing plan. The lipsticks and the powder compacts would be made separately in Japan and the USA.

The prices agreed were as the previously quoted revised prices and did not undercut the Geka USA prices. Our general manager in the USA, Wolfgang, had lost the business and was convinced we had won the contract by undercutting his prices. He was furious with me. However, we had not undercut the USA prices. It was a Proctor and Gamble/Max Factor strategic position for efficient supply and not only a pricing issue. Sometimes, there are political situations within companies that can complicate what happens.

A similar situation on intercompany pricing, but with a different outcome, occurred at Metal Box Ltd. During the 1970s, motor car engine oil was sold in metal one-pint cans at petrol stations. The product manager at the Metal Box Composite Products factory thought it would be a good idea to sell composite cans for motor oil to the big oil companies. (A composite can is a spiral wound cardboard tube with metal ends.) For motor oil, it would have a plastic laminate film coating inside and use the metal ends with the easy-peel opening strip that the existing metal cans had. The composite cans

> were proposed to the oil companies and were offered at a lower price than the metal cans. The result was that the oil companies said they wanted to keep the metal cans, but the price had to be reduced to the price offered for the composite prices, which is what happened.

That was a bit of a disaster, and I thought of that situation when quoting Max Factor. We did not want to fall into that trap of cutting prices and margins against each other's manufacturing sites just because I was unaware of the Max Factor global strategy.

As I've emphasised, it is pretty apparent that customers want reliable service and products conforming to quality standards. Nowadays, it is even more important than years ago, especially with Just-In-Time (JIT) deliveries and reduced stockholdings. The trend towards JIT and reducing the number of suppliers was gathering pace. For instance, Noxell and its Cover Girl brand, also taken over by Proctor and Gamble and Max Factor products, had stocks down to 7 to 10 days. Hence, there is not much wiggle room for any faulty products or supply delays.

This leads me to the comments made to me by the Revlon USA Vice President of Purchasing, Steve Kuppe. We were supplying Revlon USA with a dual pack (a double-ended lip gloss pack) for trialling a new product. Sales were going well, and we wanted to know the future for this new product and what sort of planning we should do. I called John, the Revlon Development Director in New York, and he assured me that the product was selling through the stores and that Revlon was not just shipping to stores and filling the 'pipeline'.

After that call, I was asked to visit Steve Kuppe at Revlon in New Jersey, USA. From the pre-meeting correspondence and my phone call with the development director, I thought I was going to a meeting with Steve to discuss a possible order for $1.0 million; obviously a massive order, so very exciting.

After the usual discussions, Steve said to me, "If I give you the order, the call-offs have to be on time. If you have any delays in shipments, I will cancel the order." I told him, "that's OK, we will deliver on time". By now, I had complete faith in the management and abilities in our factory. Planning and purchasing were excellent; production was efficient with reliable machines and planned maintenance, and the corresponding good quality systems supported the efficient production.

Deliveries were to be shipped to the Revlon manufacturing plant in Phoenix, Arizona, so quite a long way from Newcastle, England. And, if I recall, a 5-hour flight for me even from New York to Phoenix.

About two weeks after my return to the UK, our sales office supervisor came into my office and said, "I thought you would like to see this." It was an order from Revlon USA with lots of pages of the components to make up the complete colour cosmetics packs. The order was not totalled, so, excitedly, I set about adding it up myself. After about six pages of components, the total order value came to $4.8million. Wow! The order was a bit of a shock as I was anticipating we would be getting 'only' a $1.0m order. Only!

Upon receiving the order, we realised that we did not have the capacity. We called an urgent management meeting to discuss what we could and should do. Yes, we could manage a $1.0m order, but not a $4.8m order! It turned out to be an order for about 18 months of production to be followed later with repeat orders as it became a standard colour cosmetics product in the Revlon range.

Ian flew down from Newcastle, and the meeting agenda was distributed beforehand so people could be prepared to discuss the following:

1. Can we make those quantities and deliveries, or do we decline such a large order?
2. Should we offer to make half the quantity and let another supplier do the other half with our pack design?

I was understandably concerned, but Ian revealed his plan to supply the products on time during our round the table discussion. After much debate, it was agreed we should accept the order in its entirety. Ian's plan was:

- Rent a neighbouring factory unit and transfer the mascara brush-making machines freeing up the room in our factory to undertake the Revlon work.

- Put some injection moulding tools of other products out to subcontractors in England.
- Send some injection moulding tools to Geka in Germany for them to make more components for us.
- In addition, based on Revlon's assurances of demand for their product, we decided to build a new factory unit of 10,000 square feet onto our existing factory.
- Upon completing the new factory, transfer the outside work back in-house.

As you can imagine, there was a lot of discussion about the possible risks. The plan was agreed upon: we would accept the whole order. The implementation of outsourcing and relocating some production to another factory unit began immediately, and it all went (relatively!) smoothly.

The result was that all the call-off orders to Revlon were delivered on time, and we delivered on time to all our other customers, honouring all our delivery promises.

In the meantime, a new 10,000-square-foot factory unit was designed, planning permission obtained, and financing organised. The additional factory unit was built in nine months, and all the outsourced production was brought back in-house, cutting costs and improving margins.

We achieved a 100% increase in sales over one year, built a new factory unit, and invested in new machinery. The company expansion put us in a UK-published engineering magazine as the '15th fastest growing plastics and engineering company in the UK over three years.'

There needs to be more than just a sufficient number of visits to customers to increase sales. In fact, making visits rather than just relying on emails and phone calls is very important to achieve good personal contacts. This also applies to departments other than sales.

Visits And Contact With Customers

The Metal Box company had a strong record of looking after its customers. On the occasion of the Divisional Sales and Marketing conference, one of the topics was the importance of the need to reinforce customer care. Dick Addison, the divisional manager, gave us all a tie pin at the end of the conference. On it were the letters:

YCDBSOYA, which stands for: **You Can't Do Business Sitting On Your Arse.**

Over the years, I have occasionally worn this tie pin on the lapel of my jacket when seeing new people or new prospects. It is a great icebreaker as it brings a laugh after they ask you what it means! I've recalled a couple of good examples of the results possible by not sitting on our backsides. One example goes back a long time, so the message of 'visiting is best' came early in my career.

Before working for Metal Box, I was assistant to the marketing manager of a large American international company which makes valves and fittings for the water, gas and oil industries.

In London, burst water mains were regular, causing flooded streets and traffic disruptions. They were due to a weakness in the valves the water utility company was using. Our company had developed valves that could save them a lot of 'flood problems' and therefore costs and damage to their reputation. (Selling benefits). My boss spent about six months writing backwards and forwards to the chief engineer at the water utility company proposing our superior valves. There did not seem to be any progress, but eventually, the engineer agreed to a meeting, and we both went along to meet him. My boss was then able to explain face-to-face what we were offering and the benefits, rather than just sending literature and drawings. The chief engineer finally understood. He agreed he would instigate the purchasing of our valves and start using them quickly. Maybe we could have achieved that result about six months earlier? We applied YCDSOYA without realising, as it was later, at Metal Box, that I learnt the acronym.

The Geka team had close contact with Rimmel Purchasing in Kent, but we did not see the marketing people very often, so I arranged to go to London to meet with Sandra in marketing. We were chatting about business, and I noticed a sample mascara pack on the cabinet behind her desk. I asked if it was something they were looking into. Sandra passed me the pack, saying "Yes, it is something we are interested in, but is not a pack that you make is it?" I said we didn't, but I was intrigued and asked her about the quantities they would need. The conversation then turned interesting! They were looking for 400 000 a year. I reminded her that we had the upper part, a cap/rod/brush like that, but not the bottle. Then told her we could tool up for the bottle for free and make that pack for them.

"OK", Sandra said. "You can have it. Now let's discuss the price." That was amazing, mainly because we would not have obtained that order if I had not arranged that meeting.

Another significant example of a similar situation was trying to obtain a patent in the USA. Correspondence seemed to be going back and forth between the patent agents, the USA Patent Office and me. The USA government patent officer continually presented copies and drawings of other patents which bore no resemblance to our application designs! Not wishing to carry on with the slow progress and leave it for too long, I arranged via our UK patent agent for the American patent agent and me to visit the American patent officer at the USA patent office. The purpose was to provide him with clarification on our design and discuss his objections. The outcome was that he agreed to grant the patent with a bit of elucidation. I cover this in more detail in Chapter Ten: Patents And Intellectual Property Rights (IPR).

Methodology
How To Boost Performance

Two key lessons apply to YCDBSOYA (you can't do (the best) business sitting on your arse).

1. It is crucial to visit customers and build a relationship. Visits build rapport which can make doing business much smoother. If there is a problem, it can be solved more amicably, further forging a good relationship.

2. The second point is that visits for face-to-face meetings enable other opportunities to win more sales!

Remember that face-to-face doesn't always mean being in the same room (although that will always be the ideal scenario). You could also consider Skype, Zoom or Microsoft Teams calls. On many occasions, they will be more effective than an emailing...but still not as good as being in the exact location as your client or prospect. Ideally, the first proper meeting should be face to face, with follow-up meetings on video calling platforms if a phone call will not suffice. However, be aware that the opportunity to build rapport is almost impossible on a video call. You will have seen this yourself: the body language is not identifiable. The little side conversations that enable each party to get to know each other better are missing, so it is still essential to make some personal visits to customers and suppliers.

So far, much has been covered on prices, service and quality. These aspects include shorter lead times and on-time deliveries. If these aspects are achieved, and relationships are good, more business can be obtained with existing customers and potentially more business in the same market segment. I will cover more on new markets in Chapter Eight: The Marketing Function. However, for now, here is a general list of where you may find new customers to grow the business:

1. Obtain more business with existing customers (increase your share of business with them).
2. Find new customers in your target market segment.
3. Find new market segments for your products.
4. Develop new products for your market segment.
5. Modify existing products or develop new ones for new segments.

Lesson
Use these lessons for improvement:

1. Focus on sales and professional sales skills.

2. Focus on good training for pricing and price negotiations: it is fundamental for a company's success.

3. Know the costs and pricing methods. (See details in Chapter Five)

4. Focus on providing excellent customer service. A 1% improvement can keep a customer.

CHAPTER SUMMARY

From this chapter, you should better understand many aspects of the sales function. Key points are:

1. Get clear costings and set sensibly profitable prices

2. Sell benefits, not just features.

3. Use the SPIN technique to improve meeting skills in face-to-face meetings.

4. Work on improving and achieving top performance for customer service and communications.

5. How to agree or raise prices.

A 1% improvement in performance on each point can add up to an overall BIG increase in performance and results!

Chapter Four

The Production (or Supply Function) and How To Increase Productivity and Save Costs

Key Function Two: how to work in tandem with the Sales Function to win more business at more profitable prices. This chapter focuses on how using specific techniques will increase productivity and improve profits.

General Overview

The production function, or service or supply function, has to work closely with the sales function. The company has to produce its products efficiently and sell them. The two functions must be well managed through good data and good planning. If production or supply gets out of synch with sales requirements, the result can be long lead times, poor customer satisfaction, and probably lower sales and lower profitability. If the sales side is not well driven, there can be a low turnover situation leading to trading losses. The earlier Revlon story illustrates the point of good planning to manage sales and production in combination.

Good production management (product supply) and data generation depend on having a sound IT system and appropriately good software. In the early days of the Geka company turnaround, we had to improve the production planning. Therefore we needed to install a good Manufacturing Resource Planning (MRP) system. The market had to be carefully researched to identify and implement a suitable system.

The new system we obtained worked well for production planning as the main requirement. An MRP system should also have an easy-to-understand cost information system based on the direct costs of production. Unfortunately, after installing the system, we found it had a weakness that none of us realised...until a lot later. The product costing reports covered the cost of material and direct labour for each separate operation to make the product. All the operations for labour and material built up to a final costing report which could be over a few pages. The system did not summarise the total labour and total material costs. This meant that it was time-consuming to add up all the direct labour costs for each production operation and the direct materials total for all the individual operations. These separate totals are essential for calculating sales prices. In addition, the summary totals enable a quick check on production efficiencies to compare different jobs and operators' times where hand work is involved.

This lack of summary totals was not serious for the number of operations in Geka, which manufactured colour cosmetics bottles and packs. But it was very serious in a subsequent company with many more production operations.

LESSON

It is essential to research thoroughly to find an appropriate IT system that works well for all required tasks. The purchase of the IT system and the problems encountered are discussed further in Chapter Seven: IT Systems And Data Management.

Production Improvements

When a company sells products at unprofitable prices, it will not make enough money. Eventually, say in 1-5 years, it will be unable to invest in improving the business. This may mean a lack of investment in modern, more efficient machinery, IT systems, updating premises, recruiting and training to improve employee performance, and marketing the business and products.

> As I mentioned earlier, Geka in the UK had been unprofitable for ten years. One of the first production problems encountered was discovering some worn-out injection moulding tools and the long production time taken to make an order. It transpired that a 16 impression injection moulding tool was only working on seven out of the 16 cavities and 'inserts' which were used to mould the parts. In other words, it was working at less than 50% of its capacity.
>
> Nine out of the 16 inserts had been blanked off because the tool inserts needed repairing. This meant the tool took more than twice as long to make an order, and any order would have been loss-making just on the labour costs for the time taken. We immediately instigated the refurbishment of that tooling. This was the start of the turnaround in production and the drive to increase productivity and efficiency. Prices were raised to sensible and competitive levels to aim for profitability. Once we began tackling the glaring poor state of the tools, we were on the turnaround route and would soon be rocketing along.

When looking at areas for improvement (which can be called 'value stream analysis') in a turnaround situation, it is imperative to look for quick fixes that will save costs, reduce bottlenecks, and generate income.

Opportunity Cost – Opportunity Revenue

There is a major concept in economics termed **'opportunity cost'**. The definition is as follows:

> **'Opportunity costs represent the potential benefits a business misses out on when choosing one alternative over another.**

Because, by definition, they are unseen, opportunity costs can be easily overlooked if one is not careful. Understanding the potential missed opportunities foregone by choosing one investment over another allows for better decision-making.'

To clarify:

- opportunity cost is the benefit that would have been obtained by an option not chosen
- to properly evaluate opportunity costs, the costs and benefits of every option available must be considered and evaluated against the others
- evaluating the different opportunity costs can provide a guide to more profitable decision-making.

However, I find this 'opportunity cost' nomenclature and description a cumbersome way of looking at improvements and investment opportunities. I consider a more appropriate term for everyday use is... **'opportunity revenue' or 'opportunity revenue and benefits.'**

My definition is that *opportunity revenue or benefits result from a decision to achieve the fastest and best results when resources are limited and against other possible projects.*

I have found this a much easier way of explaining it to staff. So, for example, when we looked at investing in repairing the 16 cavity tool mentioned previously, the 'opportunity revenue' against expenditure was very clear and very fast. Also, the opportunity was more significant than any other potential investment at the time. The tool would produce more than twice as fast, and the labour cost per hour was more than halved. The products could be shipped to bring in income faster, and the tool and injection moulding machine could be used for other orders, doubling the output. The 'opportunity revenue' was swift and therefore was the priority before moving to investment in the next 'revenue opportunity.'

My first job when I left college on a graduate intake scheme was being trained and working in the Organisation and Methods Department for a large conglomerate of 19 companies collectively called Simms Motor and Electronics Corporation. The training I received on the department's projects has been instrumental in my success. One task I worked on was introducing 'Critical Path Analysis' for the project management in the Simms Group Research and Development company. They were developing fuel injectors and car engine turbochargers. Interestingly the project timings until then had proved unachievable, but after introducing Critical Path Analysis, (or project management), forecasts became more realistic and, of course, longer than initially estimated. But then, the engineers were better able to manage the development timescales. To be involved in the development and see the turbocharged Land Rover bustling up and down the road on the industrial estate was a satisfying experience! Now from those development times, fuel injection and turbocharging on road cars have long since become a normal situation. Working in the O&M department was a great learning experience for career development and future company management.

Further Production Improvements

To provide more information and examples of improvements at Geka, I have included some of the key areas we worked on at the factory.

As sales started increasing, we needed our first new injection moulding machine. Tony, the injection moulding department manager, advised Ian and me that a fairly small moulding machine to take six impression tools was necessary. The German factory was running similar tools on smallish moulding machines, so accordingly, we ordered a small Arburg machine of 30 tonnes operation. We took the department manager's advice and assurances of the machine's suitability and quality for our output requirements. When the machine had been installed and running for a few weeks, I was with Ian in the moulding department, and the moulding manager said to me, "why did we buy this machine?"

Ian, the factory manager, and I were disappointed by this question. I decided not to get into the implication of what was wrong with the machine's suitability or to get involved at that moment in technical arguments about the size of the machine. So I said to Tony, "because that is what you asked for; Ian and I just signed the cheque".

We didn't hear another word from him! Interestingly, our German colleagues had not said anything about their experience with the suitability of this machine for our type of work. Yet, later, we realised the machine should have been larger and, therefore, more versatile to take our other larger injection moulding tools and achieve faster output.

That was a further lesson: be careful about advice given, especially from internal technical people!

> However, we did buy modern, bigger, faster machines over the following years. On one occasion, the next machine we should purchase was discussed in a managers' meeting. The question we asked was, 'which machine would be best for our type of business? What do we really need?' We went through various manufacturers' machine specifications and compared them with our itemised requirements, and we arrived at one in particular. Tony, our mould shop manager, said, "We can't afford those machines." I replied, "Well, Tony, you tell us which machine we need to maximise production efficiencies and flexibility, and I'll tell you what we can afford and how we finance it".
>
> We then progressed to sensible detailed discussions and analyses of the cost benefits of the different manufacturers' machines. Finally, from that meeting, we focused on buying the large efficient machines that we needed. And productivity was rocketing up. Price was less of an issue than the payback; the efficiencies gained against the cost and timescales for paying for a machine.

Simplifying And Rationalising

Simplifying and rationalising some product ranges and production methods enabled huge gains. One of the most significant changes was that we had 29 injection moulding base tools and various 'inserts' for those tools. Some of the tools were for a range of sizes for a particular plastic component in our cosmetics packs. The item was the simple wiper plug in the neck of a mascara pack used to scrape the excess liquid off the rod that holds the mascara brush or applicator. Some of these smaller volume components were made on four cavity tools (for four moulded components), and there were also six and eight cavity tools...and the odd larger one. It can be understood that small injection moulding tools with a small number of cavities take much longer to mould the components. Lots of tools mean more tool changes that can consume work hours, and too much moulding time is lost. Many tools also require extra maintenance and refurbishment or replacement costs when worn out. And, a lot of tools mean more injection moulding machines are needed to run them to get the output and sales required. All this involves labour time, extra capital costs and ensuing overhead costs.

So at our next Germany/UK conference, I asked, "Why have we got a range of 29 injection moulding base tools all doing a similar job for slightly different sizes of components?" That led to a beneficial discussion, and the outcome was that some weeks later, we had designs for two large 16 impression base tools for just two sizes of the wiper plug covering about 85 to 90% of the requirements of the 29 items. It was straightforward to rationalise other components to fit the bottle packs.

When those new moulding tools had been built, they went onto our new large tonnage efficient injection moulding machines. The productivity gain was 200% to 300% just on output from the bigger tools. In addition, those tools and the injection moulding machine were operating significantly faster than the previous processing time, so our efficiency gain was a remarkable 400% plus...outstanding 'opportunity revenue and benefits.'

METHODOLOGY
How To Boost Performance

Simplifying and rationalising products enables prices to be reduced as well as profits improved. The quality can also be improved and lead times reduced for quicker deliveries. Simplifying can therefore also be a marketing benefit. These improvements can also be achieved with easier production changeovers. So it can be seen that simplifying products can lead to production improvements and support the sales function. Use these four bullet points as a rule of thumb...

1. Simplifying and rationalising products is a major production benefit.

2. It also simplifies production planning and stockholding, making it more efficient.

3. It is a significant profitability improver and efficiency benefit.

4. It is also a major marketing benefit for customers. It helps them save time when preparing orders, reduces stock holding and simplifies the customers' filling lines.

Around the time we were improving our moulding machines and looking for more efficiencies, our Financial Director Roswitha had arranged a meeting with a chap who worked with her on our business accounts. I joined them for a brief chat, and our visitor explained that he also worked on Japanese efficiency techniques in manufacturing. This interested me, so I hired him to go to the factory and see what he could advise.

The reason for sharing this seemingly unrelated fact is to highlight that sometimes, employees can worry about initiatives and change. I called the (new) moulding department manager, Raymond, about hiring the consultant to help find possible improvements in the moulding shop. One of his first comments was, "Aren't I doing a good job?" I assured him he was, "but if we could squeeze even another 1% or 2% of efficiency out of the department by using Japanese manufacturing techniques, we would all benefit and have learnt something new, and it might make your job easier". Raymond was happy with this explanation and embraced the opportunity to learn more.

Kaizen Japanese Techniques

When the consultant went to the factory, he went through the processes using the Kaizen 'Five Whys' technique. Eventually, the result was a massive improvement in the moulding department, but again, some investment was needed. Most of our investments in equipment or machines had a payback of a year or less, and implementing the Kaizen improvements identified was no exception.

I'm sure you're intrigued to know what the consultant found and what we did! Please consider that the following list was implemented many years ago. I expect many companies are now doing similar things. However, it is the techniques and outcomes that are important.

The key Japanese method investigated was SMED, which stands for Single Minute Exchange of Dies and was applied to machines and tool changes, which used to take up to four hours. The 'Five Whys' were asked: why, why, why, why, why – for each step of a task. The results were as follows:

Issue One
On moulding machines, the separate moulding tool for a product used to be bolted on using several bolts around the tool. When removing the moulding tool, four or six bolts had to be unscrewed and taken out to release one side of the tool and the same on the other side. To fit another moulding tool into the machine, the reverse process, replacing and doing up a lot of bolts, was necessary.

Result
The whole operation was reduced to two bolts for each plate on either side of the tool. These bolts were partially undone to release two swivel clamps, one on each side of the mould. The clamps were swivelled, and the tool could then be removed.

Recently, I saw a similar system in a moulding shop that supplies a current customer, so this must now be pretty common).

Issue Two
There are two backing plates, one on each side of the tool, and these fit against the clamping plates in the moulding machine. The backing plates were from different tool makers and had varying thicknesses, which affected how far out the bolts could be released, hindering the insertion of the next tool.

Result
All our tools were then made with backing plates of the same thickness, so all tools went in easily and fast, with the same number of minimum bolt turns.

Issue Three
The moulding machines had various controls and hoses on both sides, which wasted a lot of time going around both sides to detach something or reattach it.

Result
The improvement was to get all the hoses onto a manifold, which meant that multiple actions became only one operation to disconnect and connect up on only one side of a machine.

Other SMED improvements were made, some immediately and some with investment over the following months. I don't wish to bore you with further detail, as I'm sure you can see how effective the processes and results were. However, I *will* share the impressive overall outcome: **the moulding department could change tools with just one person in 30 minutes instead of four hours. Faster if two people were involved.**

At that time in our growth, we changed around 26 tools a week on the moulding machines over the three shifts. The tool changes meant we lost 104 hours of moulding per week. After SMED, the 30-minute tool changes meant we lost only 13 hours a week, saving 91 hours a week on moulding time and the operators' time. An incredible productivity boost.

Another way to look at this is that we saved the equivalent of two shifts per day on a moulding machine, so it saved us from buying another injection moulding machine at, for example, £130,000 at the prices at that time.

Finally, with good modern injection moulding machines and systems, we ran the injection moulding department with 20 machines and just four people per shift. Essentially, one operator looked after five machines. This efficiency helped generate a good gross profit.

Another feature of Kaizen we implemented was Poka-yoke, a Japanese term which translates as **"fail-safe" or "mistake-proofing".** In any business, it is critical to speedily and accurately maintain quality. Poka-yoke helps people and processes work right the first time by introducing techniques that make it impossible to make mistakes.

For us, it transpired as the use of 'go and no-go' jigs and tools used for checking product measurements. These checking jigs save all the time spent measuring with a micrometre.

Everybody at the factory felt the buzz as the changes made improvements and helped us grow. I found it fascinating to see how the changes and enhancements boosted morale. Perhaps because some people's jobs became easier and more productive, job satisfaction improved, and it demonstrated that the company was successful, providing job security.

LESSON

Focus on production efficiency, or supply efficiency and continuous improvement to improve the gross profit and make more money. Think how those multiples of 1% and higher amount improvements increased performance and results.

In the first couple of years at Geka, before we had even got to SMED techniques, we implemented many improvements, refining our customer performance. So we were thrilled to receive a letter from Boots encouraging us to get to a four week lead time. The big question was, 'How do we reduce our lead times down to four weeks?' That would take some planning and investment!

After receiving the letter from Boots, shown in **Fig 8**, I phoned Ian at the factory, and he arranged to fly down for a meeting with the management team immediately. At the meeting, we discussed at length what we needed to do. This involved machinery capacities and outputs, capital investment, planning systems, purchasing systems, raw materials stockholding, people and organisation, and even overtime possibilities. We established the outline plan and the investment required. In combination with our new MRP system, Ian and the production team then set about improving the production planning, further machine efficiency, and materials purchasing had to be sharper, and quality had to be perfect.

Within about two months, we had generally made the improvements, and we achieved the four weeks lead time target for Boots. This is an excellent example of the benefits of the speed and flexibility we were building up. Of course, the factory and process improvements also meant shorter lead times for all customers supported with on-time deliveries.

A further example of the benefit SMED brought us was when a client, Rimmel, asked to visit us at the Newcastle factory – a long trip for them from Ashford in Kent. They said they had a problem with the length of a mascara rod and brush. It was too long, touching the bottom of the mascara bottle and causing the brush to bend. (Some plastics expand when exposed to various chemicals, which was the cause in this case.) They asked if we could make the rods 3 mm shorter to stop this. While our team was in discussion, Raymond, our moulding department manager, went off to the mould shop. Half an hour later, he rejoined the meeting with samples and asked, "Are these the right length?" The Rimmel team was surprised and asked how we did it so quickly. What service and expertise! The tooling for the small product changes for Rimmel was implemented within days, ready for their next production run. Thanks to SMED, we had an impressed customer!

We wanted to tackle other slow production processes and bottlenecks, so the SMED technique was also applied to other departments in the Geka factory to boost productivity. For example, we had a mascara bottle printing machine which printed about 900 to 1000 bottles an hour. When we looked at the machine, we could see that it was cycling relatively slowly, and there was a delay in the middle of the cycle where the carriage had a long slow movement backwards and forwards. We approached the print machine manufacturer and asked for improvements in a new machine to increase output. Some months later, they came up with a design and a proposal. We agreed to buy a machine once it was built, and when it was delivered, the output to print mascara bottles increased to between 2500 and 2800 per hour. So we achieved another productivity increase of 150%. No doubt the machine manufacturer also had the benefit of being able to sell that machine elsewhere, probably to our competitors!

Other essential production improvements were made in the factory, but perhaps an external example gives a better feel for production improvements? Often it is about just looking at production processes which are not efficiently linked up. It is about removing bottlenecks and speeding up processes, and understanding that suitably trained people can undertake detailed flow process and timing analyses.

I will use Boots again. They had a conference for the Managing Directors of suppliers to tell us about their plans and progress. At one stage, we were being shown a production facility. Steve H, the Boots purchasing manager, called me over to look down at the packing line for Soltan suncream bottles. I looked at it for a few moments and said to Steve,

"You know, I can see the line is not very efficient; it's overmanned. The lady folding the carton flaps in on the filled carton is now waiting for the next carton. At the end of the line, another lady is also waiting for a carton. She then sticks on a self-adhesive label and is waiting again. The operator folding in the flaps has time to also put the label on; therefore, the one on the end of the line is not needed, which would save one person out of nine". That would be an 11% increase in productivity. Steve agreed.

To be fair, the overmanning may or may not have been valid because operators sometimes have to go and replenish the cartons or prepare new rolls of labels. Some factories have a person 'running' round the production lines helping with material supplies or giving operators some respite.

Fig 10 shows a certificate recognising our cooperation with Boots. I have not included this to 'showboat'. We started as a small, virtually bankrupt supplier to the cosmetics companies in the UK; this demonstrates what can be achieved if basic principles, methodologies, and lessons are followed.

FIG 10. *Boots Letter of Commendation*

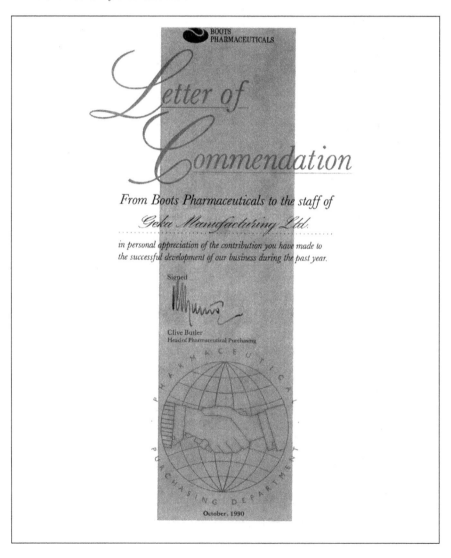

We were delighted with the enormous improvements we experienced using the Kaizen method, and I will share a further example of how it was applied within another company that also needed to improve its efficiency... Porsche. Below are the contents of a note I shared on Porsche car production with my team at Geka:

> Porsche employed a company run by two former Toyota executives to 'unclutter and change the working processes' on its production lines. The result was that the new car was built in 60 per cent of the time it took to build its predecessor.
>
> The consultants were asked to apply themselves to one of motoring's most revered names by Porsche's then-chairman, Dr Wendelin Wiedeking, who believed only " shock treatment would change the minds" of Porsche workers.
>
> The arrival of the Japanese had the desired effect. The Japanese found Porsche's factory at Zuffenhausen was piled high with parts and called it more of a warehouse than a production facility.
>
> One of the first steps was to halve the height of tall shelving to stop workers from having to reach for parts. Then they did away with the shelves. Each worker then had a metal trolley of parts that was wheeled about as jobs were completed.
>
> The number of managers has been reduced by 32 per cent, and the workforce has been cut from 9,000 to 6,500.

I read out this information at a briefing about progress and change. However, I did leave out the paragraph about, 'The number of managers and staff has been reduced!' As we grew, we needed everybody there, and more people were continually being recruited. Reading out this note was to remind the employees of the need for continuous improvement, or even major 'step improvements', both on the shop floor and in the offices to keep the company competitive and successful. Productivity gains were enabling us to win more business and create more jobs.

In order for our people to understand what we were doing and where we were going, we arranged various visits to other factories and Plastics Industry Exhibitions. Ian and I would take the moulding people to see the latest machines and see the processing rates and the high output of various modern machines. Among many efficiency improvements the team witnessed at the exhibitions and visits to companies, I remember they were particularly impressed at the rate that margarine tubs were just pouring out of a machine and along a conveyor. Fast cycling, big machines, bigger injection moulding tools, and excellent efficiency and output were what we needed. This was a fantastic way to open our operatives' minds to changes and improvements.

We arranged coach visits to Nissan Motors and Komatsu, the Japanese crane manufacturer in the North East. Everyone then could see how efficient these companies were and know how important it was for us to improve continually to survive in the future. I dislike the expression, "If it ain't broke, why fix it!" My answer to that is, "If things were not continually improved, we would still be driving around in Ford Model T cars!"

METHODOLOGY
How To Boost Performance

1. Acquire an excellent 'fit for purpose' IT system. This will boost efficiency and performance.

2. Regularly and systematically review processes, equipment and products to update and improve output and efficiencies.

CHAPTER SUMMARY

1. Get a sound IT system for sales and production/ supply management and order processing and ensure the IT system provides detailed and summary costings.

2. Work on optimum 'Opportunity Revenue' opportunities for investment.

3. Rationalise and simplify products as benefits for the company product and supply side and as benefits for customers.

4. Learn and adopt Kaizen techniques and continuous improvement.

Chapter Five

Costing And Pricing: Easy Methods To Achieve Profitable Pricing

This chapter covers how to price products by establishing simplified cost information. We then proceed to 'pitching the price'.

Data management for the all-important gross profit in both per cent and value terms has already been mentioned. But how is good gross profit generated and managed? A basic answer is through attention to good costing and pricing.

In every single company, for every type of product or service, it is imperative to ensure a sufficient gross profit margin in the selling price of products or services. The gross profit margin from every single product contributes to making the gross profit from all the sales. A sufficient gross profit then needs to be made to cover all the overheads and make a profit. Many managers seem to forget the importance of establishing a decent profit margin on an individual product. They then forget or 'have not had the time' to monitor the margin in the future. Costs do not stay constant: inflation, for example.

Many businesses seem to have unprofitable products that they continue to sell without taking any action. The MDs are often unaware that they are selling loss-making products, or they somehow think that the volume helps. Some MDs I have met often believe their low priced product is the 'right price' for the market, and generally, they are wrong. You could imagine they have been timid or had the 'Lopez Treatment' of pressure purchasing.

Several methods can be considered when calculating the selling price. These can be listed with various degrees of requirement as follows:

1. **A standard percentage margin should be applied to each new product.**

This is applied to make an overall profit for the company on the estimated sales.

2. **Every product should have a standard or minimum percentage margin in line with existing products sold.**

This percentage margin is comparable to the margins giving the company its profit. The sales price, of course, has to be acceptable to customers. It may need to be compared with competitors' pricing or the price you can achieve because your product or service and efficiency in customer satisfaction are superior to the competitors.

Generally, determining what customers will pay will soon become apparent if your prices are too high because you will not win sales in enough volume. Best prices can be learned by comparing with the prices of competitive and alternative products.

Competitive prices can occasionally be obtained by asking a third party to get a quotation from a competitor on your behalf. The typical situation where companies sell unprofitable products is because they have not calculated the required margins adequately and are selling products with low margins. I refer you to **Fig 11,** where a minimum or 'standard' margin was not achieved on nearly 50% of products sold by that company. The table has been heavily redacted, but the main coloured column shows the extent of the under-pricing.

FIG 11. GP Underpricing Spreadsheet

Last updated: 02/07/07 — Production department – Product cost / profitability analysis — 30% / 0%

Cust.	code	Description	periods 1	in hours	labour time	Labour Cost 10	labour cost (£)	Material	cost (£)	per unit	Mat cost	Last SP	Gross Profit	cost	Profit	Sales
				0.01	0.00	0.10	0.00	2.83	0.00	2.93	3.54	1.02	-187.25%	£0.00	£0.00	£0.00
				0.01	0.00	0.10	0.00	5.79	0.00	5.89	7.24	3.35	-75.82%	£0.00	£0.00	
				0.03	0.00	0.33	0.00	0.60	0.00	0.63	0.75	0.60	-55.50%	£0.00	£0.00	
				0.03	0.00	0.30	0.00	0.60	0.00	0.90	0.75	0.66	-38.46%	£0.00	£0.00	
				0.10	0.00	1.00	0.00	11.86	0.00	12.86	14.83	10.00	-28.60%	£0.00	£0.00	
				0.03	0.00	0.33	0.00	0.82	0.00	1.15	1.03	1.00	-15.30%	£0.00	£0.00	
				1.00	0.00	10.00	0.00	24.10	0.00	34.10	30.13	30.00	-13.67%	£0.00	£0.00	
				0.03	0.00	0.30	0.00	0.82	0.00	1.12	1.03	1.00	-12.00%	£0.00	£0.00	
				0.17	0.00	1.66	0.00	8.72	0.00	10.38	10.90	10.00	-3.80%	£0.00	£0.00	
				25.66	0.00	256.50	0.00	559.94	0.00	816.44	699.93	795.00	-2.70%	£0.00	£0.00	
				0.01	0.00	0.10	0.00	1.75	0.00	1.85	1.88	1.88	1.60%	£0.00	£0.00	
				2.00	0.00	20.00	0.00	44.43	0.00	64.43	55.54	66.00	2.38%	£0.00	£0.00	
				0.00	0.00	0.00	0.00	17.72	0.00	17.72	22.15	18.20	2.64%	£0.00	£0.00	
				0.50	0.00	5.00	0.00	12.94	0.00	17.94	16.18	18.50	3.03%	£0.00	£0.00	
				1.40	0.00	14.00	0.00	114.43	0.00	128.43	143.04	135.90	5.50%	£0.00	£0.00	
				0.03	0.00	0.33	0.00	13.82	0.00	14.15	17.28	15.00	5.55%	£0.00	£0.00	
				0.67	0.00	6.67	0.00	15.15	0.00	21.82	18.94	23.43	6.87%	£0.00	£0.00	
				0.01	0.00	0.10	0.00	1.75	0.00	1.85	1.99	1.99	7.04%	£0.00	£0.00	
				0.00	0.00	0.00	0.00	25.32	0.00	25.32	31.65	27.50	7.93%	£0.00	£0.00	
				2.00	0.00	20.00	0.00	44.43	0.00	64.43	56.54	70.00	7.96%	£0.00	£0.00	
				1.07	0.00	10.66	0.00	28.61	0.00	39.27	35.76	43.16	9.01%	£0.00	£0.00	
				0.01	0.00	0.10	0.00	0.80	0.00	0.90	1.00	1.00	10.00%	£0.00	£0.00	
				0.10	0.00	1.00	0.00	28.28	0.00	29.28	35.35	33.60	12.86%	£0.00	£0.00	
				0.54	0.00	5.42	0.00	6.76	0.00	12.18	8.45	14.00	13.02%	£0.00	£0.00	
				0.07	0.00	0.66	0.00	0.20	0.00	0.86	0.25	1.00	14.00%	£0.00	£0.00	
				2.00	0.00	20.00	0.00	44.43	0.00	64.43	55.54	75.00	14.09%	£0.00	£0.00	
				2.17	0.00	21.67	0.00	92.75	0.00	114.42	115.94	134.80	15.12%	£0.00	£0.00	
				0.50	0.00	5.00	0.00	7.40	0.00	12.40	9.25	14.65	15.36%	£0.00	£0.00	
				0.01	0.00	0.10	0.00	1.00	0.00	1.10	1.25	1.30	15.38%	£0.00	£0.00	
				0.37	0.00	3.66	0.00	6.39	0.00	10.06	7.99	11.98	16.11%	£0.00	£0.00	
				0.10	0.00	1.00	0.00	1.21	0.00	2.21	1.51	2.65	16.68%	£0.00	£0.00	
				0.50	0.00	5.00	0.00	24.71	0.00	29.71	30.89	35.90	17.24%	£0.00	£0.00	
				2.50	0.00	25.00	0.00	68.25	0.00	93.25	85.31	113.00	17.46%	£0.00	£0.00	
				2.00	0.00	20.00	0.00	57.29	0.00	77.29	71.61	95.00	18.54%	£0.00	£0.00	
				2.00	0.00	20.00	0.00	57.29	0.00	77.29	71.61	95.00	18.64%	£0.00	£0.00	
				0.33	0.00	3.30	0.00	6.66	0.00	9.96	8.33	12.25	18.99%	£0.00	£0.00	
				0.33	0.00	3.30	0.00	6.66	0.00	9.96	8.33	12.25	18.69%	£0.00	£0.00	

3. **A product price has to be set to compete against the competition's prices**.

The price can be set close to reasonably similar products, but volume has to be achieved to make a profit. So a price is set, and then volume is chased. Tesla is a well-known example. It is chasing volume for its cars at a 'sensible target price' for its product. The selling price is around their price and market segment group, so when target volumes have been achieved, the company calculates it will achieve profitability.

4. A unique product can have a price with a good margin applied.

This price will be very profitable for the company. Maybe it is the product itself or a service company providing a special service. Before looking at this type of price-setting requirement in more detail, let us look at how to arrive at the product cost.

The product direct cost consists of...

- the cost of materials
- the cost of direct labour
- the cost of carriage and packing.

This gives the direct cost of goods...production depreciation charges are not included.

The example is what can be shown as a **'clean direct cost'** and is very important in engineering companies or any company where direct labour and materials are used. However, it is also used for a range of other businesses, for example, a pub or bar where there could be too many bar staff for the turnover in sales.

Keeping this measurement 'clean' is essential because it enables management to track the trend over months and years. The clean gross profit figures can clearly show when action needs to be taken if there are deviations.

Some accountants want to include the depreciation for shop floor machinery and other investment in the direct costs. For clarity in the direct costs, the depreciation charge should be in the overheads with other depreciation. Alternatively, it can be shown separately above the overheads depreciation charge. Putting direct cost depreciation below the gross profit line means any additional depreciation charge from other investments will not distort the 'easy to see' trends for production efficiency.

As the depreciation charges reduce and finish, they will, over some time, look as if the gross margin has improved when in fact, it has not. The inclusion of depreciation can also distort a standardised pricing method, as I explain later in the chapter

Different companies and businesses use different ways of setting profit margins.

Pricing Method One: Multiply By A Standard Multiplication Factor

For example, in retail, the multiplication factor is generally two times. Thus, a product bought in, costing £20, is then priced for sale at £40. This times two mark up gives a gross profit margin of 50%, calculated as follows:

Direct cost £20 X 2 = £40 = the selling price (SP)

The gross profit is £20.

The gross profit margin % is calculated as cost divided by SP X 100%. (Or simply click the % button on the calculator.)

The selling price gross profit margin is arrived at as follows:

£20 divided by £40 click % = 50%. This is the cost. Then minus 100 gives a gross profit margin of 50%.

Making the example more difficult...

A retail shop that we know has a mark up of 2.55. So if they buy a product for £23, the SP is £23 X 2.55 = £58.65.

The gross profit margin is therefore:- £23 ÷ £58.65 X 100% = 39.2 Minus 100 = 60.8% gross profit margin.

To achieve a 40% gross profit margin (a useful target to have in mind), the mark up is 1.60. Therefore cost at £23 x 1.6 = £36.8 = Selling Price.

The gross profit is £ 36.8 − £23 = £13.80.

The gross profit margin percentage calculation is £13.80 divided by £23 X 100% = 60. Minus 100, and the gross profit margin is 40%.

In one of its divisions, Racal Electronics, a former big electronics company, used a standard mark up of 2.15 on its range of products. This gave them a gross profit margin of 53 per cent. Companies with different products and competition aspects can require other pricing models, depending on their overheads. For example, companies might spend heavily on advertising or research and development, so have higher overhead costs requiring a greater gross profit per cent.

Pricing Method Two: The 'Gross Margin Percentage Points Method'

This is an alternative way to set prices with the mark-up method. We favoured this method where some flexibility is required for ease of calculating different products for different customers. It allows you to arrive at a gross profit margin percentage more quickly and can be adopted with more confidence than just using the mark-up method. It can be a matter of balancing a small percentage difference to win the business against the risk of going for an unprofitable gross profit margin (GPM).

In the Pricing Method 1 example, 40% GPM on a product costing £13.80 can be arrived at by division as follows:

If a 40% GPM is required, divide £13.80 by 0.6, which is the 60% cost. Therefore £13.80 divided by 0.6 equals a selling price of £23.00.

In manufacturing, care has to be taken with the mark up if there is a very high material content and low labour content. If a standard mark up is at 1.60 to get a 40% GPM, then trying to make 40% GPM on just buying in materials and reselling them does not provide a competitive price. This is because competitors are likely to be cheaper using a lower mark up on bought-in materials. So you can lose the business on your quotation. If you are managing to sell at a higher price for some time, you are leaving yourself open to losing the business to a 'fairer pricing' competitor.

Pricing Method Three: Two-part Mark up

The competition was stronger in a couple of companies I ran, so we had to be more careful with our pricing. We set a mark-up of 1.25 for material and 1.8 for direct labour. The variation in prices between high material content and low labour content, compared to the low material content and higher labour content, could be as much as 5% or 6%. That's quite a difference in looking credible and winning or losing business. However, we already had a small mark up for overheads in the material usage, which accountants recommend. Hence, the 1.25 mark up was higher than it appears but a lot lower than the mark up of 1.8 for labour.

Target Gross Profit Margin For High Volume Orders.

A good target for high volume work was consistently achieving at least a 35% gross profit margin(GPM). The minimum GPM for high volume work for most non-retail companies could be 32% – a mark up of 1.47. To calculate, divide the direct costs by the reciprocal of the desired 32%.

So £23 direct cost ÷ 0.68= £33.82 = the selling price with 32% GPM.

If 40% GPM is required, divide the total direct cost by 0.6. This method used in price-setting quickly gives you the gross profit margin percentage. It is then easy to vary it by just one or two per cent as required. It is a simpler way of GPM percentage calculation than the mark up method if you need to play around with alternative margins when calculating prices.

Why a margin of 32%? When the monthly management accounts are produced, the transport and packing costs need to be included in the direct costs, typically between 1.5 and 2.5 %. Thus you will end up with a gross profit of 30% to cover the overheads.

Pricing Method Four: Percentage Allocations Of Overheads

There was a traditional pricing method whereby all the costs were carefully divided up and added to each product. Cost accountants were employed to calculate the square footage used for a process and its share of the rent, rates, heating, etc. This was a time consuming and cumbersome method of costing to arrive at a sales price.

In the 'old days' (up to the 1960s?), companies were more labour intensive in production and generally had lower overheads. Labour costs were used as the basis for pricing, and then the share of various overhead costs was added. The mark up on the expanded direct labour was used to arrive at a selling price. Progress has enabled more production efficiency with lower numbers of direct operatives and direct labour costs. On the other hand, overhead personnel and costs have increased. For example, there is more marketing, advertising, product development, design, customer service, and research and development. These all make the old product costing method challenging to manage and more inaccurate as a percentage share of all these overheads has to be added to each product.

These detailed costing systems can be unrealistic and can distort the reality of the business: good profitable products are discontinued while unprofitable products are continued. Moreover, the old costing systems take time and resources. That is why pricing methods 1, 2, and 3 are now used. They can provide a sales price to cover all the overheads at a stroke and save a cost accountant (or two) and somebody doing 'work study.' The MRP system should be doing most of the work by providing the direct costs.

Pitching The Price

I used to have a general rule with my sales directors that they sell at a standard for material and labour to achieve 40% GPM. However, the 40% GPM could be reduced to 32% for volume. Any pricing at that area or below to achieve high volume had to be discussed with me. Otherwise, salespeople can be tempted to sell at lower prices...and they do!

I once heard an expression, "You get the results which you incentivise." So commissions on just sales volume can lead to problems. We should not be in the habit of incentivising more sales at the expense of margins and the long term health of the company. Typically that could refer to the salespeople of Lehmann Bros and others selling sub-prime mortgages: pushing turnover and salespeople's commissions. We all know how the huge damage that did...helping cause the banking crisis and slump in 2008.

Too many companies just allow prices and margins to drop, which is the road to administration! If some sales at a lower margin are made as a reasonable objective to bring in volume, then more gross profit in money must be generated to increase the existing gross profit value. The calculated increase in money must also cover any additional overhead people and expenses. Ideally, the extra gross profit revenue coming in should not incur additional overhead costs so that the gross profit revenue generated can fall directly into the net profit.

Perhaps the extra turnover with some lower margin products can be managed with a minimum labour increase and improved efficiencies. In manufacturing, it might help increase production efficiency with improvements in machines and labour utilisation; otherwise, you end up as 'busy fools'. We covered this in Chapter Three: The Sales Function. Of course, retail companies generally run 'Money Off Sales' to dispose of older stock and bring in cash, but this is not the same as selling at silly prices and margins.

After fully evaluating the product costs and working towards the calculated margin needed to cover overheads and profit, there is then the need to win the business. This may be at the price calculated, or you may have to negotiate, and we covered it in Chapter Three, so it may be worth referring back to that chapter for a reminder.

A note on direct labour and materials costs. Some overheads in those direct costs may be calculated into the MRP costing system by your accountant, and we will cover more in the next chapter.

METHODOLOGY
How To Boost Performance

1. It is fundamental for profitable success to conduct proper costings, undertake detailed pricing and have good margins.

2. Costs and prices should be reviewed regularly because of material and labour changes.

3. An error of 1% on your costing can equate to a 3 or 4% difference to your price – either too high or too low.

CHAPTER SUMMARY

1. Four pricing methods were covered. For ease of use, focus on methods 1, 2, or 3 as appropriate and ensure the pricing is consistent and based on a consistent 'clean gross profit' measurement.

2. Establish a minimum gross profit percentage (margin) and do not go below that.

3. Be aware of any overhead allocation in the direct costs that will have a bearing on your target gross profit percentage. Ensure the total of the GP on all products sold can cover the overhead costs.

Chapter Six

Gross Profit Management: What, Why, How

Key Function 3: maximising income from production and pricing. This chapter discusses how not measuring and monitoring gross profit can result in a company's failure.

I have called it a 'function' because it is fundamental to business success. However, generally, gross profit and its management are not very well understood; therefore, I believe it is essential to cover gross profit in more detail to fully understand its importance.

I'll begin with more definitions to provide clarity:

Gross Profit. The general definition is that gross profit tells you the profit in value after deducting the company's cost of goods. (Also referred to as cost of sales.)

Gross Profit Margin. The general definition is that it tells you the profit percentage after deducting the company's cost of goods.

What is gross profit as a measurement? It examines production efficiency by comparing direct production costs, or product supply costs, to the sales income. The measurement should be in both value and a percentage for monitoring purposes.

Gross profit value, or the amount of money made, tells you how much money you are making to cover the overhead costs.

If the company sells only bought-in products or services, the same applies; they need to make sufficient gross profit in money to cover the overheads. The percentage figure enables the company to monitor the trend over current months and compare it to the previous years. If an analysis shows a trend, particularly a downward trend, corrective action must be taken. In some cases, this needs to be done urgently once the gross profit percentage trend is clear, perhaps in just a 3-month timescale allowing for fluctuations.

Gross profit measurement is used to look at total production efficiency and to measure the company's income trend from the sale of all the individual products. The gross profit generated is the amount of money derived from the sales prices of all the individual product margins added together. That sounds basic, but so many companies seem to forget about the margins on individual products.

However the gross profit percentage measurements are not always comparable between companies because **there is no standard definition of Cost of Goods/Cost of Sales.**

The accountancy standard Rule FRS 102 paragraph 13.8 states:

'Reporting entities will also include a systematic allocation of fixed and variable production overheads which they incur in manufacturing overheads from turning raw materials into finished goods.'

For example, some companies may put 5% or 10% on the raw material costs, and therefore it could be more or less according to what the accountant decides. If you mark up the material costs by 25% for pricing purposes, you will already have an element of cost recovery towards the selling price you are calculating.

The same applies to the direct labour wages costs. For example, if an operative is paid £12 per hour, the company might cost the labour at £25 or £50 per hour or more. The result is that the mark up to achieve the selling price can vary depending on how much overhead costs are applied to the direct costs. The main thing for the individual company is to keep the costing consistent so that the trend over time can be adequately monitored. The trend analysis is a measurement of the efficiency being achieved over time.

If one company has a higher gross profit margin than another, maybe only a per cent or two, that company may not be more efficient; they may just have a lower overhead mark up on their direct costs to arrive at a selling price.

Another common situation regarding the definition of cost of goods is that each accountant may put in different or too many cost items, especially for direct production costs. Some even leave out direct wages and just lump all wages and salaries as one sum below the gross profit line in the Profit & Loss account. This, of course, means that the GP shown is not a proper measurement of production efficiency. It is merely the measurement of the difference between the total sales and the cost of materials. In non-manufacturing, this measurement is critical because the goods are usually bought in and then resold. Hence, the gross profit in money terms is what is available to pay all the personnel and the overheads.

However, retail and service companies still need to measure the labour costs of retail shop floor staff in money, the percentage to sales, and the percentage trend.

Why should we focus on gross profit measurement? Because it enables us to understand the company's fundamental performance and its efficiency in producing the products or services. Therefore, it is the basis for the company's success or failure at the net profit level.

The gross profit relating to the amount of money made shows how much has been made to cover all the overheads and to make a profit.

Lesson

1. **When reading the profit and loss account, remember that DOWN to the gross profit line shows how much money you have made. BELOW the gross profit figure shows where you spend it.**

2. **The other significant use of the gross profit figures is to show how the company performs over time. It shows** *where you were, where you are now and where you are going.*

A further important point about the gross profit percentage figure is that it can show if a company is performing poorly before the gross profit line in the accounts or is performing badly after the gross profit percentage.

If a company is unprofitable, the overall problems could lie in the two areas derived from the 'two halves' of the P&L accounts.

1. If the accounts show a low gross profit, the unprofitability causes lie above the GP line. This is the most common cause of problems.
2. If the GP percentage and money are good and the company is unprofitable, the problems lie below the GP line because of excess overhead costs. (However, maybe the planned turnover has not yet been achieved, and it will become profitable?)
3. Quite often, unprofitability is a combination of both 'halves' of the figures in the P&L accounts.

The gross profit layout in the accounts was shown in the previous chapter, and further information is shown in Chapter Eleven: Financial Accounts and Reporting. As a reminder, the gross profit layout is as follows:

> **Total Sales:**
> Less direct Materials or product costs
> Less Production consumables
> Less Direct wages
> Less Transport and Packing
> Gives **Gross Profit £ and %.**

How Does Gross Profit Show A Trend And Even Foretell The Future?

Usually, you can look at the previous year's financial accounts, which will also have the prior previous year's figures, i.e. two years' figures. The trend in percentage terms each for labour and material can be analysed for the last two years and then compared with the current year. If the direct materials per cent compared to the sales income is declining, it can indicate that the sales prices have been reduced or material and direct costs have increased (or a combination of both). If the margin is reduced in the current year to date, then the forecast for the rest of the year is that the gross profit and probably the net profit will be reduced. Therefore the forecast for the following year will likely show a decline unless action is taken.

To be very clear, the decline of income in the gross profit means less and less money is available to cover the remaining costs of salaries and overheads.

What About Direct Labour Costs?

If the trend is increasing in percentage terms, say direct wages were 15% two years ago, and now they are 18 %, what are the reasons, and what should be done? Here are a few 'possible' reasons:

- sales prices have been forced down by competitors who have more efficient production
- sales are down so that the labour is not producing enough output and that the production function is now overmanned
- there is too much inefficient production and overtime costs
- maybe there were wage rises to keep the operatives.

So, it is possible to see the trend, and if action is not taken to make improvements in the current year, there will be a poorer performance than the previous year. The following year's results could also be worse, whether manufacturing, a service company, or a product reseller.

Regarding Trends And The Future.

Fig 12 shows the Thomas Cook Travel Company's retail travel operation trend. The 5-year trend in gross profit to 2018 shows annual declining results with apparently insufficient or no corrective action being achieved. The lack of action against a clear declining trend resulted in the failure of the company. This chart shows the importance of monitoring GP in large *and* smaller companies. The chart powerfully highlights the need to monitor the gross profit and take urgent action.

FIG 12. T.Cook's GP Trend to Overheads

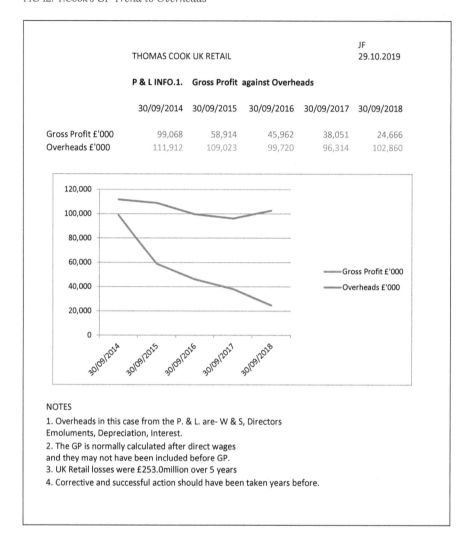

NOTES
1. Overheads in this case from the P. & L. are- W & S, Directors Emoluments, Depreciation, Interest.
2. The GP is normally calculated after direct wages and they may not have been included before GP.
3. UK Retail losses were £253.0million over 5 years
4. Corrective and successful action should have been taken years before.

Fig 13 shows the continuing decline in gross profit percentage as the sales declined in percentage terms. The sales income and the gross profit were dropping every year for five years. There is no indication of significant corrective action to improve gross profit. However, in Fig 12, we can see some reduction in overheads in 2017, but then an increase in 2018.

FIG 13. T.Cook's GP Trend to Sales

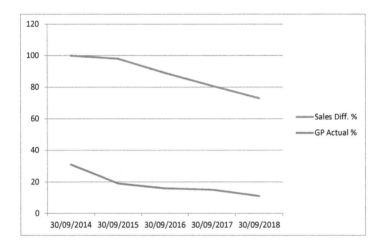

Fig 13

THOMAS COOK UK RETAIL   JF29.10.2019
P & L INFO
Percentage changes from 2014 for Sales, versus actual GP

Sales £'000	317,059	310,903	282,311	257,777	232,005
	30/09/2014	30/09/2015	30/09/2016	30/09/2017	30/09/2018
Sales Diff. %	100	98	89	81	73
GP Actual %	31	19	16	15	11

NOTES

1. Sales declined by 27% from 2014.

2. GP percent of 30/31 % should have been maintained and overheads reduced.

3.The drop in GP from 31% to 11% over five years is a 20 points difference. This 20% GP on Sales is a reduction of £46.4m on GP, on sales of £232.0m in 2018, let alone the loss in GP over the previous 4 years.

4. Very few, if any, companies can survive with a GP of 20% and less; T. Cook retail did not.

5. Corrective action should have been taken years ago. Why was it not? Or not successful?

Lesson

The question of 'how does the measurement of GP foretell the future' is clearly shown in these charts with the annual decline into bankruptcy of Thomas Cook, and I believe we can take the two key lessons below from Thomas Cook's experience.

Thomas Cook's gross profit trends are also covered in further detail in Chapter Twelve: Management And Percentages Management.

Lesson One: How To Maximise The Money At The Gross Profit Line Of The P&L Accounts

1. Regarding the direct costs and material usage percentages, these figures are compared to the sales income, achieved by careful and considered pricing of the products to be sold. 2. In addition, the material usage, or supply usage, has to be managed by good purchasing and supply efficiencies. In Thomas Cook's case, they probably needed to better manage both the supply and sales prices, direct people numbers, and office/overhead costs. These charts are just for their Retail business and do not include the airline and hotel arms.

To maintain gross profit income, the margins on all products must be regularly reviewed. As shown in Figs 12 and 13, such results are surprisingly common (as mentioned earlier).

It is important to ensure that any analysis of product and customer sales margins is ranked with the results from worst to best. The poor performers will then catch your and everyone else's attention.

Other Direct Material Costs

The clear presentation of direct costs enables management to identify possibilities for good savings. At our engineering company, which manufactured stainless steel assemblies, we used thousands of pounds a month of cutting tools used in the milling machines. It was too involved to cost the cutting tools for each job because they were not always worn out and could be used on the next job. We put a percentage cost in for cutting tools depending on the job hours on the machines.

The key aspect of the cutting tools is that we worked on the accounts to show this cost separately in the monthly P&L accounts below the material usage. When we had separated out the 'general other costs' included in the figures, it was surprising to see the high cost of cutting tools.

It is said, 'If you can't measure it, you cannot improve it'. So we looked at each project concerning the life of the tools from various suppliers. We evaluated the cutting speeds and the length of life of different cutting tools from several manufacturers. Some tools were more expensive, but they were more efficient. After evaluation, we decided to purchase the more expensive tools as they saved costs by cutting faster and lasting longer. The net gain was to cut costs by some £30,000 to £40,000 p.a. and improve output. The increase in gross profit margin was two per cent, a very beneficial improvement. Previously at that company, there were also a lot of costs simply lumped in together by the accountant as 'other direct costs', which correctly included oils for lubricating the cutting of steel. But we also found sundries like toilet rolls, light bulbs and similar odd items were lumped into other direct costs. When they were split out, we could see where improvements could be made and which costs should actually be in the overheads. Since we are looking at data and its management, I must emphasise that the same principles apply to large and small companies. And the large companies don't always show important information clearly, so it cannot be analysed for them to manage the company efficiently.

Lesson Two: Clean Gross Profit

The 'clean Gross Profit ' indicates whether other areas can be improved. It provides clear information for management to make cost savings and efficiency improvements.

Manufacturing Depreciation Charge

To reiterate: a depreciation charge on production can distort the gross profit percentage trend at the monthly reporting stage of the cost of goods. The depreciation charge adds no beneficial information, especially if the company grows fast and continually invests.

Preferably, the depreciation total should be towards the bottom of the P&L. In that position, the depreciation charge can be quickly noticed and added to the net profit to show the 'Funds Generated'. The funds generated are the net profit and the depreciation charge added together.

I have frequently had to explain to SME clients that depreciation is, in effect, a 'savings pot'. This means allocating the money into the 'savings pot' called depreciation, which reduces the net profit. If there is no profit, the depreciation account is still in the accounts as a 'charge' or a 'savings pot' because no money is actually spent. Adding the depreciation back in at the end of the P&L can be encouraging during low sales months and holiday times if looking for 'funds generated' for future payments to creditors.

An example of the depreciation charge is as follows. A company spends £50,000 on, for example, a machine, computers, or premises refurbishment. The £50,000 may be spent out of cash or funded in other ways. If the company depreciates or gradually 'writes off' the value of the investment over five years, then £10,000 per annum is entered into the depreciation account in the P&L. In the Balance Sheet, the investment of £50,000 is added to the Tangible Assets sum. This figure is then written down as £10,000 a year. After five years, the asset disappears off the balance sheet, and the annual 'charge' of £10,000 is no longer entered into the depreciation account in the P&L. Showing production depreciation as a cost of goods does not help in analysing trends. Moreover, it can distort the pricing model of 'mark up' on the 'cost of goods'

I have mentioned that it is not helpful putting depreciation in the cost of goods, but of course, some companies do. Therefore their GP may be less than yours if you check your competitors through their accounts in UK Companies House. Consequently, it could be that they appear less efficient in production than you because they are putting more costs into cost of goods. Likewise, if you look at competitors who appear more efficient, there may be different cost allocations.

Remember that there is no standard definition of cost of goods/cost of sales in the accountancy rule book.

METHODOLOGY
How To Boost Performance

1. Thomas Cook's demise dramatically shows the importance of monitoring and managing the gross profit per cent and value, or amount of money coming in to cover the overheads. Just think that every 1% drop in GP on Cook's £300m of sales was a loss of £3m gross profit towards covering overheads.

2. The fundamental importance of maintaining typically around 32% to 40 % gross profit has been covered previously. This critical management aspect generally applies to nearly all Small and Medium Size Enterprise companies: that's 90% of companies in the UK! So around 5.0m companies...of which 300,000 are classed as manufacturing. This manufacturing sector is larger when companies of 250 employees and more are included.

3. For larger companies, there are always exceptions to the general observation that SMEs aim for 40% GP. The significant exceptions are the giant multinational companies. Because of huge sales that cover the overhead costs, their accounts usually show thy operate with a GP of 20% and even less. Automotive manufacturing companies and supermarket chains are examples. Thomas Cook (on the retail side) used to have a GP of 31% in 2014 and then allowed it to drop to 11%. Maybe if it had cut its overheads, as just one aspect of control, it could have survived on just 20% GP?

4. The establishment and understanding of Clean Gross Profit are fundamental to business success and must be properly monitored and managed. It should be clear from the previous sections that

to run a company successfully, gross profit management is of
fundamental importance.

5. Follow this recommended cost of goods format to provide a basis for
easier and more successful company management:

Action

A team can be set up to oversee the current gross profit performance and
establish ongoing plans concerning the gross profit forecasts. The team
could be the MD/CEO, Production Director, Sales Director, and Finance
Director. The team would meet every three months to review in detail
what does not get reviewed in the regular monthly Board or Management
Meetings. The agenda would include the following:

1. The margins per customer and per product from the sales director.
2. The customer and product costings from the production or operations
    director.
3. The gross profit trend and forecast trend from the finance director.
4. Forecast cash flow with investment plans by the finance director.
5. Overview of the reports; the agreed action requirements and direction
    for plans and timings by the CEO/MD.

Result

Establishing a top team brings gross profit management into a 'function'
that can be diligently managed to drive company success. (I have called Gross
Profit Management a function, although it is not actually a department.)

CHAPTER SUMMARY

1.   Gross profit measurement should be with a 'clean gross profit' on direct costs. Follow the recommended format for the layout of GP and direct costs in the accounts.

2.   There is no legal definition in the UK of Gross Profit. Gross profit figures (if consistently 'clean') tell you where you were – where you are – and where you are going. Every 1% loss in GP value can soon have a devastating effect on a company's performance.

3.   Ensure the gross profit is clearly set out every month. If necessary senior managers need to review and take action.

Chapter Seven
IT Systems And Data Management

Key Function Four: avoiding a basic weakness in an IT system. This chapter covers how getting a comprehensive software system is essential to prevent any significant problems in costing, pricing and stock control.

To improve the production planning at Geka, we needed to install a good MRP (Manufacturing Resource Planning) system. The Manufacturing Resource Planning (MRP) system was referred to in Chapter Five, but we will now explore it more deeply. Note: another term for MRP is ERP, Enterprise Resource Planning.

We employed an experienced, knowledgeable consultant, Ivor, to help us find a good system and help us define our requirements: manufacturing planning, stock management, accounts, email, order processing, sales processing, and, most importantly, a costing system. He advised that, at that time, we would not find a suitable off-the-shelf system at a reasonable cost...perhaps we could achieve 90-95% of our requirements. A list of providers was compiled, which we whittled down to five. Then Ivor, Ian Stavert, Roswitha and I visited the suppliers. We also saw a couple of customers to obtain user viewpoints.

One of the suitable companies identified had a good system but was a relatively small company in the south of England, 300 miles from Newcastle, so we discounted that one based on distance and service aspects. Another good supplier had a manufacturing customer in Gateshead, near Newcastle, so we all visited with our production planner. She went through the system with their planner and was satisfied with the performance.

We agreed that this MRP supplier and system matched most of our requirements, so we decided on that company. However, Roswitha preferred another accounts system, so we chose to have a separate accounts package 'bolted on', which worked well after installation.

The MRP system worked well for production planning as the main requirement. Another key requirement was to have a good cost information system. However, shortly after installing the system, we found it had an application weakness. The product costing reports for a single product showed the cost of material and cost of labour for every single operation in the manufacturing cycle on a line-by-line basis. All the separate functions for labour and material built up to a final costing report listed over several pages, with a total cost shown on the last page. Ideally, we only needed the total labour and total material cost – shown separately, and then with the total of the two costs together; just three lines on one 'output' on the computer screen or printout.

However, as it was, if we wanted to know in one figure the total material cost for a product, we had to plough through a few pages, whether on screen or as a hard copy and add up the totals from each individual operation.

When the total product cost with separate costs for labour and materials can be shown, it is extremely useful and time-saving for analysing production efficiency and pricing. For example, if the analysis indicates that the total material costs and total labour costs vary between production runs or between similar products, the individual totals of labour and material costs can be investigated to look where improvements could be made.

Also, with a summary total, costs can quickly be found when quoting prices for that or similar products. Fortunately, there were not too many operations in the production of Geka products; but for some products, there were undoubtedly a few pages to look at for all the operations! Typically there could be eight operations covering two of three pages of printout. The failure of the system to provide the subtotals also meant that product pricing took us longer, which wasted time.

The MRP system in Geka was installed with a very user-friendly coding system; devised by our product development engineer, Colin. It enabled us to identify a product by its alphanumerical code. And we could look at the sum of individual components on total manufactured quantities. This information could be compared to machine utilisation and capacities for different products. It also could show any machine bottlenecks in the next year's production budget by showing if volumes exceeded the capacities of specific items made on specific machines. We could easily do 'far forward' production planning using Colin's alphanumerical coding system. Each product code included three-letter abbreviations for the product name and the numerical code for the individual item. Having a product code for groups of products meant it was possible to look at the order book and align sales forecasts to available machine capacities.

One of the excellent features of the selected MRP system was when there was a material price rise. When entered into the system, the price increase was updated for every product on the computer. The same applied when the wages were increased: the hourly rates on labour costs per product could be quickly updated on all products. I recognise this is all regular stuff today compared to some years ago, but the information on requirements might help when looking for a new system today or an upgrade.

I think the MRP company must have been subsequently taken over as I considered using them to replace the MRP system for an engineering company I worked with in 2015. The MRP system in the engineering company had the same flaw of not showing total labour and material costs separately per product. In that company, there were labour-intensive products: one product took over 200 operations to produce, so if we wanted to check the production costs, there could be up to 50 pages to review. It was difficult to add up on the computer screen and write figures down by hand, and a multipage hard copy was often needed to see where production variations occurred. Needless to say, costings had not been reviewed because it was too laborious and time-consuming, so many products were being sold at a loss. Unfortunately, the former MRP company no longer existed, so I had to look elsewhere.

Finding a solution for that engineering company was essential. It was laborious to see overall variations in the production of products and then drill down into specific operations to find out what variations and possible inefficiencies were occurring. The inefficiencies we found ranged from high material costs, not fully trained employees who take longer than planned in manual operations, difficulties with machines needing renewal or servicing, to finding out about downtime for machine repairs or materials not available. We made many products a month with multiple operations, so it was time-consuming. Consequently, it was not done.

As mentioned in the previous chapter, some products to the main customer had not had a price rise for nine years. We might think, 'how dumb can you get', but the MRP system was a significant problem. The MRP supplier to the engineering company said they could adjust the software to enable the individual product costings per operation to be totalled. Their customer sales engineer ran some tests and fixes, telling us it was "All done!" – but after he left, it still had errors in the output. His changes also affected the results by adding some total labour costs to the monthly report's total production material usage figures. We tried hard to get the supplier's engineer to come back to fix the problem, but the MRP company said they did not want to service that software anymore and that we should buy a new system from them. And rather than come back to fix what they had done, they wanted to charge another £800 per day, with the real possibility he would not revisit us for many weeks! This is the sort of thing that can kill both a company and their supplier. Perhaps the problem was not necessarily that the MRP software needed updating; instead, maybe it was the engineer's programming skills? He could have come back quickly and put it back to how it was. Enough said.

To illustrate the difficulty described, **Fig 14** is the cost of goods monthly printout summary for labour and materials in 2015. After the engineer left, you can see that the labour and material figures went haywire. The highlighted area clearly shows that the labour usage figures were going into the material content from July onwards and that the figures were incorrect.

FIG 14. *MRP Problem*

MRP: Copy of Cost of Goods Screenshot
IT Problem of System and Supplier Support

Month	Invoice cost £	Material cost	Material %	Labour cost	Labour %	Total Sales £
JAN	135,094	41,966	20.05	85,464	40.83	209,313
FEB	102,065	32,002	15.69	65,587	32.16	203,958
MAR	125,013	42,383	23.66	74,664	41.69	179,103
APR	93,392	24,225	15.81	66,746	42.91	153,231
MAY	81,536	24,183	18.38	51,395	39.07	131,552
JUN	130,194	33,647	17.62	85,097	34.55	191,003
JUL	117,777	89,665	49.84	24,750	13.76	179,917
AUG	77,808	58,406	45.45	13,927	10.84	128,512
SEP	121,786	85,091	42.87	36,995	18.64	198,490
OCT	133,331	95,257	46.64	26,311	12.88	204,238
NOV	84,464	65,033	43.38	20,826	13.89	149,919
DEC	72,321	48,850	41.98	17,447	14.99	116,377
TOTALS	1,276,789	640,714	31.32	568,215	27.78	2,045,618

Note: The highlighted area shows the incorrect transfer by the IT system of a high proportion of the labour costs to the material costs.

After the problematic update, it was not an easy task to use this MRP system to find out the main production costs. Then when the sales engineer screwed it up, what chance had we of looking at costs and margins to review production efficiency and look at costings for pricing purposes?

A company needs to know its monthly material usage, whether this is calculated manually or by the MRP system or another IT programme. The information is then used in the monthly management accounts; anomalies and trends can be identified, and any action taken as necessary.

The direct costs for the monthly management reports could be found in the actual wages paid out. The material usage had to be calculated more approximately. Having to do regular stock takes and adjustments is no way to run a company efficiently when an IT system is meant to help stock control.

There were other inefficiencies too, and I will share one further example. The technical director had to load in all the Bills of Material (BOMs) to see the costs before determining a price for a sales quotation. That was all right until a quote was not accepted. Then, all the BOMs had to be erased; otherwise, they built up and clogged the system. If you have many operations for a product and are doing quite a few quotes per week, then a lot of time was wasted removing the BOMs.

An inadequate system can result in significant inefficiencies in the company's operations, higher costs, loss of profit and momentum, and incorrect prices. When I spoke to the Technical Director about why they first bought the system, he said, "Because it was the least expensive". A terrible mistake, I thought! Especially as the service left much to be desired.

That MRP company was, I understand, subsequently taken over, and the new owner has said that the system has been updated and that it can summarise the costs of multi operations. I recently found about 1000 Manufacturing Resource Planning and Enterprise Resource Planning systems listed under a search website. So plenty to choose from, and hopefully, get the most appropriate system for your company.

LESSON

1. Buy an MRP system that summarises the total cost of labour and material for each product on ONE sheet of paper and is separated into three lines: Total material, Total Labour and Grand Total.

2. This is essential for multi-operation products. It is also very important to ensure that the MRP system is the best for all company activities. Otherwise, you could regret it for years, and maybe the company will not survive. The MRP system is the mainstay in production planning costs and pricing and the integration with the sales and the accounts.

3. Remember: 1% or more improvement in the system can be the winning factor for time-saving efficiency and extra profit.

Further demonstrating the benefits of using an MRP system for planning and data provision, the MRP system at Geka enabled us (with just two people planning and two in purchasing) to achieve an £8 million turnover a year; the current 2020 sales value would be approximately £12 million, so we were able to run a lean operation in the overheads and at the same time be efficient with quick turnaround of orders.

As with many other manufacturing companies, multiple operations were needed to produce all the components for one product. The MRP system does the material planning and can plan numerous production operations. However, this can be complicated to operate. The system we had could do 'Rough cut planning', which the factory tended to use. Then the detailed operations on different machines could be worked out manually on a planning board, which everyone could easily see. I encountered some substantial companies which also worked in this way.

The established production times for each product are kept in a database for timings when planning the machine loadings. That means the labour time and material costs for each operation need to be monitored and kept up to date. If a new product has not been made, the team is brought in to discuss and assess production processes and timings. If any manual operations are required, manual tests were carried out, and appropriate timings were used for the costings. Then if production for a new product order commences, the actual timings and costs can be reviewed against the quotation. Any deviations in production cost compared to the quote can then be compared and worked on to be improved where possible.

Chapter Four covered the requirement that accurate costs are critical for the sales department to set profitable and competitive prices. Salespeople must know the costs to set accurate prices which they will not go below. If the costing is sloppy and inaccurate, the salesperson can sell at what they believe is a good margin, only for the product to be loss-making. I have found several companies with 'sloppy costing', so I conclude it is relatively common. Similarly, I have encountered companies where the MD does his costing by guesswork on the back of an envelope or scrap of paper, then the cost inevitably ends up being incorrect, and too low a price is charged.

One government-funded body we used to supply as an engineering company had to purchase at the lowest price available from eight approved suppliers. By experimenting with the gross profit margins on various quotations, we found the best margins for us to win the business – and won about 30% of the contracts available! We would regularly speak to the purchasing manager, who would say the winner was cheaper by 'x' amount, and then add that the company who won the order moaned they were not making any money on that price. Others regularly had prices which were too high. According to the purchasing manager, some companies bid too low against their costings to get the business because they needed it. Of course, all engineering companies have different machines and capabilities...maybe also different costing models. So although they may be similar, the prices will vary as the products may be produced differently. We never went for business at too low a price to achieve volume for the sake of it.

This chapter on IT Systems and Data Management is about a Key Function. 'IT Systems' is not necessarily a stand-alone function in smaller companies that tend to outsource IT support. However, I refer to it as a function because of its fundamental importance. The example below also concerns management aspects as it is both an IT and Management aspect. This anecdote is with reference to **Fig 11** regarding costings and pricings. I am covering the story in more detail here as it concerns Data Management.

A Chartered Accountant who owned his own accountancy company was a member of our business networking groups. He told me he used to be the Financial Director of a company with thousands of retail outlets, so he was familiar with the accounts of running a business. At a regular network meeting, the accountant said the MD of a client company had agreed for me to go in and have a chat. The company was not profitable, and the MD wanted to do a sales drive to increase sales and profits. The accountant said he was also trying to raise a £150,000 mortgage on the factory premises to reduce the bank overdraft caused by losses over the previous three years.

Before my late-morning meeting with the MD, I dropped by the accountant's office to see the latest management accounts. I took a couple of minutes to check them and saw that they had been losing money for three years and had a meagre gross profit of around 18-24%. In other words, the company was losing money, mounting up their overdraft and bank loans to fund the losses. The accountant's plan was to help raise a mortgage to finance the losses.

On arriving at the company, I settled down with the MD to look at his accounts. I highlighted that his gross profit margin was too low – it should be much higher. Then we discussed that he wanted a sales drive to increase turnover and make the company profitable. I asked which products he intended to drive sales, then told him that we needed to know the margins on the products to sell because there was no point selling more of any loss-making products. I asked what the margins were, but he did not have that information. So I asked how we could find that out. He suggested we see the production manager as "he should know".

I trotted off downstairs and saw the production manager. He had the information available: products, labour, materials, and margins. I was surprised this information was not readily available to the MD or that he was not fully aware of it! I asked for a spreadsheet of the sales and margins by product for the financial year to date, which was six months. When the computer spreadsheet came up, I saw many loss-makers (products with a gross margin of 20% and less).

I then asked for the spreadsheet to be re-calculated, starting with loss-making products at the top. The results showed that around 50% of products sold in the first six months were loss-makers or low margin (if less than 30% gross margin). Fig 11 shows how bad the situation was.

Also, the gross margins were shown on the high side because the total monthly labour costs, which were paid monthly, were not included. Later, the MD and I checked the cumulative direct wages sum with the total direct labour on the costing summary, and of course, the actual wages paid were higher. This is because direct labour waiting time, inefficiencies, and social costs are not included in costings. This is fairly common. One way of overcoming it is to look at the percentage difference between the costings and the total wages paid, then add that percentage difference to the job costings.

Fig 11 is the production manager's spreadsheet on the production costs and margins ranked by top loss-makers for the YTD (Year to Date). After that first spreadsheet, I asked the production manager if he could also do the same for the products on the outstanding order book. Similar forecast losses were revealed for the next six months of the order book, again with 50 per cent of products being unprofitable.

I took these two hard copy spreadsheets to the MD. Luckily he was strong enough to take the shock! So immediately, price rises were needed. I came back two weeks later in line with the two weekly visits for our agreed business support programme. After I arrived, I discussed progress with the MD, and he said he had already implemented some significant price rises. One of his biggest customers was a major oil company that had agreed to immediate big price increases on the range of products.

We had not talked about techniques for price discussions and raising prices, so I was a little concerned. I asked how it had gone with the oil company. He told me it had been "fine", but I dug deeper and asked exactly what happened. "I have other big orders to follow on those we already have," he said. That was good news.

That price rise, combined with the price rises to other customers, meant the company could return to profit in a few weeks. An astounding turnaround, and they maintained it. The application for the £150,000 mortgage was cancelled, and the company became profitable and was able to trade its way out of the bank overdraft.

Part of my original discussion with the MD was to rank his key people out of 10. For his chief design engineer, he gave a nine. After discovering the low margin products, I asked how this could have happened. He replied, "We kept putting in design improvements for the customers but did not cost them or review the prices". I did not ask him what his new ranking out of 10 would be for his chief designer! I thought that would not be fair, and obviously, it was not necessarily all the design engineer's fault. I was confident it wouldn't happen again in the future.

After our discussion, the MD then planned to review the processes, lines of communication, the supply of KPIs (Key Performance Indicators) and good management information. This all contributed to setting the company on the road to recovery. The MD said he had really learned about improving his management skills and setting up appropriate interdepartmental meetings.

Lesson

1. Management must keep the costings up to date with all product costs and monitor the margins and overall gross profit value and per cent.

2. They should check product improvements and changes to maintain margins (or increases or decreases).

3. Ensure good communication between all departments: designers, engineers, production, sales and management, when innovating and making product improvements.

METHODOLOGY
How To Boost Performance

Establish regular joint team meetings to ensure good communications, decision-making, and necessary management actions.

Figs 12 and **13** showed the analysis and comments on the GP trend for Thomas Cook Retail operations. For years, there was declining GP, which management should have recognised and taken appropriate action. The IT and data management systems must be set up to show important 'clean information' for easy monitoring.

If margins and gross profit are measured and tracked and necessary actions are taken, the benefits are there for small and large companies. The annual accounts of competitors, showing P&L and gross profit, can be checked in UK Companies House. Thomas Cook's Retail Operations charts came from their annual accounts figures at Companies House. The clues are there to see for companies in difficulty or declining into bankruptcy due to poor pricing, margins and low GP both as a per cent and value generated.

Again, Thomas Cook's demise dramatically shows the importance of having established IT and data management systems to monitor and manage gross profit clearly. I trust these anecdotes sufficiently emphasise the importance of using a 'fit for purpose' IT and MRP system for accurate information for costings, pricing and the 'clean gross profit' in the P&L.

Lesson

1. Ensure the MRP system is easy to use and accurately summarises total monthly labour and materials costs.

2. Furthermore, ensure that individual product costs with multiple operations can be summarised in three lines: labour, material, and total cost per product.

3. The accounts system must show a 'clean gross profit' including other significant direct costs and transport and packing.

METHODOLOGY
How To Boost Performance

1. Acquire an IT system as suitable as possible for data capture for all functions.

2. Ensure the presentation of information is clear and easy to read.

3. Ensure there are summary costs of individual products, product groups and for customers.

CHAPTER SUMMARY

1. Do not buy the cheapest system unless it is the right system for your particular company.

2. Find a professional IT consultant to help you define all your requirements, and then conduct a full evaluation of systems with a shortlist of suitable suppliers.

3. A key requirement of an MRP system is to ensure accurate material usage per product, precise capture of direct labour, clear costs per product, and a summary three-line cost per product comprising of labour, materials and the total direct cost.

4. Ensure the system has clear information for stock usage and control with flexibility for cost changes and product group analyses.

5. Adopt an alphanumerical product coding system to easily identify and analyse product groups for profitability, sales trends, and forward planning.

6. Ensure monthly management reports have 'clean gross profit' figures.

Chapter Eight

The Marketing Function: How To Achieve Improvements To Increase Enquiries

This chapter covers what marketing is: what it does, how to do it, and how it supports both sales and production, or service, to achieve those 1% improvements to increase results and success.

At a meeting with the MD of a small company, we chatted about his business in the usual progressive questioning format. The MD said he wanted more sales, so I asked him what marketing he undertook. And as mentioned earlier in Chapter Three: The Sales Function, he replied that he had tried the local directory, and it did not work!

The point is that he had little idea about marketing, nor had he done any sales training.

I had a similar meeting with the MD of another company, and we discussed his company literature. After I had looked over it for a few moments, I asked him if he had any literature from his competitors. "Ah, that's a good idea," he said, now keen on the discussion. He invited his sales director to the meeting, and together, we compared the company literature with their competitors'. I then asked the MD, "with both sets of literature in front of you, as a potential customer, which company would you choose to contact?" After a bit of thought, he answered, "this one, my competitor's".

It was good that he had recognised the difference between both examples and that he needed to improve his material to win more business. When a company has inferior literature or a website that poorly presents the 'benefits', it might be necessary to quote a lower price than it would like to get a sales opportunity. The MD had answered for himself what was one of the first things he needed to do to improve his sales opportunities.

Companies need to have an excellent website. It must quickly and clearly state what the company sells and show, with confidence, how its products or services will benefit the customer. If this is not immediately clear, research has shown that people often log off in 10 to 20 seconds. So clarity on the company offering on the landing page or home page is critical.

However, this is not as straightforward as it could be for some. Over many years I have worked with numerous MDs and their teams. When the conversation inevitably moves to benefits, I have found that many find it challenging to grasp the difference between a feature and a benefit, even when the difference is explained.

For example, I remember an occasion when I was due to meet the MD of a manufacturing company. The night before the visit, I had a look at his website. His product offering was unclear, the entire content was woolly, and when I left the site, I was no clearer about what they offered than when I had entered! At the meeting the next day, during the discussion and questions, the MD said, " I have had 12,000 hits on my website since April" (about five months). I agreed that was indeed a great result. But when I asked how many orders had been generated from those visits, the answer was, "None". No orders, no enquiries, no sales. He began to look a bit uncomfortable.

I asked if he knew at which page people logged off. I was surprised he knew the answer but unsurprised when I heard it was on the products page. I told him that was exactly where I had logged off too, as I didn't understand it.

He agreed the website was unclear and needed completely re-vamping before he could expect to generate any valuable enquiries or interest from it. He said he would work on the website himself. Interestingly he also wanted some help with the improvements necessary on production processes, so we moved on to that subject.

Often, companies just need a bit of help to start improving even a few things to better market their company; then, the opportunities increase for growing their business. *Everything* needs to be done as well as possible to be successful. Even if it is only a one or two per cent improvement here and a few per cent there, the momentum starts to build. Investment in good support services and perhaps investment in an advisor is usually worth the expense.

Fig15 shows the overall objectives for marketing in a simple overview.

FIG 15. *Overall Marketing Objectives*

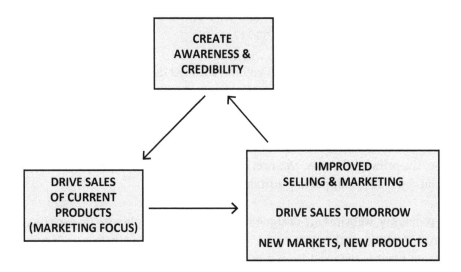

OVERALL MARKETING OBJECTIVES

As an interesting point, there has been much debate on whether Henry Ford was a production man or a marketing man in developing the high output production line. What's your initial thought?

Many people have been influenced to think he was a production man. However, the argument goes that he was a marketing man because he recognised that he would sell a 'helluva lot more' if he could make his cars cheaper. Henry Ford also standardised his models to be made cheaper; he said, "you can have any colour you like as long as it is black" because black dried quicker than other colours. Originally the cars were painted green.

The standardised colour black kept the costs down and the price down so he could sell more.

Ford was brought up on a farm. His vision for the automobile was to make it available for as many people as possible, especially in the isolated communities: providing transport to get into town. The Model T originally sold for $850 in 1908. Other manufacturers' prices were around $2000 per car. After the production improvements, the price came down to $360. The Model T initially took 12.5 hours per vehicle. After introducing the production line, the time per vehicle came down to 5.5 hours. Finally, with more production efficiencies, the production time came down to 93 minutes per vehicle, and Ford could sell even more cars. At $360 per car, this price was roughly three months' wages for his employees, so they could also buy the Model T. Fifteen million Model T's were sold before a new car design, the Model A, was announced in 1927.

Henry Ford generated enough volume with his decreased prices to ensure he covered all his overhead costs and could make a good profit. You can be sure that careful planning between pricing and overhead costs ensured those excellent results.

So, the principle here is, **'Marketing supports sales *and* production'**. And you could add, **'supports profitability'**.

Frequently, websites are designed and written by people with no experience in marketing…such as the owner's son or daughter. Too little is understood about what is required from a marketing and a customer's point of view. For example, using the right words and phrases and judgment about the consequences of what is written.

One company I started working with had a website that quite disappointed me with the naivety of the content. Here are a couple of poor examples to demonstrate why:

1. After describing two of the salespeople and their titles, such as northern region salesman and southern region salesman, the following statement said, *"And there is Fred Bloggs who also does sales."* Had the salesman no title? Why not give a title such as 'special

accounts' salesman, something to at least make the company and website look professional.

2. The worst statement after introducing the key employees was this, *"This is Paul the MD, he spends most of his time on his other company."*

This read as if the MD was not very interested in the company, and it indicated there was no drive behind it if there were any problems or whether he was worth contacting if there were any issues that needed solving. That statement would be off-putting to prospects.

Those were just two off-puts in amongst banal descriptions. Websites and literature often use phrases such as "we offer" and include many "we's." However, there should be as many "you's" written as "we's". In other words, there should be no more than 50% of "we's" to get the balance right.

A phrase to avoid is, "We also do...". The 'also' implies it is occasional work, not important, or they are not skilled in it. That particular product or service can be listed as a complete offering to inspire the prospective client, providing an additional small but useful turnover for the company.

Marketing materials need to involve the reader and create personal interest for them. Rather than "We offer," the following phrases are a better way to start:

- Your choice of products...
- Products available for you are ...
- Products for you to choose from...
- Services provided are...

One of the cleverest, and simplest advertisements I have seen, which covered 'you' and the relevant subject, was an advertisement to visit India, **Fig 16.** And it did not even have any pictures of India. I am sure you can agree that it is a very clever and powerful advertisement!

FIG 16. *Visit India*

INDIA

Important information for Travellers

1. **Bring a camera**
   You'll only kick yourself if you don't.
2. **Read a guidebook or two**
   It's a big place and you won't want to miss anything.
3. **Don't pack too much**
   You'll need the space to bring home everything you bought in the markets.

**Call your tour operator today, and you can
safely expect the holiday of a lifetime.**

LESSON

1. Have a well-written website. The offer must be instantly clear, and the benefits sold. There should be 'you's and no more than 50% 'we's.'

2. However, one must be aware that websites are very different from traditional sales and marketing literature. Although the wording may be similar, it is essential to use certain words that enable Search Engine Optimisation to find your website and bring it as near to the top of the subject listing as possible.

Next, a more detailed overview and aide-mémoire for what elements are involved in marketing. **Fig 17** shows THE MARKETING FOCUS and the key aspects that need to be focused upon to improve them, then link them all together to grow the business and sustain it.

FIG 17. *The Marketing Focus*

THE MARKETING FOCUS

There are dozens of marketing books, but I shall provide a focused overview in this chapter, covering some key aspects. The reasoning behind this is: that I have not met many MDs or owners of smaller companies who have the time or inclination to read business books; or have been on even a one-day seminar on Sales or Marketing. And, in my opinion, this is a mistake.

It also surprises me when I ask someone in a sales role if they have had any sales or marketing training, been on a course, or read anything, and I find out they have not. Often, technical people are appointed to a sales role and get no sales training. This means they don't know about the major key thing in selling and marketing: **sell benefits – not just features.**

Technical people know specific details about their products, but they often can't answer the questions, "Why should I buy from your company" and "What are the benefits of your company and products for the prospective customer?"

There is a need to be clear about which are features, and which are benefits... and the differences. Interestingly, the advertisement for visiting India does not list any sightseeing features such as the Taj Mahal or a game reserve. It lists *guide points* to achieve *benefits* to make the most of a trip to India, and with only three travel guide points, it is an excellent example of how to sell benefits.

Notice that the centre of the chart in **Fig 17** says people should be trained and motivated. That's the first big point on the Sales and Marketing front. Learning about selling benefits is a significant starting point. **Fig 17** also shows the key focus items, but they all need to intertwine with each other to achieve maximum marketing focus. Training is required on each focus aspect and needs to be understood in relation to the other focus elements. Therefore as we now consider each focus aspect, there may also be a reference to another focus aspect.

1. Products And Services

This is the basis of the business. What is being offered and supplied? Are there customers for your products, and are they in sufficient numbers to grow your business? Some basic Marketing Research may be required to establish if there is further business potential for the product. The company may be in a specialist market with few customers, so understanding this situation is vital for forward planning.

Benefits, as well as features, need to be clearly defined at this stage.

2. Features And Benefits

Think of a feature as something that applies to your product, whereas a benefit will interest the customer or prospect, encouraging them to buy.

Next are some general examples of benefits over features; however, be aware that there is a difference between retail selling and industrial selling.

Feature. Our lead time is two weeks.

Benefit. Delivery to you is an industry-leading two weeks, so you will not have to wait long.

Feature. (If true) We are a quality manufacturer.

Benefit. Every product is carefully checked before shipment to ensure you will not be disappointed.

Benefit. In the unlikely event that you are not fully satisfied with your purchase, you can return it for a full refund.

Feature. We have service engineers on callout.

Benefit. Should your new product develop a problem, our engineer will be with you the same day or within 24 hours to minimise any inconvenience to you.

Feature. We have an extensive range of products.

Benefit. There is an extensive range of products for you to choose from.

Feature. We have a large range of colours.

Benefit. The large colour range has been specially developed to suit your requirements and is fade-free for your long-lasting enjoyment.

And so on. The benefits could be briefer if required but are longer here to emphasise the point.

3. Competition Information And Market Information

This focus area overlaps with Customers and Prospects, and also Customer needs, and Product Development. Some marketing research can obtain information about your competitors and your market opportunities.

There is a step process to find the information that is needed for the business to:

- provide information for the sales personnel
- satisfy existing customers with their needs
- obtain information for targeting sales growth
- obtain knowledge of your competitors to provide ammunition in sales meetings. This means you sometimes have to counter lies about your company and products put out by competitors
- obtain information to help in product improvement and/or new product development.

Seven steps can be used to obtain competitor and market information. The Market Information Research Process points cover a wide range of businesses, so not all of them are necessarily appropriate for smaller and niche SMEs.

Step One. The Wider Market

What is the broad market that you operate within? What defines it, and what are its boundaries?

Step Two. The Focus

Within the broader market, what segments are of most interest for you?

Which are likely to be the most profitable and the most appropriate?

Note: segmentation is one of the most critical aspects of marketing.

Step Three. The Detailed Research

Collect and analyse the data relevant to the target segments.

Who are the potential customers; what are their needs and wants?

How are you performing with your existing customers? Are you delivering on time and with defect-free products and services? If the 'on time' deliveries are 'out,' and you have rejects or service problems, it will be difficult to win new business and keep existing customers.

Step Four. The Competitors

Which competitors are serving these segments, and how good are their lead times, servicing and pricing? It may be possible to find this information from prospects and existing customers. Pricing can be tested from the quotes supplied to prospects and customers and getting some feedback from the prospective buyers on how competitive your quote is.

Step Five. The Analysis

From the research, determine the profile of each relevant sector. Write up the types of customers and their buying patterns. Do a SWOT analysis (Strengths, Weaknesses, Opportunities and Threats analysis) of the competition.

Step Six. The Decision

This is the crunch. You will now know what the target segments look like, what they want and who is currently servicing those needs. The question now is, does your company have the will, the resources and the capability to chase that segment? If the answer is 'yes', proceed to the next step... The Plan.

Step Seven. The Plan

Establish a Marketing Plan (and a production plan) to suit the target segments. Highlight the features and benefits that create the perception you desire and can deliver. Determine the best methods of reaching the target groups and implement the plan.

4. Customers And Prospects

This focus point covers two aspects. First, information and controls are needed for existing customers. Secondly, the same controls should be used when research identifies new prospects to be targeted. Controls should, for example, cover the following, and then later more or different information according to the business:

- Customers are ranked alphabetically and by turnover to find them quickly by name or importance. This is easy to do with Excel, a good IT or Customer Relationship Management system (CRM).
- Top customers and Key Accounts should be identified for a target visit every 4 to 6 weeks.
- Second and third-ranked customers can be targeted for less frequent visits.
- Frequency of orders. When was the last order?
- The records should include all contact names and their superiors for reference if required in the future (subject to GDPR guidance).
- Potential product sales and customers you have not won yet, with an assessment of potential by value and quantity.

5. Customer Needs

To use a good example from my previous customers in the cosmetics market: the large companies (our major customers) needed to be visited every 4 to 6 weeks. Our sales manager regularly visited Rimmel/Coty in Ashford, Kent, and occasionally I accompanied him or went alone.

On a visit to Rimmel to see the purchasing chief (later the European Purchasing Director), and as we sat down, he waved down his chest and joked, "I should be wearing a T-Shirt saying, **Price – Quality – Service**".

The customer will never say that your prices are excellent, but they should be able to say that the quality and service are excellent. This can be summarised as, 'customers want a competitive price, faultless quality and exemplary service.' Working with Rimmel, we developed a new range of colour cosmetics packs for mascaras, eyeliners, and lipgloss and designed a standard range for them to rationalise 16 or so packs to about eight but with variations for the different European brands.

This rationalisation then enabled us to build bigger tools to make more units at a time and automate more. The increased volumes and rationalisation created efficiencies for us in longer, faster production runs. The result for Rimmel/Coty for their European sales was more competitive lower prices from us, and they could also fill and cap the bottles more efficiently, by much longer runs on the filling lines.

The result for us was that we were shipping about one million components a week. Moreover, there were no complaints of rejects or quality problems for years from the launch, and then ongoing. So Rimmel got good prices and excellent quality and service from us. We also obtained significant sales increases from rationalisation and the combination with other brand packs.

On joining Geka, we found we were one of three or four suppliers to Boots for their No 7 and No 17 colour cosmetics ranges. To date, service and on-time deliveries had been poor. So with Boots' recommendation, we set out to reduce lead times and improve quality and on-time deliveries. Remarkably it was not just us pushing to improve things. As you read in the letter in Chapter Three, Boots told us how we could get a bigger share of their business. **Fig 18** shows another letter from Boots, two years after the previous one. I'm happy to say we had not become complacent!

FIG 18. *Boots Letter Regarding Customer Service*

Dear John,

Thank you for the letter referring to the arrangements you have made to ensure that service continues through the present transport disruptions and look forward to deliveries as normal.

I have just received from our Airdrie Quality Control Department details of their findings on their recent visit to your factory, and must congratulate you and your staff on the excellent rating they have given you. I hope you will transmit this information to all those involved in your organisation.

Yours sincerely
Packaging Materials Purchasing Manager.

There are several key points arising from this letter.

1. We kept our customer informed. This is essential in difficult times, so they don't worry about whether production materials will arrive on time.
2. The factory obtained an excellent rating. It was always important to have a clean, tidy and well-organised factory because that generated a lot of sales after customer visits. A clean, tidy, busy production facility is a good selling tool. As a broad brush statement, we had calculated that a customer or prospect visit to our factory was worth at least £100,000 of extra business per visit.
3. This letter was used at a briefing meeting after the Boots visit to inform and motivate people.

Another point about this customer experience is; that it shows that you can succeed whatever the size of your company or your customer's size.

LESSON

1. You can succeed whatever the size of the customer if you set about the task with the requisite sales skills, enthusiasm, determination and professionalism.

2. Keep your customers informed.

3. Quality products and excellent customer service are essential.

4. Good planning and well-managed implementation are required.

5. Motivate employees with good communication...always.

There is a range of aspects of service: personal service, communication and sensitivity to customers' individual needs are essential. As I expect many of you know, our German friends tend to drive rather fast on the autobahns. Also, some of them seem to drive too quickly on snowy, icy roads in the winter, even around town.

I was in our German factory to meet with Revlon's Vice President of Purchasing, who was visiting from the USA. He was picked up at the hotel and driven rather too quickly on the icy roads to the factory. After a car journey that involved sliding around street corners, some of which were cobbled streets, he arrived looking very unhappy. He mentioned the 'scary' drive to me, and I relayed it to the German Product Development Director who had lived in the USA. Over the years, I had experienced that in England, the American visitors were not used to speeding along our narrow country lanes, and it disturbed them. I suggested that they should be more considerate to overseas visitors and drive slower. However, he dismissed my point

That, to me, is counterproductive and not good business sense. The last thing you should do is upset customers, especially if trying to build rapport at the start of a day of productive meetings. In the example I've shared, you could argue that perhaps some customers might not want to risk doing business with suppliers who are reckless in their driving – they may be reckless or lacking in judgement in running the company?

Below is a missive from the product development manager at Revlon USA, who sent this amusing, but concerned email from a previous experience of a visit to Germany and driving with our German friends.

Email: Wolfgang (of Geka) to Rob at Revlon, New York–

Subject: Visit to Bologna Fair.

Your visit on April 21 is o.k. We will come back to you again regarding ground transportation. You can get a ride with somebody from us (from Germany to Bologna in Italy), i.e. Wilhelm on April 22nd.

Do you have a hotel reservation? This might be the most important thing for the Bologna Fair. – Please advise.

Regards

Wolfgang

Rob's reply:

Have a hotel reservation in Bologna, do not have auto insurance to travel with Wilhelm.... previous experience suggests need to be followed closely by Medivac...! Seriously, how long is the drive and when are you heading out. I would like to travel down by car but may be lousy company given the jet lag.... Does Wilhelm have airbags all round? Is he wanted in any southern European states, Interpol and all that...!

I will call you...Rob.

So there it is; quite amusing, but it *is* important to look after your customers with politeness and consideration in all aspects...including how they are chauffeured!

6. The Sales Proposition (USP)

The acronym USP stands for 'Unique Selling Proposition'. You can turn this phrase around and say, what is the 'Unique Buying Proposition'. That is, 'why buy from you?'

You have to be clear on your product and service offering and be clear about selling the benefits, not just the features. And you should ideally be able to demonstrate your benefits with visual aids and examples. It helps at a sales meeting if the prospect can handle any visual aids and get involved.

7. Literature, Website, PR, Etc.

I explained earlier in the book that there are overlaps between some Functions, and literature is one example. Literature is essential. It is about the company, and if it's not good, your company can look small, unprofitable and perhaps not competent and reliable.

The use of literature during a presentation can be compelling in helping to win the business. Yet, today, too many business owners and managers think all you need is a website. In industrial selling, I have found that it is still essential to have a brochure, or at least a flyer or 'leave behind'. Because if you say, "have a look at our website", a busy buyer or manager cannot immediately do so and will soon forget as they have put your Business Card down 'somewhere'! The opportunity for making a better impression is then lost. Therefore, one piece of well-executed literature left in an office is a reminder to encourage prospective customers to look at your website when they have a spare moment. It is also possible the literature will be passed to another staff member with a, "here, have a look at this".

In my experience, it is always beneficial when prospects can become more involved in a meeting by handling and discussing literature, samples or pictures. Research on competitors should reveal all the information you need to sharpen up the content in your literature and website and enable you to compete from a higher vantage point.

8. Pricing

I have left this focus point until this point in the chapter because the other key points needed to be clarified first. If you just want to sell on price, so be it; it's your choice.

But if you want to be able to charge the maximum prices and make a reasonable profit, then you must be:

- clear on your benefits
- have the best possible website
- your 'leave behind' must be expertly produced
- samples and pictures should be available (maybe a video too) to show products supplied to existing customers.

Only then will you maximise your chances of success at a sales meeting. Armed with target prices and clarity on the lowest price you can go to, you have a good chance of success with this chapter's acquired knowledge and weapons. If a salesperson is not fully trained and prepared, the competition may well be and will gain the advantage over you and your company.

9. Product Development And Innovations

Product Development is shown in the Marketing Focus chart as a key point linked to marketing. However, it is an important topic and is therefore covered extensively in Chapter Nine.

METHODOLOGY
How To Boost Performance

1. Review all the above focus points to look for required and possible improvements.

2. Prioritise the areas for improvement. This could be for quick fixes and also ones for the greatest benefits to be achieved.

3. Tackle the top three to five choices as the first priorities.

CHAPTER SUMMARY

1. Marketing focuses on benefits and helps support and increase sales and profitability.

2. Marketing sharpens the company's outward-facing visibility using website (online) and literature (offline) advertising.

3. Marketing addresses customer needs such as price, quality, service and product improvements.

4. Marketing prompts research to develop or introduce new products and understand customers' needs.

Chapter Nine
Product Development And New Products

This chapter focuses on avoiding wasteful time and effort on potential failures. It describes four ways to develop new products, how to manage new product development, and explores the reasons why new products fail.

When a company is not making continuous improvements, it isn't 'standing still'; it is, instead, going backwards. Be assured that many competitors will be improving their products and service, so continuous improvement of products is often a necessity to ensure the company does not get left behind.

What does product development involve in simple terms? Here are four key points:

1. **Improving the existing products**. This can be for market benefits, production efficiencies, aesthetics, environmentally friendly materials, or to satisfy regulations such as for health and safety.
2. **Developing new types of existing products as a range extension**. This will increase sales.
3. **Developing different products to add to your range**. The enlarged range can extend your customer base and increase sales to existing customers.
4. **Developing a completely new product for new markets**. Those products can also sell to existing customers.

Some straightforward examples follow.

Improving Existing Products

A good example from our company experience was a product benefit achieved for our customers and the women who use colour cosmetics.

Mascaras generally had caps which screwed down onto the bottle with 2.5 turns. During my first two weeks as MD of the company, I asked why there were so many turns to screw the cap/rod/brush back onto the bottle? It wasn't user-friendly: fewer turns to close would make the mascara easier and quicker to open and close. The technical people told me the 'extra' turns ensured the caps did not vibrate undone during transport. However, I was keen to pursue the idea.

After talking to a couple of our customers in cosmetics manufacturing and some female users, we learned that if we could reduce the number of turns to screw the cap on and off, women using mascara and similar packs would find this more convenient. We could then sell this as a benefit to the colour cosmetics manufacturers, giving us a benefit our competitors weren't offering.

Some 'pushing and shoving' of the development director in Germany led to an agreement to start developing a design for caps that could be screwed on with 1.5 turns. Our German colleagues developed and incorporated a 'click close' feature for the cap as a further improvement. This ensures the caps are fully closed to provide a seal and preserve the contents. In addition, the packs stay safely closed during transit. It was an excellent, convenient result for the end-users and the cosmetics companies.

The new designs were carefully developed and tested to show they worked well. Soon we were making mascara and similar product packs with closures of one and a half turns and a 'click close'. The feature provided faster opening and closing and gave the user confidence that the pack was correctly closed. The development gave us a competitive advantage and demonstrated continuous improvement.

Many of the company designs of mascara packs had caps glued onto the rod, which then had the mascara brush attached. The production method to glue the caps meant using special glue application machines. These needed engineers to maintain them; glue needed to be bought which cost money; purchasing and administration time was required, and storage costs and administration were also required.

There were also the capital costs in replacing worn-out glueing machines; also, quality checks were needed to check that caps were glued on correctly. Accordingly, we worked on eliminating the glueing of caps. The plan was to have all new products and convert many old ones to be manufactured with either press fitted or snap-on caps. We achieved the changes and obtained the internal cost and efficiency savings we were looking for.

The revised mascara cap products improved our production, factory efficiency, and profitability. They gave us an advantage over competitors and enabled us to sell more to our customers.

Other good examples of product improvement were undertaken at Autotype International, which helped grow the company sales by 40% per annum year on year.

Company growth by continuous product improvement and new products was achieved in tandem with solid sales and promotional activities. Those were quite exciting times for everyone as they were all involved in this rocketing success. At one stage, when we won the Queen's Award for Export, we were testing development products in South Africa, California, Germany and Holland.

The Autotype products are more technical to explain than the mascara cap example, but the product development examples are noteworthy. Some of the products are used in the printing industry for the preparation and layout of images and text before print production. Others are used for printing a range of products like magazines, and screen printing films are used for point-of-sale products, electronics printed circuit boards and instrument dials. Screen printing films are used to produce 'water slide transfers' which are used in pottery manufacturing for chinaware. Many famous name tableware manufacturers use Autotype films.

Feedback from the market indicated that an aspect of one of the print preparation products needed improvement. This was on the tensile or breaking strength of a membrane coating on a polyester film base of a product called masking film: one of our major sales products.

We had received comments from our customer visits, especially in Germany and Sweden, that the competitors' product was easier to use when cutting masks for planning the printing plates. The competitors' membrane was stronger and easier to peel off the polyester plastic sheet without breaking. Accordingly, we asked our technical service department to test our films against those of our competitors' films.

The report showed that our film membrane was weaker and had to be handled more carefully, which slowed up planning the artwork for printing. I spoke with our production director and asked whether development could start on achieving an increase in tensile strength of the membrane to exceed the competitors' specifications. There was a detailed discussion about our different chemistry and production processes and the difficulty in changing or making improvements. Also, as we were busy doing production trials and developments on other new products, it would make sense to add it to the Research and Development Department (R&D) programme at a later date.

Eventually, at the end of the discussion, it was agreed we *should* do something as this was one of our major products. Therefore, although R&D was already overstretched, the additional product development project was added to the list. After a few months of R&D work and trials, we had an improved product. We could not quite achieve our aim of making a tensile strength superior to the competitor's product, but the result was a significant improvement when added to our other existing product benefits.

We launched the improved product to our agents around the world. The result was that the agents could sell it more easily, and sales increased by approximately 25%. This is only one of the many product improvements we made for existing products, for the wider markets, and for our customers: prompted by talking to them.

Lesson

To improve products, talk to customers! Then conduct competitive product analysis and brainstorming sessions.

Developing New Products As A Range Extension

There is a further excellent example from Autotype. I was given an intensive induction and product training programme on joining the company. During the product training, a film (a membrane on a polyester film base) was demonstrated for colour separation for the printing of solid colours. This film was used for hand cutting the membrane with a scalpel type knife around an image to be printed. I asked if it could be made light-sensitive to UV light (used in the printing industry). If it could, it would be a great film for the market. A quick exposure in the UV lightbox and 'film developing' would save lengthy hand cutting time. I was told, 'No, this can't be done'. But about four years later, our competitors came out with just such an ultraviolet sensitive screen printing film which could generally replace the time-consuming hand cutting work.

Our technical services department evaluated the competitor product, and a report was issued that said the product performance regarding the result for the printed image was 'not that good'. The report suggested it would not amount to much as far as sales were concerned. The technical report underplayed the convenience for screen printers and the potential competition against our other big selling screen printing films. Several internal follow-up meetings took place. Those of us in the marketing department argued that the competitor product would be strong competition. We should not accept the technical report nor ignore the threat from this new film. The product idea was good, but as far as we thought needed to be technically improved. We argued to start the development of our own product, which the board agreed upon. It was developed, market-tested, and launched as a completely new product, and within 12 to 18 months, it achieved annual sales of over £3 million and continued its fast growth. It was a significant contributor to our 40%

year on year growth without being detrimental to our existing screen printing films.

From this example (and the previous one about quick closing caps on bottles), I learned that we need to be careful what the 'experts' in a company tell us. To reinforce this viewpoint, I will share a further example from when I was a product manager in the Flexible Packaging Division in Metal Box Ltd, an international packaging company with a billion pound a year turnover. At that time, another plastics film manufacturing company developed a metallised polyester film used to wrap consumer products such as chocolate bars. The film looked like aluminium foil, and I wondered if it could be of interest for Metal Box to use for the products of our food manufacturing customers. I spoke to the technical packaging engineers and was told that metallised polyester film looked good but wouldn't be any good for food wrapping because the barrier properties are not as good as silver foil.

In short, I accepted their argument, so the opportunity was not followed up. Today, this film is used for wrapping plenty of different products everywhere. The engineers were thinking only technically, not looking at the marketing or cost-saving possibilities for packaging and for niche sales.

Lesson

1. Develop and improve both existing and new products to add to your existing ones for current customers and to extend your customer base and markets.

2. Make customer visits. Discuss the products. Obtain feedback.

3. Be mindful of technical experts and their sometimes biased assessments. I coined the saying (and have used it frequently): be careful of in-company experts and their advice because they can tend to tell you erroneously and without sufficiently strong evidence why you can't do something.

I am aware that point three sounds negative. However, it is more a prompt to get you to pursue ideas perhaps a bit further. Keep asking and enquiring until you find the benefits and possibilities and whether they can be made to happen. At least *try* some product development, and if it does not work, at least you put it to bed and move on to other ideas.

Product development can be driven by the research and development department or by identifying the market and customer needs. Then those needs can be developed into a new product at a profit-earning price. The price will depend on the volume you can expect, balanced by the price you can get.

At Autotype, as I mentioned previously, the main products were coated polyester films for the printing industry. We also sold some associated chemicals used in cleaning or preparing silk screens for mounting the films onto before screen printing. A type of competitor product to the screen printing films that does not achieve such a fine print result is called a 'direct emulsion'. This is a 'two pot' system of a liquid emulsion that has to be made sensitive to UV light with the additive of a catalyst. This is added by the operator and stirred into the pot of emulsion just before use, so is a bit time-consuming for the operator. To add to our range, we developed a one-pot 'ready sensitised' emulsion to make the system easier for general screen printers.

The new product worked well enough to be a marketable product technically. The only trouble with our development product was when the tub was opened; the emulsion had a powerful and unpleasant smell of solvents.

The key point about this product development was whether it was suitable for the market. We had an important distributor visiting us at the factory, and we decided to show him the product. The customer benefit for ease-of-use was evident, and we considered the performance for screen printing was sufficiently good, but it had this one major drawback; it smelt very badly. We told our distributor that it had a strong smell and that we wondered if it was acceptable and whether it would sell.

Our distributor made a wonderful, very amusing marketing comment. He said, "You tell me how much it costs, and I'll tell you how badly it smells!".

In the end, we all agreed the selling price would be too high for customers to tolerate the strong smell, and we would not be able to sell enough volume at the price we needed. Therefore it was decided the launch would be aborted. However, it is an interesting example of almost everything being right with a new product but not *quite* good enough: so back to the 'drawing board'.

Developing A Completely New Product For New Markets

Although...they might also appeal to existing customers, as demonstrated by the Apple SmartWatch. Unlike a mobile phone or computer, it still uses Apple's electronics expertise. Although a different product and potential target market, it appeals to existing customers whilst attracting new ones to the Apple brand. The key aspect of the SmartWatch is that it is electronically based and can be a stand-alone product and linked to Apple's other products.

Similarly, a boat building company I knew made racing dinghies using fibreglass. They branched out into making special fibreglass bowls and baths for the UK National Health Service. This became a big part of their business – using existing expertise to produce a new product for a new market.

The tricky thing for companies is finding new ideas and new markets, then getting the whole plan to succeed. Often smaller companies are too busy with their day-to-day work to be able to look at ideas for expansion. Or maybe they don't have 'ideas' people in the company. However, with in-house brainstorming sessions and market and product research to explore any ideas generated, plus examining competitive and alternative products, it *is* achievable.

One way to succeed in this area for expansion is to buy an existing company specialising in the new target area you've settled on. This is, of course, easier for larger companies with better access to raising finance. Often, much work goes into targeting a prospective company before buying it. However, opportunities can arise, so don't dismiss this idea or place it in the 'too difficult' box.

When working in the marketing department at Metal Box Ltd, I received a call from a company that wanted to buy plastic tubes, which are widely used for toothpaste, cosmetics, and food pastes. When the enquiry came, I could easily have said "we do not make them" and put the phone down. However, I immediately thought, 'this sounds interesting. I wonder what the story behind it is?'. So I said, "We don't manufacture plastics and laminated tubes, so I'm wondering, what prompted your call to us?"

The conversation revealed that the current lead time for tubes in the UK was six months. So there seemed to be a demand but a lack of capacity. I discussed this with my boss. We decided to ask our internal market research team to explore information on products packed in tubes, total estimated current demand, number of suppliers, and details on their company size and probable customers. Fortunately, we had many food and non-food customers the researchers could talk to. So in just a few weeks, we had a complete report on the UK market for plastic tubes.

The report showed a significant usage for a wide range of products...and very few suppliers. Further research on current manufacturers identified a company in France called Valerflax. The company owner had indicated that he was interested in selling the company.

A proposal to purchase Valerflax was presented to the Board and approved. Under the Metal Box banner, Valerflax became an important supplier of plastic tubes to the UK and European markets. Interestingly, this acquisition and the new product began as an incoming phone call: we listened to the reasons behind the call, asked the right questions, conducted the necessary research...and took the opportunity presented.

LESSON

Always ask a few extra questions – it can lead to helpful information and sometimes big opportunities.

After the acquisition of Valerflax, Tony, the General Manager of one of the metal can making divisions, was appointed to be the General Manager in France. The day Tony left, I helped him load up his car at the head office in Reading, saying goodbye and wishing him good luck in France. That was the last I saw of Tony until he contacted me regarding a patent situation ten years later. This story is covered in Chapter Ten: Patents And Intellectual Property Rights (IPR).

As mentioned, Geka manufactured colour cosmetics packs (bottles and closures) and was an injection moulding and bottle blowing company. With this expertise, it obviously could manufacture new products and new markets.

I was approached by a small company start-up, a spin-off from Newcastle University. They had invented and made a prototype of a toothbrush combined with a rigid plastic dispenser tube to hold the toothpaste. The product had a press lever to open the nozzle, which allowed the toothpaste to be ejected onto the toothbrush bristles; releasing the press lever closed the dispensing nozzle. The toothbrush with toothpaste on it was then ready to use, making it very quick and convenient.

We were certainly interested in manufacturing this if there was market demand. The Managing Director could not confirm customer interest to me but said he had patent applied status. I thought I would check out the potential and called two large companies, one of which was Colgate. I was told at a senior level that Colgate was not interested because they sold toothpaste and did not want to be linked to any particular type or brand of toothbrush. They did not want (at that time) a lot of variants with different toothbrushes, such as hard, medium, or soft and with various bristle designs and with varying varieties of toothpaste. The contact said that Colgate's business was volume manufacturing and marketing toothpaste, not toothbrushes, so they were not interested.

My next call was to a toothbrush manufacturer. The marketing department told me exactly the same story as Colgate, but in reverse. They are toothbrush manufacturers and not into promoting their products with a specific toothpaste manufacturer, so they were not interested. So, neither was I anymore! That took just two phone calls.

I reported this information back to the disconsolate MD. I did say that maybe a small marketing company could be interested and that they could use a contract filling company which does short runs for special products, perhaps for travel or airlines. I have never seen the product on the market, so I expect it 'died at birth'. And, because of the lack of market research, not making a few phone calls and visits and not using a non-disclosure agreement (NDA), a lot of time and money was wasted on developing and applying for a patent.

LESSON

To save a lot of money and time wasted on progressing new product ideas – and to achieve success – it is necessary to undertake initial marketing research to establish possible demand and distribution. Ensure the research is appropriately targeted and thorough.

The next example was an 'interesting' disaster for a company that had raised finance to launch a new product. I received a call from Tom, an accountant I knew from our consultant contacts; he was now the Financial Director of a new company. He said the company was burning cash at a high rate of knots and that the MD did not seem to know what he was doing – could we come in and help?

I called the MD, and he said he primarily wanted help on the sales side. He then sent me a fairly thick report on his market research for the product he was selling, which I duly read before seeing him. I did not find it convincing. I took Ron, a consultant colleague with me who was a former General Sales Director interested in helping on the sales side. When we arrived, the MD wanted to tell us about his 45-foot yacht. This went on for over an hour, with several other distractions thrown in for good measure. As Tom had indicated, the MD had no focus. Eventually, we got him back on track.

The Report that the MD had sent me centred around the potential of a Customer Relationship Management (CRM) software system being sold in America. This was in the early 2000s, and various systems were already on the market in the UK. The marketing report was filled with many assumptions and no real worthwhile evidence. I was not convinced about the suggested potential for this particular product. Moreover, there was no meaningful mention of competing products in the UK. A significant point of this example was that the MD had raised £6.0 million on the UK AIM market to launch and push an American CRM system for which he had taken a licence, and he was burning through the cash at more than £100,000 a month.

Ron and I started asking questions. "What is the annual sales target you want to achieve?" The response was £20 million a year. Next question, "How many competitors do you have?" The answer was ten. I then asked, "What is the turnover of the largest of these competitors?" He replied, "No more than £1.0 million".

I then said, "So if you buy up all your competitors, you would still have under £10 million turnover. You are competing with ten other competitors with an American system to get some market share in the UK. From what you say, none of the others seems to be achieving good sales yet".

And what was the market growth? He thought that whatever the growth, he would compete against those competitors. Finally, we listened to how he was trying to organise and motivate the sales team, which sounded grossly ineffective. Sadly, neither Ron nor I thought this company could be helped. I did have another look at CRM systems about a year or two later, and I counted 37, so now there is even more competition.

This cautionary tale is also about investors putting £6 million into a new company based on a 'wishy washy' marketing report. We did not know how investors could believe it. Tom, the Financial Director, called me a few months later to say that the company had folded eight months after our visit. I don't believe the investors got any money back.

Managing New Product Development

It is vital to have a process or structure for managing and developing new products, innovations, and manufacturing improvements.

At the various companies I've worked in and with, we have generally established regular meetings to include sales, marketing, R&D, production, and sometimes purchasing personnel called in as needed. We called the committee meeting the 'Manufacturing and Product Development Meeting,' or MPD. The agenda for these meetings was to review the progress of all product developments and the impact on various departments, review timescales and raise and discuss other new ideas. There certainly needs to be good communication between R&D, marketing and manufacturing. In between and just before these bigger meetings, there were smaller inter-department meetings to be clear and correct on reporting progress at the larger 'all departments' meetings. The MPD meetings were approximately every six to 10 weeks, depending on whether any product would soon be launched.

The other key aspect in managing new product development is for the project manager to use software for critical path project management. This keeps the development people and management team more aware of progress and timescales. Innovation can consist of small steps to improve existing products and also small changes to products which can improve production efficiency, and timescales still need to be considered.

At Autotype, our fast growth was significantly helped by new products and product improvements. Our customers tested many prototype products, including in overseas markets, and some new product developments had to go back into R&D for changes before the next production trial.

Generally, companies think innovations are for products for the market. However, innovations can be for internal gain to improve them for production and even administration benefits. At Geka, we ran a suggestion scheme for improvements in the factory. Every month we paid £10 (at today's rate) for every sensible approved suggestion and £100 for the best suggestion of the month if it could be implemented. We also paid 10 per cent of any big savings idea implemented. One lady in production had an idea to reduce three people to two in one production process, which resulted in her receiving a four-figure sum.

At an MPD Meeting (at Geka), the purchasing manager showed a mascara pack component of a metal ferrule that had a curled edge at one end instead of being a parallel-sided open tube shape. The supplier had offered this because it was cheaper than the straight edge tube version. This was because a metal cap was used, which then had the centre of the cap top punched out rather than the tube being specially cut in a different operation. The supplier's easier process meant a considerable price reduction. However, it was not what we were using at that time.

There was a debate on how it would look on a double-end mascara pack. Would the consumer dislike it, or would they even notice it? What would *our* customers think? For our production, the printed ferrule had to be oriented and assembled correctly. The curled end printed ferrule would actually make assembly easier by indicating which way round the ferrule should be assembled. The alternative component was offered to us at a 10 per cent lower price. When we calculated it would also cut costs for assembly, we decided we could split the cost-saving between the customer and us to encourage them to accept it. The sales manager, called the development manager in America, proposed the idea and offered a price reduction on the pack. The sample was posted off, and approval came from the customer within a week. Another good result from a new idea, this time from purchasing.

A similar but different production improvement was discussed for a second time at the MPD committee meeting concerning the difficulty in the assembly of one particular design of mascara cap. When going down the assembly conveyor line, the tapered top end of the cap would regularly stick inside the mouth of the cap it was following. In other words, we could not get smooth production, only 'stop start' with the operator having to unjam the sticking caps. Whatever was tried in production did not work. Finally, we discussed that if the cap was wider at the top, that would stop each cap from sticking into the 'mouth' of the one in front. We agreed to get samples made and sent to the customer. They would need to check whether the slightly wider caps at the top of the cap would be all right on their filling lines and whether the mascara pack would still fit if a carton was used. The sales director called the customer development director to discuss what we proposed. The customer director thought that would be fine, and we sent off samples for him to see. The customer approved the slightly wider top to the caps, and our production efficiency improved accordingly.

Company development meetings can result in all-around benefits for the production and sales teams, marketing, and customers and boost morale through interest and involvement. The Product Development meetings can also be used for brainstorming sessions to spark other ideas.

LESSON

1. **Regular Manufacturing and Product Development or Product Improvement Meetings ensure that developments and ideas can be discussed and pushed through to production or supply and to the market more efficiently.**

2. **These meetings can lead to improved performance and profitability. Just 1% improvement here and there can soon make a big difference.**

3. **These meetings also provide a good forum for exploring and discussing costs and pricing to improve profitability.**

Reasons Why New Products Fail

Before Launch And After Launch

The examples mentioned previously should give some idea of why new products fail. The failure rate of new products is extremely high. Various estimates put it at 70% and above. The next chart offers reasons why many new products fail. The biggest reasons are usually Insufficient Demand and Alternatives, followed by Pricing and other factors.

When clients show me new product ideas I always ask "what is the competition?" I frequently get the answer "there is no competition". I then ask "what is the alternative" and get the answer "there is no alternative".

However, there is usually a different product which is doing the job and almost invariably I could find that there is an alternative or substitute. That is why when doing the market evaluation, researchers have to be thorough, ask the 'drill down' questions, and explore possible alternatives and usage.

The key reasons why new products fail are through poor research and planning at the inception stage. Fig 19 shows the main reasons.

FIG 19. *Causes of unsuccessful products before launch*

REASONS WHY NEW PRODUCTS FAIL
Reasons Before Launch

INSUFFICIENT DEMAND (SMALL MARKET)	COMPETITION, ALTERNATIVES & SUBSTITUTES	INSUFFICIENT MARKET RESEARCH
POOR PRODUCT DESIGN & MANUFACTURE	WRONG PRICE LEVEL	POOR DISTRIBUTION PLANNING

FIG 20. *Causes of unsuccessful products after launch*

REASONS WHY NEW PRODUCTS FAIL
Reasons After Launch

POOR/NO MARKETING RESEARCH	DIFFICULT MANUFACTURE OR SERVICE	POOR TEST MARKETING
INCORRECT PRICING	LACK OF / TOO MUCH QUALITY	POOR PROMOTIONAL MARKETING

If a product is launched and does not do well, there could be several reasons, as shown in **Fig 20**.

I have intentionally shown 'Poor Marketing Research' and 'Insufficient Marketing Research' in each of the two charts because there is an overlap with how well test marketing is conducted after the product is developed. Failure can be due to lack of demand, difficult and high manufacturing costs, quality issues, and promotional and pricing issues. Incorrect pricing can lead to selling unprofitably. There could also be insufficient funds for sales and promotion.

Test and trial marketing depends on the product's stage of development: test marketing of a prototype and further test marketing with a finished product. Pre-full production 'prototypes' can be tested with a few customers.

A limited production run to sell in a particular geographical area can be undertaken like the FMCG companies do (Fast Moving Consumer Goods companies), or selling initially through just a few dealers or selected customers to check out any glitches. A small test production run for the sales will also test the 'start up' of the production process.

A recent example of two causes for failure, pricing and manufacturing, is that of a completely new product by the Dyson company. In 2020 Dyson announced the cancellation of the development of their SUV electric seven-seater vehicle after spending £500 million on its development. The reason given was that Dyson found they could not produce the car for under £150,000. The car could have been suitable for the market and able to compete against Tesla, for example, but the problem was the high sales price needed because of the high manufacturing cost. Dyson would probably have sold some but not in sufficient volume. And the low volumes would have pushed the price even higher. So it was cancelled.

METHODOLOGY
How To Boost Performance

1. Involve all functions in product development and innovations by establishing appropriate regular meetings.

2. Fully investigate the alternatives and substitutes to know the benefits of the new product and what the potential sales could be.

3. Establish an outline of production costs and investments needed as early as possible.

CHAPTER SUMMARY

1. There are four types of new product development. Do research first. Talk to customers and target markets to assess realistic interest and look at alternatives...that's VERY important!

2. Assess production costs and probable pricing before product completion. Manage and monitor NPD progress.

3. Use Project Management software (like Microsoft Project).

4. Consider the general reasons why new products fail so you can try and avoid them.

Chapter Ten

Patents And Intellectual Property Rights (IPR)

This chapter will inform you about aspects to consider if applying for a patent and demonstrate **how to improve applications' success and avoid failures.** Typical problems arising in patent applications are included, so you can avoid them and save a lot of money and time.

Patents and Intellectual Property Rights are an essential part of life for many businesses. Many patents are applied for and granted, then achieve hardly any sales or none at all. It can be a waste of time and money to apply for them in many cases.

Other patents achieve successful sales volumes, and the products are protected from competition. However, a company may be forced to defend their patent rights against an imitator, which can cost huge sums of money. In between these extremes, various other scenarios occur to a greater or lesser degree.

Three things apply when obtaining a patent. You could say 'should apply', but this is not always the case. The three things are:

1. The application should be for something which has not been invented before.
2. It should be inventive, not something which a person 'skilled in the art' or experienced in the business area, could not easily have thought of.
3. It should be commercially viable.

I have provided some examples of different applications and situations from my own experiences: providing food for thought for companies or individuals involved in seeking a patent. In Chapter Nine: Product Development And New Products there is also the development of the combined toothpaste and toothbrush dispenser example; which although innovative was not 'commercially viable', so was a waste of money.

Straightforward Patent Application

The Flexible Packaging Division at Metal Box Ltd manufactured plastics films, and we were working on the 'stand-up pack', a flexible plastics film pack. It is a plastic pack with a gusset or additional plastic fold in the base, so it stands up and is used everywhere now for all sorts of products. The stand-up feature is helpful for the consumer to use at home and for display and product selection on the shelves of retail shops.

Our prototypes of this pack were difficult to open. The pack could not be torn open across the top because of the film's orientation (direction of the grain). The pack could be torn down the side, which was not good, as all the contents spilt out. Otherwise, the pack needed scissors to cut the top seal off, so it was not very convenient for the end-user.

I had realised that if the pack could be made with the grain running across rather than along it, then the top, with nicks at either side, could be torn open by hand. The next thought was that with a different heat seal shape to close the pack after filling; it could be opened by hand by tearing across the top, leaving only a small aperture for a straw for a drink.

A person 'skilled in the art' could not easily have thought of this because they know that the film is extruded and blown with the 'grain' running forward. Also, film packs were sealed after product filling using a heated bar across the top of the plastics packs

At the time, the company was also working on blowing film, which was 'biaxially orientated'. This means the film was pulled sideways as well as forward during the manufacturing extrusion process. This meant there could be an improvement in the ease of tearability across the top of the sealed pack, which might solve the problem.

We applied for a patent through our internal company patent agent. The application was for the 'stand up pack' to have the actual film of the pack be orientated horizontally instead of vertically with a 'nick' on either side at the top so the pack could be torn open by hand. In addition, the application was for shaped heat sealing at the top for apertures for pouring different types of product. Alternative reseal ideas such as gripper re-closure seals were also included in the patent application.

The application was successful, and the stand-up pack is now universally used today. However, it seemed to take some years before these packs became popular and universal. Metal Box sold off its plastics division, and maybe the patent hindered other manufacturers from bringing it to market until the patent expired. Also, the product filling machinery needed development to increase filling speeds to make the pack more economical to use compared to other packaging being filled on faster machinery. This sort of patent application met the main criteria and was quickly accepted by the patent office.

A More Difficult Patent Application

This example concerns the officers at the patent offices and how strict they might be on granting or refusing a patent. (This could be in the UK or USA.)

This anecdote concerns the American patent office in Silver City. We applied for a patent for a colour cosmetics pack component on something completely inventive that would be new for cosmetics consumers and benefit the cosmetics manufacturers.

In co-operation with their agent in the USA, our patent agent in London applied to get a patent in the USA and Europe. The USA Patent Officer kept finding objections to the application and sending back letters and information about other patents that he thought we were infringing. These other patents covered nothing like what we were applying for. This went on several times, and of course, it was expensive with our agents in the USA and England working on it and time-consuming for us.

In the end, I was going to New York for a cosmetics packaging exhibition and thought a visit at the same time to the Patent Officer in Silver City would be useful. A visit was therefore arranged.

We showed the officer the product prototypes and referred to the patents he was using as objections, which had no bearing on our patent application. After a fairly short chat, he 'saw the light', leant back in his chair and said, "Oh, I see now."

This was an immediate relief as we did not know how the meeting would go after so much correspondence. We just needed to alter a few words in the application and send the updated application back to him so he could sign it off. Job done, meeting over, successful outcome. Otherwise, this could have gone on for more months, and we may not have had the patent granted at all.

So, getting a patent can be a bit difficult, even if meeting the criteria. The application can depend on the Patent Officer, how good your patent agent is, and how well the patent is written. I thought our patent agents were good, but it was a difficult process with that particular patent officer in the USA.

The application can also depend on what prior art and patents are available for a patent officer to compare. This is well covered with the further example below.

Bad Patent With A Bad Outcome

This is about a patent being granted that did not meet the first two criteria, which were:

- something inventive that a person skilled in the art could not have thought of
- something which had not been done before.

Along the way, this application involved some poor executive judgement and a patent officer who was probably less strict than the one I had visited in Silver City.

The story goes back to the Metal Box acquisition of Valerflax in France mentioned in Chapter Nine. The person chosen to run the French company was Toby, a divisional manager at Metal Box. Ten years after helping him load his car in Reading, I did not imagine that we would end up in what I refer to as 'a stupid patent fight'.

Toby ran the plastics tube manufacturer in France for a few years; then when I met him again, he was the Chief Executive Officer (CEO) of a cosmetics packaging company in the USA. I was running Geka in the UK when he contacted me to say he was coming over to England and wanted to meet. We met up for lunch, and Toby proceeded to tell me that he had just applied for a patent in the USA for a new hollow centre filament, or fibre, for use in mascara brushes. The hollow fibre was made by Dupont in the USA, and samples had been issued to various manufacturers already, including Geka. They could be used for all sorts of brushes as well as mascara brushes.

Toby's patent application was to use this hollow fibre for mascara brushes to achieve a 'closed surface' effect. The characteristic of this fibre is that during brush manufacture, when the fibres are squeezed between the twisted wire being used to form the brush, then the hollow centre of the fibre is crushed, and the fibres splay out in random directions. The splayed out fibres cause the resultant brush to become a 'closed surface brush' – or uniform looking brush. The closed surface is achieved in the brush making machine with a few extra twists of the wire. If fewer twists are used in the manufacture of the brush, then the closed surface is not achieved. This 'closed surface' was a bit different from brushes showing the usual 'spiral twist' of the fibres.

Toby wanted to inform me that if the patent application was granted in America, he would then apply to have it granted in Europe. He would then expect us to pay an upfront fee of $100,000 and Royalties for selling hollow fibre mascara brushes and a minimum payment per year.

Dupont had sent sample fibres out to all types of brush makers, and I told Toby that we were already using the fibre and selling 'closed surface' mascara brushes. Therefore we had 'prior art', and anyway, there was nothing inventive in always trying and using new fibres. The original sample fibres were just sent out by Dupont for general use. There was no secrecy, and any person 'skilled in the art' could use these filaments and make a 'closed surface brush' by adjusting the setting for the number of twists in the mascara brush machine.

I also told Toby that in addition to the Dupont hollow fibre, which we were already using for 'closed surface brushes,' we had another fibre which we used to give a closed surface brush. Moreover, in the 1950s, Geka supplied Max Factor with 'closed surface' brushes using natural fibres.

"Toby", I said, "I cannot believe the patent will be granted because of previous prior art, meaning we are using it. Anybody skilled in the art could do it, and it is not sufficiently inventive". Toby insisted he was going to push on with the application in the USA because 'closed surface' mascara brushes using hollow fibre were going to be 'the big thing' for mascara packs. Despite my information for him, Toby said if the application is granted in the USA, he will carry on with an application in Europe. He would then be demanding sales royalty fees from us for selling hollow fibre mascara brushes as well as the upfront fee.

Some months later, I was on a visit to Rimmel when I had a call from our office saying Toby had been granted the patent in the USA and would be applying for the patent in Europe. He wanted us to stop selling hollow fibre mascara brushes immediately and planned to take out an injunction to stop us. "Mmm, a bit worrying," I thought. "That sounds like hassle coming up".

When I got back to the office, I called our patent agent to discuss the situation. He advised approaching a London firm of lawyers he had worked with. I called the firm and explained the situation to Graham, a partner at the firm. I said we wanted to fight any injunction and fight the European patent application. I asked how much it might cost us to do that. Graham informed me he thought it would be about £30,000 (more than 20 years ago). After discussing with my colleagues in Germany, it was agreed we would jointly proceed with the legal action as this spurious patent could affect the whole Geka Group (which was obviously Toby's intention so he could gain a competitive advantage).

Of course, the correspondence goes back and forth once lawyers get involved! Evidence had to be hunted out. Statements have to be read and changed. There was a claim from Toby's side that the hollow fibre samples were sent out in confidence by Dupont. We had contacted the Dupont Technical director, who disputed that claim and was prepared to come to court in England to support us by confirming samples were sent to many brush making customers.

A date was eventually set for the court case. A few weeks before the case came to court, a meeting was arranged in Germany between the two sides. The outcome of the meeting was that it was agreed that both sides wanted to settle before the case came to court, as it would cost even more legal fees if the case went to appeal. After the meeting, documents from the other side kept being received by our lawyers while we were winding down the legal work. The former Technical Director of Dupont fibres had come to London by this stage. The trouble was that he wanted to stay in the Dorchester Hotel, so his costs and the lawyers' costs at this time were £20,000 per week!

During the evidence gathering, I had sent our lawyers a selection of hollow fibre mascara brushes at a fairly early stage, each with a different number of twists of the wire in the brush. The samples started off with a smaller number of twists, say 12 twists for the mascara brush, and the brushes showed the usual spiral effect and were not 'closed surface'. Then as the twists were increased to 16 twists, so the filaments splayed out more. At a certain number of twists, the brush had a 'closed surface'. Just before that point, one twist or two twists less, the brushes were not quite closed surface. I asked Graham (our lawyer) to send the brush samples to Toby's lawyers with the question, 'which number of twists infringed his patent, and which did not'. Something as simple as that is not really patent worthy. You cannot have something as simple as a number of wire twists which nearly meet the patent claim but do not infringe it for a matter of two twists of wire. Did the USA lawyers ever ask Toby and his team? Our lawyers did not get an answer. Their lawyers carried on mounting up the costs for Toby and us.

Although there was an agreement in principle to settle out of court, we were running out of time before the court date, which was just three weeks away. My German colleagues thought Toby's lawyers were getting us to stop work so that we would be unprepared for the court case, and then they could win it. I called Graham and asked him what was happening. He said whatever he wrote and proposed to Toby's lawyers in London got a non-constructive reply that did not show any urgency towards an agreement before the court hearing. This could have gone on for weeks and was costing a lot. I told Graham he needed to meet with Toby's lawyers and thrash it out, but Graham felt they would never agree. I said I would call Toby in America and ask him to tell his lawyers to meet you 'tomorrow'. I did that, and asked him if he wanted to settle. He said he did. I explained the situation between the lawyers and how I thought we could probably settle quickly with a meeting between them as they were located no more than a mile apart in London. Toby agreed to instruct his lawyers to set up a meeting the next day. It transpired the meeting took place a day after that – but at least it did happen.

I briefed Graham in advance, saying I wanted the other party to agree on five points and provided my 'fallback' position on those five points – just in case. Graham was pessimistic about getting an agreeable resolution. However, he at least had a day to prepare!

After the meeting, Graham called me immediately to tell me, "Everything has been agreed upon, and we are settling". I asked about my five points, and he reassured me that Toby's lawyers had agreed to all five of them. I asked if that was 'in full or the fallback positions'. He said, "They agreed in full to all the five demands".

That was great news. We got it wrapped up and saved some more tens of thousands of pounds a week. I had offered them a small royalty fee on sales, no upfront payments, and no annual minimum sales. Plus, our existing closed surface brush fibre was left out of the royalty deal. The agreement was quickly written up, and the patent fight was over. The main objective had been achieved (to stop the huge costs this was incurring), but we would also be able to continue selling hollow fibre brushes if we wanted to at a slight cost increase.

As a result of the agreement, I was determined not to pay royalty fees to Toby's company. We changed the brush specification with clients who used the Dupont hollow fibre brushes back to our own 'closed surface' brush fibre. There was only one customer who decided not to change. Therefore any fees payable from us to Toby's company were minimal. We could continue supplying all our customers and future customers with brushes and fibres to meet all mascara formulation requirements.

Some months after settlement, Toby was in England and wanted to meet up again. I agreed. I thought it would be interesting to hear what he had to say. Over lunch, Toby bemoaned the patent fight and the whole situation. I reminded him that I had warned him at our previous meeting that he had an extremely weak case for a patent, that it did not meet the basic criteria, and that we were already making hollow fibre brushes for customers. The statement claiming Dupont had sent out the fibres in secrecy was plainly 'fake news'. In fact, we also discovered a patent in the UK for a closed surface brush going back donkey's years...to the First World War.

Toby was a bit disconsolate and said, "Well, I have learnt a lot about lawyers. I let them get on with it, then finally, with the date for the court hearing looming, they told me they did not think we could win". After what I told Toby previously, I was amazed that he had allowed the lawyers to 'just get on with it'. An excellent way to shovel money out of the company! Toby had been under the impression that this nice looking 'closed surface' brush would be used for all mascara formulations. I pointed out that closed surface brushes were only suitable for thin liquid formulations that could flow between the fibres and be combed onto the eyelashes. Thicker formulations did not work well with 'closed surface brushes' because there was not enough 'pick up', so open surface brushes were needed for thicker formulations – which were the majority. The demand for closed surface brushes was far less than he thought! I told Toby that I reckoned his settlement with us would take him about 18-20 years to get a payback on his lawyers' fees. Toby did agree with this and said rather gloomily, "I think you are probably right." I added that if and when we changed that last customer to another brush, he would get no Royalties from us at all.

The next I heard of Toby was that he was back in the UK running a small sales office. We reckoned the patent fight and the money spent might have caused him problems with the company's owners in the USA. It had cost us some £360,000 (£685,000 at 2020 prices), so for Tony, I reckon the cost may have been up to $800,000 or $900,000 or more for nothing.

The difficulty with this patent application, I suspect, is that the patent officer could not find any prior art and would not have understood the brush making industry. So, he had been lenient in the granting of the patent. Perhaps when Tony said he was applying for a patent, we should have kept an eye open on patent applications and objected straight away to the USA patent office. We just could not believe a patent would be granted in the USA for such a flimsy case and no inventiveness.

As you can see, this perfectly demonstrates a bad patent application. Unfortunately for Toby (and us), it got granted. It cost our two firms, both of which were part of a group of companies, a lot of money.

LESSON

Bad or weak patents can be granted against your business.

A No-no In Patent Applications

I once worked with a small electronics firm. The MDO had been sent a new electronic device from one of his suppliers, complementing his own products. It was a more compact unit than the ones he was currently using in his equipment.

On discussion with the MDO, we thought that the electronic product could be used for a new application using only the electronic workings, which could be built into other equipment. We discussed that perhaps the application could be patented as it was different equipment for a new market application. The MDO mentioned this to his supplier, but although the manufacturer did not believe it could be patented, my customer thought it was worth pursuing.

The MDO, an electronics engineer and his colleague, got the patent application written up and involved me. When I saw the drafts, I realised the MDO was not only proposing to put his own name on the patent but also the name of his supplier/manufacturer. I told him not to put the manufacturer's name on it. The MDO said, "I have no reason to distrust him. He has been supplying me with products for my current market segment for years". I told him that it was unwise and served no useful purpose. However, my advice was ignored.

The patent was granted. He then had a contract drawn up between himself and his supplier whereby my customer would have worldwide rights to sell this modified electronics device internationally for its particular application in domestic appliances.

We visited several companies together, and the device was successfully sold. In particular to one large multinational, so some income from the patent was generated from the first orders. After that success, my customer's supplier went direct to my client's customer, undercut the MDO's price, and then approached other potential users. The MD could do nothing unless he wanted to go to court over the exclusivity contract. Knowing the potential cost, it was decided there was no point in fighting it.

If the MDO had put his name alone on the patent, it is likely he would still be getting an income from all the repeat business for the unit.

I was suspicious of the supplier at an early stage. For example, when a meeting between the MDO and supplier was arranged to discuss the draft contract, the MDO called me afterwards to tell me how it went. I asked what comments or changes to the contract the supplier had discussed and was told the supplier did not say much and agreed with everything. My view later was that the supplier had agreed to everything or did not ask any questions, thinking he could later ignore it if he wanted to because the MDO's company was not large enough to have the resources to fight it. Although the MDO had been a general manager of a large multinational electronics group and was very well qualified, on this occasion, he had been just a bit naïve about such a complex situation.

LESSON

Never put anybody else's name on a patent, even if you are business partners in the same firm.

If business partners split up, then, without an explicit agreement in place, each could use it.

Patents should be covered in employment contracts as belonging to the company, not the employee.

The patent lawyer at Metal Box asked if I wanted my name on the patent for the 'stand up pack'; I said no, it did not matter to me as the patent belonged to Metal Box. However, the patent that we obtained at Silver City in the USA has my name on it, and I have the patent letter here in my office. However, the patent rights under my employment contract belong to the Geka Group, which is as it should be.

Protecting Your IPR

When undertaking product development, it is always advisable to use a Non Disclosure Agreement (NDA) when sharing the details of the project. An application must be kept secret before a patent application is made; otherwise, it can be objected to, or the idea can be stolen.

Our colleagues in Germany were visited at the factory by the product development people from a large French international cosmetics company. The visitors were shown an exciting development which was underway and which they liked. Some weeks later, Norbert, the Geka Germany product development director, saw a patent application had been filed by the patent person on the development side of the French cosmetics company. Norbert wrote to the Patent Office objecting to the patent application and citing our prior art and details. The patent office sent the objection to the French company. They then wrote to Norbert, stating that if Geka wanted to do future business with them, he would have to rescind his objection. So we had to do that!

LESSON

Do not show anybody, especially customers or suppliers, any new ideas or development work...and certainly not without an NDA or if in a position of 'patent applied for.' A patent granted is the best protection.

I mentioned in Chapter Four how we had improved output at Geka UK. The group had developed special machinery for handling specific components, and we ensured these machines had covers on them so visitors could not see the workings. In addition, on specially developed machines, I had the manufacturers' nameplates taken off and filed away. This would preserve our advantages for as long as possible.

Buyers often like to have a second supplier, so if they get information to help another supplier and, therefore, some leverage in pricing, they might pass on the information. I did not want to provide an opportunity for this to happen.

Compared to losing a possible patent claim, we did have a much better experience with an American cosmetics company. Geka Germany developed a new mascara brush design and patented it. The brush was shown to the customer, who wanted to use it but did not want to rely on just one supplier. So just in case of any future supply difficulties, they wanted to own the patent. The company paid $500,000 for the patent rights and then bought the mascara products with that brush from Geka Germany. Geka would then be the sole supplier for that product for as long as the customer was happy with the group's performance. That was a satisfactory outcome for the patent obtained, and both the customer and Geka were satisfied.

METHODOLOGY
How To Boost Performance

1. It could be good insurance to ask a patent agent to monitor all new applications pertaining to your business area. There is then the opportunity to object and have the application refused; this is far cheaper than going to court.

2. Be aware that bad or weak patents can be granted against your business.

3. Be aware that if you have a patent, you might have to defend it. This is generally very expensive.

4. If a weak patent gets granted against your business, have you got the resources to fight it?

5. Always use an NDA. Protect your in-house knowledge and expertise.

CHAPTER SUMMARY

1. I have highlighted the three things that need to be considered when deciding to proceed with a patent application. Also, look out for what 'prior art' exists.

2. Be aware that patents can be granted even if 'prior art' products exist.

3. Also explained was what *not* to do in patent applications, product development, and specialist know-how.

Chapter Eleven
Financial Accounts And Reporting

This chapter demonstrates **how to achieve effective and meaningful reporting** and set out clearer, compelling and informative reports for management to enable faster remedial action.

You will further learn about special and highly significant methods to manage gross profit to achieve success.

Gross Profit

The importance of the 'clean gross profit' measurement was covered in Chapter Six, and the links to costing and pricing have been explained. A business has to focus on making a sensible margin on the product or service and make a good gross profit to cover the overhead costs. Obtaining a good gross profit is essential to making a net profit. Therefore, it is imperative to measure the 'clean gross profit' monthly and continue to monitor the percentage trend. The monthly accounts should show the key costs in the Cost of Goods (as previously explained) and so show the 'clean gross profit.'

Before proceeding to reporting aspects, I want to repeat some points on gross profit I highlighted in Chapter Six.

> **Before net profit, the most important figures are the 'clean gross profit' figures.**

> **The continual measurement and careful management of gross profit are essential for the survival and growth of a company.**

To also repeat, the reason for this statement is that the GP figures tell you:

- **where you were**
- **where you are**
- **where you are going.**

If the figures show 'where you are going' and you don't take action to influence it, you might arrive where you do not want to be. Just one significant example is Thomas Cook Fig 12 & Fig 13. The gross profit figures mean both the value and the percentage; both statistics must be measured and monitored.

Over the years, I have found that many accountants and many SME MDs do not have a good understanding of the gross profit measurement. I have frequently had to explain to MDs its significance in their P&L accounts. For example...

> **'Down at the gross profit figure, this shows where you have made money; below that, it is where you spend the money.'**

If the gross profit in money for the month or the year does not cover all the indirect costs below the gross profit line, the company is making a loss in that month or year.

The gross profit money earned should cover all the overheads, such as indirect staffing of sales, marketing, accounts, administration, variable costs, rent and rates, depreciation, and so on, leaving enough money left over for profit.

Yet, many accounting books just show, 'Sales less Cost of Goods equals Gross Profit.'

The big reason why different accountants use different figures in the Cost of Goods column and why this results in many companies not understanding it (as already covered in Chapter Six) is because **there is no set legal definition for Cost of Goods, so different accountants show different items.**

What some accountants call Cost of Goods and Cost of Sales can include a range of costs. And some accountants show the gross profit as simply,

'Sales price less materials'. They then put the direct labour cost below the gross profit line. This is entirely wrong for measuring production or service efficiency; it does not inform management of the critical 'clean cost of goods', the relevant percentages, how efficient and consistent the labour costs are compared to the sales revenue, and of course, any changes in the trend. So, it is essential to have a 'clean gross profit' in the monthly management accounts. It should look like this to manage for success:

Total Sales:
- less direct Materials
- less Production consumables
- less Direct wages
- less Transport and Packing
- **equals Gross Profit £ and %.**

Fig 21. Example 1. This business plan shows the direct cost of goods layout and the gross profit figures in value and per cent layout from a small telecoms equipment reseller.

The chart shows the year-end accounts and the plan for the following year. The P&L format makes planning by percentages and money very quick and easy. We set the accounts up for clarity on the sales income, materials, and direct labour. A nice gross profit margin of 57% is achieved, with a gross profit of £371,623. This value fully covered all the overheads of £327,423 and made an operating profit of £44,200 with a margin of 6.8%. However, you can see that this private company declared a loss because the MD took out dividends of £77,639.

Some of this dividend was taken over the year. Also, some may not have been taken out of the business, but it can be in a director's loan account. The dividends are partly funded by the depreciation charge account of £12,917 and by quick payment by debtors, and perhaps slowing a few payments to suppliers.

FIG 21. XYZ P&L and Budget Plan

XYZ BUSINESS PLAN P & L 2005

	ACTUAL YR TO DEC 04	% OF SALES	BUDGET 2005	% OF SALES
1. SALES			Plus 52%	
1. Hardware	527870	82		
2. Maintenance	63540	10		
3. Lcr commissions	42370	7		
4. Consultancy sales	13902	2		
TOTAL SALES	**647682**	**100**	**984,000**	**100**
2. DIRECT COSTS				
Systems purchases	197029	30		
Maintenance	17119	3		
Engineer labour	61911	10		
TOTAL DIRECT COSTS	**276059**	**43**	**423000**	**43**
3. GROSS PROFIT	**371623**	**57**	**561000**	**57**
4. INDIRECT COSTS				
Salaries, ni & comms	187723	**29**	**218000**	**22**
Variable costs	77900	12	88000	9
Fixed costs	31509	5	33500	3
Professional costs	12180	2	14000	
Bank charges/interest	5194	0.8	5300	
Depreciation/amortis'n	12917	2	12950	
TOTAL INDIRECT COST	**327423**	**51**	**371750**	**38**
5. TOTAL COSTS	**603482**	**93.2**	**794750**	**81**
6. OPERATING PROFIT	**44200**	**6.8**	**189250**	**19**
Dividends/drawings	77639	13.4	100000	10
7. NET PROFIT(LOSS)	**-33439**	**-5%**	**89250**	**9**
8. TAXATION T.B.C.				

Fig 21 is the clear layout for the 2004 accounts showing the various product group sales, gross profit, overheads, how much profit was made, and the drawings taken out, leaving a net loss. As can be seen, the clear accounts layout made it easy and quick to plan for the following year. If the gross profit of 57% in 2004 is also the target for the next year, then projections are easy. Just increase overall sales to achieve the same GP margin.

The accounts show a loss, but actually, this was a good going concern. Over the next few years, it achieved a turnover of £5 million per annum with an excellent net profit. Later on, the MD sold the company for £4.4 million. He was delighted with the fantastic sales price (and permitted me to publish the information). This result was assisted by the fact that the clean gross profit and easy to read accounts enabled more focus on other things that mattered, such as increasing sales at the right margins.

Planning And Budgeting

Trying to predict different sales of different products is not always a productive use of time. However, where contract or repeat sales are made, individual customer product sales can more easily be planned for the year ahead.

Once the budget for sales is set, and the gross profit amount in pounds is planned, then planning for the remaining costs and people required is more straightforward. The forward planning is based on the previous year's percentage costs and probable additional required costs. For instance, it can be seen in Fig 21 that the forecast increase in overhead costs would result in costs of 38% of sales compared to 51% in the 'current' year.

The emphasis has been made on the importance of monitoring the performance and trends in the costs and percentages of direct labour and materials. **Fig 21** is a simple layout of sales and GP. The following example has more direct costs involved in the gross profit calculation. These additional direct costs can also be very important to monitor. The following example, **Fig 22**, shows a manufacturing company's P&L layout after we had managed to clean up the figures in the 'cost of goods'.

FIG 22. *Triple Y Engineering P&L*

Triple YYY Engineering Limited

	Current Month		Year to Date	
	£	% to Sales	£	% to Sales
Sales				
UK sales	162,400	96		
Export sales	4,000	2.4		
Carriage & packing Charged	1,600	1		
Total Sales	168,000	100		
Cost of Direct Materials	38,000	23		
Gross Profit 1	130,000	77		
Production Costs excl. Depreciation				
Direct Labour	55,500	33		
Sub Contractors	1,700	1		
General tooling	1,400	1		
Cutting Tools	2,500	2		
Production consumables	950	1		
Plant repairs	1,000	1		
Carriage & Packing	3,250	2		
Total Labour & production costs	63,050	37.5		
Total Production costs	101,050	62		
Gross profit 2	67,300	38		

The most critical costs are:

- the cost of Direct Materials at 22.6% of sales
- the cost of Direct labour at 33% of sales
- the Gross Profit margin figure at 38% of sales.

The 38% GP (in this case, £67,300) is what is available that month to cover all the overheads and depreciation and to make a profit. These three figures of materials, labour, and GP need to be closely monitored and improved wherever possible.

In the example in Fig 22, a line is shown as GP1 with direct material costs shown above. This clearly measures the material usage and the amount of gross profit margin made at this stage. The description of Gross Profit 1 can be used at this point and makes it quite clear to the MD and directors the materials costs compared to sales income and the trend in the cost of the raw materials. The figures can also indicate the trend in any materials price increases. There is a focus on the 23% material usage in this company. The management had achieved this percentage through price rises on unprofitable products. Those percentage figures are the sum of all the *Individual Sales Prices and Individual Product Margins added together.*

If prices are reduced or margins are reduced because of material cost increases or customer pressures, the key percentages will worsen. If they get worse for, say, three months or more, it is imperative to look at possible actions to take before things deteriorate even further.

In the chart of Triple YYY Engineering, the production consumables figure is very important. A significant consumable is 'cutting tools'. Initially, we struggled to get to grips with the accounts; they were unclear and difficult to understand. We discovered that the previous accountant had included items such as light bulbs, toilet paper, company cleaning materials, and other miscellaneous items. These were mainly indirect costs but entered as production consumables. This took some sorting out in the ledgers and the accounts to understand the GP situation and trend. When the cutting tool costs were clarified, they showed up as costs of approximately £84,000 per year...a high cost. After some investigation, we found that the buyer was quite logically purchasing the cheapest cutting tools from two suppliers. We started doing trials with more expensive and better cutting tools and found that the more expensive cutting tools lasted longer and did not need replacing so often. This enabled us to reduce the costs of the cutting tools significantly. We also found an increase in productivity because the new tools cut faster.

In **Fig 22**, where the monthly cost for cutting tools is £2500, this was a low production month but showed a cost of only 2% on sales compared to previous monthly figures of up to 4% of sales. So costs were halved, saving approximately £40,000 a year. That was a significant cost reduction and improvement in productivity. This achievement was realised by having clean gross profit monthly accounts, so we could closely analyse and monitor expenditure and trends and instigate actions where we saw they were possible.

The Depreciation Charge

In our example, it can be seen that there is no depreciation charge put in the production costs for the depreciation of machinery. Some accountants like to put that charge in as a direct cost. However, depreciation is not a cost, it is a 'charge', or simply a 'savings account for future investment.' You could think of it as the money taken out of profits and entered into a savings account called 'depreciation.' I have had to explain this to several small company MDs. And of course, you can argue this point with the accountant, as there is no set rule for the definition of Cost of Goods to arrive at the gross profit.

If a depreciation charge is shown in direct costs, it reduces the real gross profit and reduces the actual trend. The depreciation charge has to be added back in below the gross profit line to know how much money has been made for the month and whether the gross profit covers the overhead costs.

The other thing about a depreciation charge being included in the production costs is that it distorts the trend, which otherwise could more clearly indicate the necessity for action. For instance, as a machine or investment drops out of having a depreciation charge, i.e. it is written off, then the gross profit would go up. Perhaps later, after some further investment and an increased depreciation charge, there is a reduction in the GP percentage margin.

LESSON

The depreciation charge entered before Gross Profit serves no useful purpose and only confuses the trend.

Other Direct Costs

In Fig 22, the accountant has included plant repairs in the cost of sales. This is only 1% of sales, so it is not too significant. The trouble with the entry of plant repairs is that there can be expensive months with thousands of pounds for repairs and other months with no cost. Large variations can affect the GP trend. It can sometimes be better to put plant repairs in the overheads and keep an eye on them there. In reality, it is a production cost, and if costs are going up, something needs to be done to make improvements. The costs and trends in plant repairs can be covered in the monthly production report and accounts report.

The key requirement in looking at production efficiency is the measurement of the total direct cost and the individual important items of material usage and direct wages. There is huge importance in measuring the gross profit and the margin of material usage or bought-in products. Some material costs, such as plastics based on oil, have tended to increase every few months in the past. All the plastics products suppliers conduct price rise negotiations regularly because, if prices were not raised because of inflation of material costs, a company would soon end up in grave difficulties. Years ago, there was a period of considerable increases in the price of copper used in the manufacture of metal goods such as valves and tubes for the water, gas and oil industries. I was once told that the copper came from mines in Zambia, and every time there was a wage rise of 'just a penny an hour', (I don't know if that was the true figure), that then caused a largish increase in the price of copper. Regardless, I was busy at the valve manufacturer working on costings and raising prices every three months.

The two examples in Figs 21 and 22 show a layout for the 'Sales and Cost of Goods' information to arrive at the 'clean gross profit' value and margin. It is then easy to monitor these critical figures.

As mentioned, the P&L accounts in some companies add the direct wages to the overhead personnel costs to show total wages and salaries below the GP line. As can be envisaged, this is of no help in understanding the efficiency and trend in the use of direct labour. This seemed to be the case with the company's former owner in Fig 22.

To summarise, it is crucial to have a 'clean gross profit' to focus on measuring production efficiencies in the Cost of Goods. It is also essential to keep an eye on the total sales value and on the prices and margins of individual products. Attention also needs to be kept on the overall margins on sales to individual customers and the individual products supplied to them.

A further comment on Fig 22 and the monitoring of gross profit and the margins of individual customers. Previously, I mentioned the customer who had not had price rises for nine years! The figures in Fig 22 were after increasing prices to that customer and tackling some production inefficiencies. The company was then starting to get back on track to profit and sales growth.

Having gone through the accounts layout and the items for gross profit measurement in some detail, **Fig 23** is an overview chart showing what has been covered down to the gross profit line. The chart shows the 'four circles' that have to be well managed to make money in manufacturing. It also applies to other industries to various degrees.

FIG 23. Production Efficiency Maximisation

OVERVIEW OF PRODUCTION EFFICIENCY MAXIMISATION

1. THE KEY ELEMENTS OF COST OF PRODUCTION ARE SHOWN BELOW:

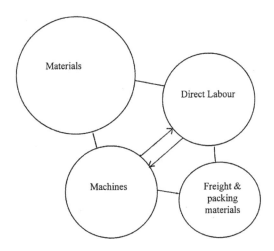

The elements closely interreact. Machines and labour are the most interdependent. Machines with high output, high quality output, high utilisation and minimum labour are needed.

---

2. MATERIALS AND DIRECT LABOUR ARE THE BIGGEST COSTS IN PRODUCTION.

Materials - Apply best purchasing practises. This is fairly straight forward and generally well understood.

---

3. DIRECT LABOUR AND MACHINES - This is an area where normally huge improvements can be made.

---

4. ADDITIONALLY - Review sales prices and costs to see if some products should be discontinued or prices increased.
- Review short run work for costs / contribution and discontinue or subcontract out.

The production process can be described as: **'the output of Men, Materials and Machines'**, (or maybe these days, People, Purchases, and Production equipment?) and then including freight and packing materials.

With some repetition for emphasis, the chart shows a circle called materials, which represents Direct Materials. The Direct Materials costs vary on a month to month basis according to the use of different company operations and with different products.

What is important to watch is the costs on the main items; that the percentage margin on direct materials to sales is being maintained; in addition, monitor that the direct labour percentage costs to sales are not creeping up.

Other production costs such as plant repairs and their trend can be monitored in the overheads figures to look at investment requirements and planned maintenance.

Overhead Costs

In larger companies, qualified accountants are employed. They write the monthly reports to explain costs and variances for the month by looking at the detailed accounts behind the summary management accounts. It is also essential that the person in charge of the accounts in smaller companies should still do a report or add comments to the accounts.

However, it is advantageous to an MD to have the overheads set out in the accounts in a way they can be read quickly, easily understood and queried if necessary. The key section in the overhead costs is the overhead wages and salaries, which can quickly be kept an eye on in relation to sales trends and profitability.

In **Fig 24,** the format of three accounts pages is a good way of presenting clear and meaningful accounts. Some key points to notice are:

Page 1 covers the sales and cost of goods down to the gross profit.

Page 2 covers the overhead accounts for the P and L. It is sensible to put the variable, fixed and professional costs into separate groupings for convenience. This makes for easier and faster reading and understanding.

Trends can always be seen by reference to costs as a percentage to sales.

The Variable costs should be ranked as best as possible at the start of the year from highest cost to lowest cost, again to quickly read and identify any cost variances, especially those of significance. Preparing the layout at the start of the year ensures the same familiar format for the year.

The overheads of the Fixed and Professional costs are each grouped into separate blocks. These costs do not vary much, so time is saved by not having to review them unnecessarily every single month among a sea of numbers.

FIG 24. XYZ Accounts Layout

XYZ Ltd   Profit Loss Account

YEAR:	March 2005 to February 2006			Period:	Oct-05	
				Month:	8	
Sales	This Month	Sales Ratio % of Turnover		Year to Date	Sales Ratio % of Turnover	
Hardware	24,356	33.0%		274,160	41.2%	
Leasing	21,336	28.9%		80,393	12.1%	
Maintenance	11,112	15.1%		90,721	13.6%	
Commissions	2,730	3.7%		43,577	6.6%	
Labour	9,773	13.2%		137,438	20.7%	
Maintenenance New Sales	1,655	2.2%		14,138	2.1%	
Progressive Maintenance	2,643	3.6%		5,254	0.8%	
Information on Hold		0.0%		1,000	0.2%	
Sales to RBC	122	0.2%		18,429	2.8%	
Interest Received	37	0.1%		316	0.0%	
Sale of Assets		0.0%		-129	0.0%	
Total Sales	**£73,764**	100.0%		**£665,297**	100.0%	
Purchases	This Month	Purchase Ratio % of Turnover		Year to Date	Purchase Ratio % of Turnover	
Purchases	22,541	30.6%		204,016	30.7%	
Purchase Charges	392	0.5%		3,287	0.5%	
Late Invoices		0.0%			0.0%	
Total Purchases	**£22,933**	31.1%		**£207,303**	31.2%	
Direct Expenses	This Month	Direct Expenses Ratio % of Turnover		Year to Date	Direct Expenses Ratio % of Turnover	
Labour & Sub Contractors	700	0.9%		3,007	0.5%	
Commissions	995	1.3%		1,835	0.3%	
Direct Salaries	19,365	26.3%		149,417	22.5%	
Total Direct Expenses	**£21,060**	28.6%		**£154,259**	23.2%	
	This Month	Gross Profit Ratio % of Turnover		Year to Date	Gross Profit Ratio % of Turnover	
Gross Profit / (Loss)	**£29,771**	40.4%		**£303,735**	45.7%	

XYZ Ltd   **Profit Loss Account**

Overheads	This Month	Overheads Ratio % of Turnover		Year to Date	Overheads Ratio % of Turnover
Variable Costs					
Wages & Salaries	12,909	17.5%		99,611	15.0%
Motor Expenses	1,839	2.5%		18,568	2.8%
Mal Consultancy Fees	0	0.0%		10,256	1.5%
Travel & Entertaining	1,622	2.2%		16,260	2.4%
Parking	492	0.7%		2,563	0.4%
Mileage	2,699	3.7%		19,503	2.9%
Congestion Charging	170	0.2%		1,196	0.2%
Mobile Phone	995	1.3%		7,133	1.1%
Telephone & Fax	394	0.5%		2,752	0.4%
Internet / Website	87	0.1%		1,776	0.3%
Training Cost	2,898	3.9%		10,781	1.6%
Post & Carriage	219	0.3%		1,217	0.2%
Stationery	257	0.3%		4,165	0.6%
Computer Costs	434	0.6%		1,255	0.2%
Staff Welfare	76	0.1%		927	0.1%
Staff Entertainment	0	0.0%		424	0.1%
Maintenance (Premises)	26	0.0%		686	0.1%
Misc. Expenses	0	0.0%		455	0.1%
Insurance Claim Costs	0	0.0%		0	0.0%
Sales Promotions	0	0.0%		0	0.0%
Advertising	119	0.2%		1,573	0.2%
Gifts	0	0.0%		435	0.1%
Disposal of Assets	0	0.0%		0	0.0%
Bad Debts	-2	0.0%		6,897	1.0%
Suspense Account	-603	-0.8%		27	0.0%
Sub Total	**24,631**	**33.4%**		**208,460**	**31.3%**
Fixed Costs					
Rent & Rates	3,527	4.8%		26,933	4.0%
Depreciation	1,402	1.9%		21,422	3.2%
Directors Pension	600	0.8%		5,200	0.8%
Directors Insurance	23	0.0%		186	0.0%
Insurance Claim Costs	278	0.4%		1,667	0.3%
Heat, Light & Power	291	0.4%		659	0.1%
Sub Total	**6,121**	**8.3%**		**56,067**	**8.4%**
Professional Costs					
Audit & Accountancy	0	0.0%		10,536	1.6%
Bank Charges & Interest	365	0.5%		1,603	0.2%
Legal Fees	0	0.0%		2,700	0.4%
Professional Fees	0	0.0%		250	0.0%
Late Invoices	0	0.0%		0	0.0%
Sub Total	**365**	**0.5%**		**15,089**	**2.3%**
Total Overheads	**£31,117**	**42.2%**		**£279,616**	**42.0%**
Directors Dividends	This Month	Overheads Ratio % of Turnover		Year to Date	Overheads Ratio % of Turnover
Dividends	0	0.0%		0	0.0%
Total Dividends	0	0.0%		0	0.0%
	This Month	Net Profit Ratio % of Turnover		Year to Date	Net Profit Ratio % of Turnover
Net Profit / (Loss)	**-£1,346**	**-1.8%**		**£24,119**	**3.6%**

XYZ Ltd   Balance sheet KPI's

	This Month			Year to Date	
	Current Assets	Current Liabs.		Current Assets	Current Liabs.
	£14,771	£13,685		£206,975	£246,552
Working Capital Ratio	1.08	1.00		0.84	1.00

Should be   2:1

	This Month			Year to Date	
	Liquid Assets	Current Liabs.		Liquid Assets	Current Liabs.
	£14,771	£13,685		£171,975	£246,552
Liquid Capital Ratio	1.08	1.00		0.70	1.00

Should be   1:1

	This Month		Year to Date	
Stock	£0		£35,000	

	This Month		Year to Date	
Total Assets	£12,339		£418,857	
Total Liabilities	£13,685		£346,558	
Net Worth	-£1,346		£72,299	

	This Month		Year to Date	
Net Profit	-£1,346		£24,119	
Capital 01/03/2005	£45,028		£45,028	
Return on Capital Invested %			54%	

		Debtor Days
Debtors	£116,787	64.1

		Creditor Days
Creditors	£142,723	245.6

XYZ Ltd   Balance sheet KPI's

	This Month			Year to Date	
	Current Assets	Current Liabs.		Current Assets	Current Liabs.
	£14,771	£13,685		£206,975	£246,552
Working Capital Ratio	1.08	1.00		0.84	1.00

Should be   2:1

	This Month			Year to Date	
	Liquid Assets	Current Liabs.		Liquid Assets	Current Liabs.
	£14,771	£13,685		£171,975	£246,552
Liquid Capital Ratio	1.08	1.00		0.70	1.00

Should be   1:1

	This Month		Year to Date	
Stock	£0		£35,000	

	This Month		Year to Date	
Total Assets	£12,339		£418,857	
Total Liabilities	£13,685		£346,558	
Net Worth	-£1,346		£72,299	

	This Month		Year to Date	
Net Profit	-£1,346		£24,119	
Capital 01/03/2005	£45,028		£45,028	
Return on Capital Invested %			54%	

		Debtor Days
Debtors	£116,787	64.1

		Creditor Days
Creditors	£142,723	245.6

LESSON

The accounts layout in Figs 24/1/2/3 shows a useful layout of the monthly accounts for easy and quick reading, especially in smaller companies.

Depreciation And Funds Generated

One point to notice in Fig 24/2 is that depreciation has been put under Fixed Costs. It can be better there as a single 'charge' item rather than split into production depreciation and overhead depreciation.

As mentioned previously, depreciation is a 'charge' and not a real cost. It is a deduction from the profit and is a 'savings account for future investment'. The depreciation charge is added to the net profit to arrive at the **funds generated** for the month and year. So looking at the year figures for Period 8...

Net Profit: £24,119

Plus Depreciation: £21,442

Funds generated: £45,561 giving a figure of 6.8% on sales for the year to date.

Depreciation is not taxed at the corporate tax level on profit. There are tax allowances for the depreciation charge to encourage investment.

There is also another reason for the depreciation charge. It gives a focus on whether the company is investing in the future. To maintain the value of a company it is generally recommended that the same percentage amount of money that it is depreciating each year should be invested. If there is only a minimal depreciation charge, it is likely to be one of the following:

- the company cannot afford investing (so possibly in trouble?)
- the owners are being complacent, or,
- they are milking the profit, which will adversely affect the company in the future.

Another reason for a decreasing depreciation charge can be that a considerable investment programme of refurbishing has been undertaken, so the depreciation amount is declining each year because little extra investment is currently required.

The depreciation situation is especially important in manufacturing companies.

Balance Sheet Items

For the sake of completion in covering XYZ's accounts in Fig 24/3, the accounts supervisor added the balance sheet information to the monthly P&L accounts and also presented pie charts and graphs for most of the accounts information. This made for excellent quick visual details for the MD, and it was easier for him to ask questions and understand the progress of his companies.

The figures I've shown are for one of the three companies the Managing Director Owner (MDO) was running, so with three sets of figures like this, there was a clear picture for him to see of the performance of the companies.

Net Profit

The most important measure of a company's success is the net profit, often referred to as Return on Sales, or ROS. This ROS figure is not always a true figure on how a company is performing and can give a misleading view.

If you are looking at a company's balance sheet, some figures can lead to an untrue balance sheet overview. It may be that stock valuation is inflated or undervalued, depreciation is altered, or intangible assets are not written off as they should be. Thomas Cook's accounts are a prime example of this.

Their Balance Sheet and P&L needed to be read carefully to understand the real situation properly. (See more in Appendix 2).

These variations can be included or omitted in the P&L account and can affect the net profit *and* the figures on the Balance Sheet. A minimum depreciation charge that does not reduce goodwill, for instance, and obsolescent assets not written down, will show a larger net profit or a net profit when a loss should be declared.

The depreciation charge can be high by writing off redundant assets of machines and computers, for example, although these write-offs can be shown as a 'special write down', reducing the profits.

If the old stocks left in the stores are not written down, this inflates the profit situation or just reduces the losses declared. Are these 'adjustments' or 'non-adjustments' important? Yes, for several reasons. In smaller companies, better figures can help keep the bank manager happy or help secure a loan or increase an overdraft.

The Telecoms reseller company in Fig 21 showed a year-end loss but actually was a good going concern. This result was assisted by the fact that the clean gross profit and easy to read accounts enabled the MD to understand the business's finances.

Auditors And Annual Accounts

I have mentioned that a company's accounts, which have to be filed annually in the UK, can be checked at Companies House. However, it is important to understand that gross profit figures in the annual accounts are not always comparable between different companies. This is usually because of the different ways of presenting the figures by the auditors.

When starting at Geka, the company's accounts and the auditing were not clear or useful. Roswitha and I looked for a new auditor/accountancy firm. We chose Chantry Vellacott, the 24th largest ranked auditing firm in the country. They looked at our accounts before taking over as auditor. I liked that they gave us a 'Weakness List', which was a great help for areas to improve on the accounts. We did not get one from the previous auditors.

A couple of years later, after the annual audit and checking their report, I saw that the figure that Chantry Vellacott reported as our gross profit bore little resemblance to what we actually achieved. The GP was very low. I phoned William, the Senior Partner, to enquire about the difference. He told me that if I wanted a true representation of our GP, he would amend our annual report to show the true figure. This surprised me, but I asked him to leave it as I did not want competitors to be able to judge our results or efficiency. Obviously, the auditors put a lot of costs in the 'Cost of Goods.' As some accountants call that part of the accounts the 'Cost of Sales', they put in lots of other costs and overhead costs, maybe even including finance costs on production investments, the costs of toilet rolls, window cleaning, factory cleaners etc.

So annual accounts of companies can vary for comparison purposes between companies and probably between auditors. The key thing is to look at the yearly trends, not just at one year and look at other benchmark figures such as sales per employee when trying to understand a competitor's or customer's business. Public Companies generally do not want people to know too much about the business. One reason is that too much information could cause volatility in the share prices and have consequences.

METHODOLOGY
How To Boost Performance

1. Adopt the suggested formats which are devised to help management easily understand them and help run the business. There are no detailed rules to be followed for the 'Cost of Goods'.

2. When looking for competitive comparisons, the annual year-end accounts that auditors send to the UK Government's Companies House are set out according to their own rules or normal practice. Those accounts include summarised totals and compilations of several costs, so they usually have to be scrutinised with an open mind.

CHAPTER SUMMARY

1. It was highlighted that a good clean gross profit layout in the accounts is a fundamental requirement. There is no legal definition of 'Cost of Goods', so the layout is down to individual choice but should be clear.

2. Good examples of account P&L layouts were demonstrated in Figs 21, 22 and 24.

3. Use careful assessment and sensibility in the positioning of depreciation in the accounts.

4. In the accounts, rank overhead variable costs from highest to lowest for easy management review and to focus on the important items and variations.

Chapter Twelve

Management
And Percentages
Management

Key Function 5. How To Effectively Control The Business. This chapter explores the importance of:

- measuring percentages and trends in gross profit percentages
- the presentation of management reports with percentages
- the use of KPI snapshot
- a simple business plan layout

...and shares analysis and reasons for the demise of Thomas Cook, the travel company, and the importance of benchmarking overheads.

Company Management

The focus until now has been on several principles and methods where the Rocketship Management concept applies to propel a company forward. The following information is relevant for measuring and managing performance.

A useful method for measuring and interpreting information is to use graphs, both for actual numbers and percentages. These provide a simple way to see trends that indicate when action is needed, and this is especially true when percentage figures are used.

Looking further at gross profit and the importance of trend monitoring and analysis, **Fig 25** is an example of a year position at Geka with the trends over two years. The 1998 percentages and the trends show that improvements needed to be undertaken to arrest the gross profit per cent decline. Actions that were undertaken then led to the improved results in 1999. The chart shows the importance of measuring the percentages.

FIG 25. *Geka Trend in GP %*

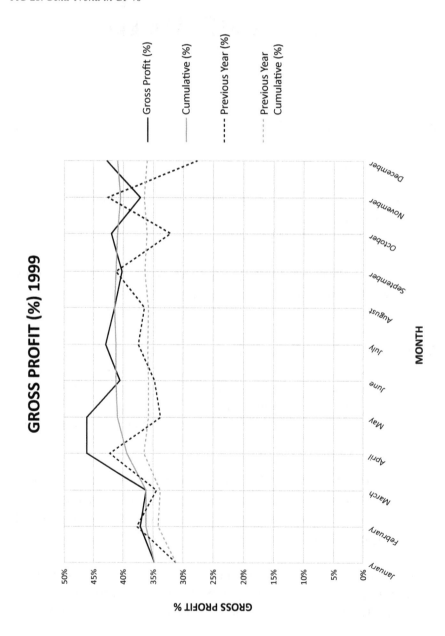

NOTES:

In the 'previous year' (1998), the gross profit per cent line runs with a few peaks and troughs over the months. Variations generally depend on the product mix for the month. The cumulative gross profit percentage averaged out consistently at an acceptable 36%. However, in the previous year from April 1998 onwards the chart shows the gross profit per cent is starting to level off. It also shows the drop in GP% per month more clearly with the cumulative figures for the 'previous year', when comparing 1999 to 1998.

During 1998 the company needed to invest in additional efficient machines to increase output speeds and save labour costs, as the hourly wage rates had significantly increased compared to 1997. (More on this later.) From January 1999 after investments in 1998, it can be seen that the monthly GP% starts at 35% and then exceeds this each month. The cumulative GP% ends the year at 41%, nearly six percentage points higher than the previous year. The improvement resulted from new machines, a new building to bring outsourced work back 'in-house', and extra turnover from improved margins. The additional six percentage points of gross profit improvement were a value of £470,000. A huge improvement towards paying for the overheads and contributing to increased net profit.

Fig 26 then shows the gross profit and sales by value. The key points and trends repeat some of the previous points made, but in value rather than percentages:

1. For the 'previous year,' the 1998 dotted line for gross profit by value (£) shows a decline in the last three months and the first few months of 1999. It then starts to increase in May 1999 above the previous year as production investments and the extra turnover begin to take effect.
2. In addition, it can be seen that sales increased in 1999 from September to December, bringing in more gross profit at a higher percentage through the improved efficiencies and including the extra volumes.

It took some months before the cumulative gross profit value in 1999 grew above 1998. This was after sales increased in the last four months of the year. See **Fig 26**

FIG 26. Geka Trend in GP £

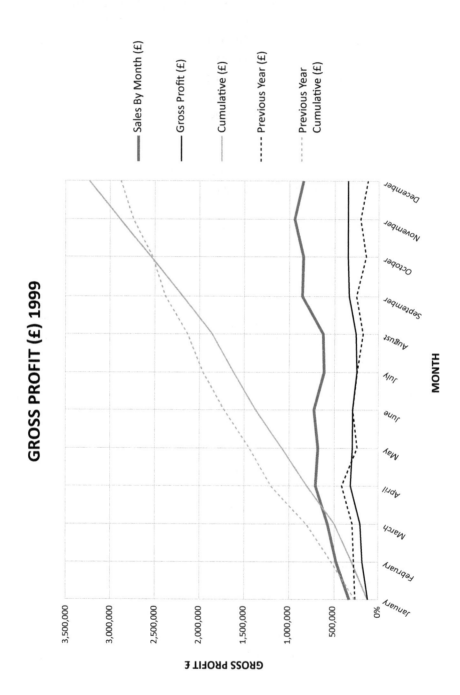

There is a major reason behind the 'down and up trends' in the two above charts. In 1997, at a monthly Board Meeting, Ian, the factory manager, reported that the company had lost a couple of the production operators to another company on the industrial estate. They had obtained a 20% wage increase. In addition, Ian had asked about the working conditions. The other company operated a 4.5-day week with Friday afternoons off. This was especially tempting for the female employees because they could get their shopping and preparations done before the weekend. Ian found out that our company was the only company out of 19 on the industrial estate that worked a whole five-day week. There had been a stable workforce for a long time, and it was important not to lose people. So, at the management meeting, shock, horror, I suggested, "OK, let's increase the shop floor wages by 20 % and make other pay adjustments among the pay scales". But I added a caveat that we must invest more in further automation and the latest machines to offset the wage increases and maintain our gross profit per cent and gross profit money income.

We then discussed and planned what we needed to do to implement changes to the working hours and days to make the changes as smooth as possible.

> At the factory, we had introduced a very worthwhile committee meeting which kept employees informed and motivated. We called it the SWAT committee, standing for Social, Welfare and Activities Team. A great acronym that the factory employees themselves came up with. Ian ran regular meetings with representatives from management and employees. The agenda included subjects like Christmas parties and any outings.

With regard to changing the work times, Ian said, "I'll organise a survey on what people prefer for the daily working hours, and we'll go for the most popular choices".

The company-wide survey determined that most people would be happy to start at 8.15 a.m., reduce the break times a little to keep the same hours for the week and finish at 2.30 pm on a Friday. This was implemented and worked very well. The reduction to a four and a half day working week combined with a 20% wage rise meant that the workforce turnover dropped to a minimum once more and was a great morale booster.

Regarding the pay rises, the intention for the future was to keep the direct labour costs close to the same 'percentage to sales' each year. Obviously, in the short term, the direct labour costs in both money and percentage terms would increase, reducing the gross profit. The plan was to reduce the forecast increase in percentage points with extra automation.

The 20% wage rise only hurt us for a few months, as shown by the GP in Fig 25 and especially Fig 26. Both the GP income and the GP percentage soon increased despite the large wage rises.

The graph in Fig 26 shows the gross profit in money made from the sales. So, to be a bit repetitious here (in case you have skipped chapters!), a company needs to make enough money at the GP level to pay for all the overheads and make a profit. If sales can be grown and the gross profit revenue increases in tandem, that will lead to success. Then if during this time, the overhead costs can remain level or be constrained, the company becomes even more profitable.

To reiterate: when monitoring the gross profit per cent and observing the trend, if a poor trend has continued after three months, it is definitely time to consider what action can be taken. In our situation, we were winning new higher volume business at a slightly lower margin, but we calculated that the volume would bring in more gross profit in revenue if we automated further and increased efficiencies. This we did, and the results in sales growth, gross profit income growth, and then net profitability increased further.

By managing the product gross margins and the gross profit revenue, we drove the company to a much-improved result.

METHODOLOGY
How To Boost Performance

1. The graphs in Figs 25 and 26 demonstrate that measuring 'clean gross profit' in both percentages and value can provide clear information of where you are.

2. The GP percentage trend also tells you where you could be going if you do not act on any adverse information indicated.

Some further points on the importance of closely monitoring monthly gross profit figures and the trends: the graphs show typical monthly GP variations. The reasons can be as follows:

1. Sometimes, the monthly labour cost will be higher in percentage terms because the sales value is lower for the month or if there are products in that month with a lower gross profit margin.
2. More overtime may be worked, increasing labour costs because of the overtime premium payments.
3. There can also be higher labour costs if occasionally some rework is needed, so labour time is wasted.

While the company was growing fast, we frequently put on Saturday and Sunday shifts even though we already worked a three-shift 24 hours a day five days a week system.

Transport And Packing Cost (T&P)

This cost is typically 2% of sales, but it *can* be 1.5 % or 3 or 4%. You might think this small percentage cost is not worth bothering with. However, a variation in the percentage can tell you a lot. I once asked a financial director, "What does it tell you if the Transport and Packing percentage has increased for the month in question?" His reply? "It tells you that the transport company has increased its prices." He could not think of anything else, so I told him it could indicate that investigation could be needed as follows:

1. You are making extra shipments because of part shipments. This could mean the transport company is unreliable. For instance, it does not turn up, so you need to arrange other transport and part ship. Or maybe they can only load half the shipment – for whatever reason.

2. It could mean you are not making to schedule because of machine breakdowns or labour issues such as sickness. If machines need maintenance or repair, you have to part ship, raising costs.

3. Deliveries are running late because of poor production planning. Materials or components are not available because of poor purchasing, so you are running late for deliveries. So special deliveries have to be made at extra cost.

4. Suppliers are letting you down because of poor vendor management, so special deliveries have to be made to speed up delivery.

5. It could be the customer has ordered late, so you help him out with special deliveries at no extra charge, for goodwill.

6. Finally, it can be because the salesman promises unrealistic delivery lead times, which causes urgent, costly transport or part shipments. It also increases factory costs, such as overtime to meet the tight delivery dates.

LESSON

It can be well worth drilling down into the reasons for higher transport costs to find out the underlying causes and take action.

The Geka overhead costs were controlled so that the net profit at the year-end increased by 57% to 9.4% ROS. The company then became in the top bracket of plastics and engineering companies. In 1998 the company was the 15th fastest growing plastics and engineering company in the UK over three years.

Fig 27 is a chart of Return on Sales which shows the net profit situation.

FIG 27. *Geka Trend in ROS*

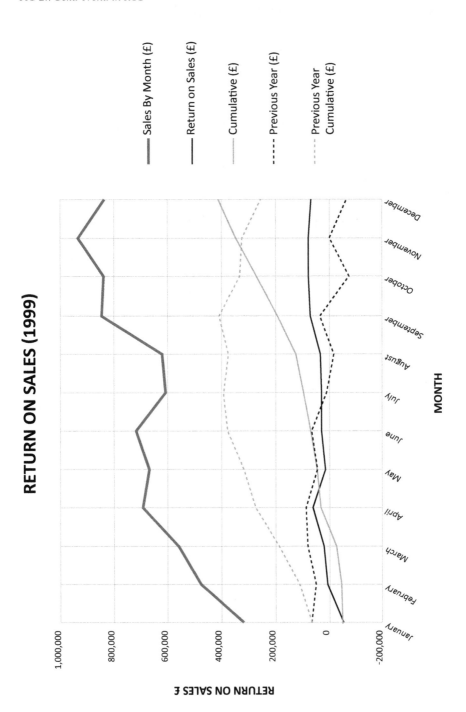

Presentation Of Management Reports

If a company is not large, the variable and overhead costs can be presented monthly in detail, as shown previously in Fig 24. However, when a company is large, information on variable costs becomes too detailed and perhaps unnecessary for senior management to wade through. The information needs to be summarised, and, as mentioned previously, the accountant should report separately on important variations in the monthly report. The sales function and the manufacturing function should provide separate reports.

NOTE: I am not divulging any proprietary information on Geka or more recent information on any company without permission if they are still in existence. Most of the example companies have changed ownership. I am showing the Geka UK information because it is outdated but clearly demonstrates the use of percentages measurements. The parent company was sold in 2000, and the UK company was sold off in 2006. Since the initial sale of the group, it has changed ownership more than once.

Fig 28 is the year-end P&L showing the month and year-end accounts with summaries of the cost groupings. There is a lot to read about in an £8 million turnover company or larger. We could not get all the columns we wanted on one page, so we left off the column for 'percentage figures for the previous year'. These percentage figures can be calculated separately if required. (Normally, Fig 28 was prepared in Landscape.)

FIG 28. Geka P&L Report

GEKA UK FINANCIAL REPORT **CUMULATIVE DECEMBER 1999**

	ACTUAL CUM £	% OF SALES	BUDGET CUM	% OF SALES	DIFF TO BUDGET £	DIFF TO BUDGET %	PREV. YR CUM £	DIFF TO PREV YR %
1.SALES								
MFG Production UK	6,043,887	74.4	5,075,340	70.1	968,547	19.1	5,926,256	2.0
Geka D	1,081,196	13.3	1,088,120	15.0	-6,924	-0.6	1,242,764	-13.0
Total Production	7,125,083	87.7	6,163,460	85.1	961,623	15.6	7,169,020	-0.6
Wholesale	1,003,436	12.3	1,076,040	14.9	-72,604	-6.7	1,028,716	-2.4
TOTAL SALES	8,128,519	100%	7,239,500	100%	768,532	10.8	8,197,736	-0.8
Sales Bonus							-71,429	
Sundry Inc (Tooling)	27,700				27,700		23,573	17.5
Grants	21,553	0.27	44,000	0.62	-22,447	-51.0	22,241	-3.1
Commission on Sales	-273,140		-147,400		-125,740		-201,270	36
TOTAL INCOME	7,904,632		7,136,100		768,532	10.8	7,970,851	-0.8
2. COSTS								
Prod.Material	2,214,492	31.1	1,946,250	31.6	268,242	13.8	2,632,021	-15.9
Sub contract work	78,126	1.1	38,350	0.6	41,776	114.9	153,339	-49
Production wages	1,358,403	19.1	1,143,480	18.6	214,923	18.8	1,317,983	3.1
Transport/Packing	193,866	2.4	144,000	2.0	49,866	34.6	180,446	7.4
TOTAL PROD. COST	3,844,887	54.0	3,270,080	53.0	574,807	17.6	4,283,789	-10.2
Wholesale Purchase	850,592	84.8	983.15	91.4	-132,558	-13.5	786.3	8.2
GROSS PROFIT PROD.	3,280,196	46.0	2,893,380	46.9	386,816	13.4	2,885,231	14.0
GROSS PROFIT	3,209,153	40.6	2,882,870	40.4	326,283	11.3	2,900,745	11.0
Personnel Cost	815,361	10.3	753,400	10.6	61,961	8.2	841,130	-3.1
Variable Costs	481,719	6.1	532,200	7.5	-50,481	-9.9	598,993	-19.6
Fixed Costs	348,196	4.4	349,140	4.9	-944	-0.3	365,716	-4.8
Depreciation	617,709	7.8	611,200	8.6	6,509	1.1	475,734	29.8
TOTAL OTHER COST	2,262,985	28.6	2,245,940	31.5	17,045	0.8	2,281,573	-0.8
3. RESULT								
Operating Profit	948,168	12.0	636,930	8.9	309,238	48.6	619,172	52.8
Head Office Charges	300,000	3.8	300,000	4.2	0	0	214,356	40.0
Interest on Loans	201,800	2.6	168,000	2.4	33,800	20.1	147,210	37.1
PROFIT	444,368	5.6	168,930	2.4	275,438	163.1	257,606	72.5

Some key points from Fig 28 are as follows:

- Actual cum for 1999 of 'clean gross profit' on production is £3.280 million at 46%. The Previous year, gross profit on production was 40%. The six percentage points improvement was a value increase of £394,000 on similar production sales.
  How was this achieved? Look at the material usage for the previous year at £2.632 million; it is 36.7%. In 1999 material usage was £2.214

million, or 31% of sales. A key reason for this improvement was major new products at a higher margin. In addition, we achieved good material savings from a supplier by changing the specification of a component with the customer's approval. We reduced subcontract material work by £75,000 by investing and bringing work in-house at only an extra 0.69% increase in production wages.

- Having made a good production gross profit margin of 46% and net production margin after 'wholesale products' of 40.6%, we had a net gross profit of £3.209 million.
- Notice that wholesale sales and purchases are itemised separately to keep an eye on maintaining those wholesale percentage margins of Germany-made products at just 15%. Keeping wholesale sales out of production costs enabled us to keep the 'Clean Gross Profit' and its measurements.
- How did we spend or save it? The overhead personnel costs were reduced as a percentage as also variable costs. Fixed costs dropped £17,000 to £348,196. The reasons for that were reductions in banking and professional charges and rented buildings. More on that later.
- Depreciation charge (against profits) has increased from £475,734 at 6% to 7.8% because of capital investments. This amount is not unusual. One company where I consulted invested £40 million a year or 7% of turnover around their many European factories, and their depreciation charge was at the same percentage each year.
- The interest on loans to build the new factory unit is quite high at £202,000 for the year, but at 2.6% of sales are typical for many growth manufacturing companies.
- It can be seen that the German parent company could take £300,000 in 'Head Office charges'. As we had a good year, they also took another £70,000 as 'R&D support'. This figure appears as an extra £70,000 commission on sales over the previous year.
- So, what are the Funds Generated? They are as follows:

Depreciation: £617,709
Profit: £444,368
Add back H.O. Charge: £300,000
Add back sales commission charge: £70,000
Total Funds Generated: £1,432,077, which is 18% of Total Income.

Fig 28 is an overall summary. If more detail was required, for instance, on some of the previous year's percentages, these could be calculated separately. The chart shows how a company can grow after 10 years of losses and after achieving a turnaround.

METHODOLOGY
How To Boost Performance

1. As an overview, the Geka company turnaround was achieved by initially analysing and improving product margins and the gross profit.

2. Improvement was achieved by better costing, price rises, and production improvements.

3. The target was to achieve top performance in quality and service.

4. Further performance improvements were obtained by better sales performance, marketing, and product developments.

5. Overhead costs and team numbers were carefully managed.

Overheads

The monitoring of percentages for overheads is also important. These are less straightforward to manage because longer timescales can be involved. However, the percentages can show if the company is drifting away from being 'lean and efficient'.

Fig 29 shows Geka UK's percentages for the overheads, taken from Fig 28. The trend down in Personnel costs meant we ran 'lean and mean' with process improvements also helped by IT. We outsourced many activities such as tool making, IT support, transport, and car renting. HR was managed in-house with the factory manager because Ian had all the reference books with the HR regulations (which he liked using!).

FIG 29. *Geka UK Trend in Overheads %*

GEKA UK OVERHEAD COSTS TRENDS
PERCENTAGES TO TOTAL SALES

	1995	1998	1999
Personnel costs	13.1	10.5	10.3
Variable costs	5.8	7.5	6.1
Fixed costs	7.7	4.6	4.4
Total Overhead costs	26.6	22.6	20.8
Depreciation charge	7.7	6.0	7.8
Totals Other Costs	**34.3**	**28.6**	**28.6**

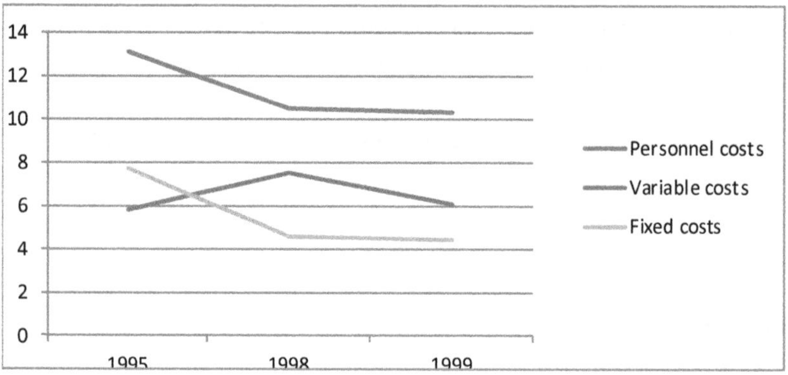

Just a note on the higher variable costs in 1998. These were higher because costs were included for the new factory and production reorganisation. If required, some costs could have been capitalised to increase the profit declared and the assets value on the balance sheet.

METHODOLOGY
How To Boost Performance

1. Monitor the overhead costs and manage the percentages.

2. Undertake the continuous improvement of processes, including overhead administration.

3. Set a percentage target to maintain for overhead costs.

4. Benchmark overhead percentages against competitors or similar companies.

Snapshot Of Key Performance Indicators

In addition to the P&L report, it is also beneficial for a managing director to have a Snapshot of the Key Performance Indicators (KPIs) and essential to have the key information at one's fingertips, so it's not necessary to keep trawling through the computer or asking the accounts department.

Moreover, you can't ask these questions when you have some thinking time away from the office and you don't want to trawl through the laptop. One of the important aspects of the snapshot is that you can quickly see important trends on one page for several items.

A lot of information will be on the IT system, but keeping a hard copy Snapshot handy, saves time and keeps you up to date. It is always helpful to have a copy, whether in the briefcase or laptop, to review on the plane or at home. The Snapshot KPIs example is in Fig 30.

The MDs with whom I suggest the Snapshot find it really useful. The Snapshot items of information will vary from company to company depending on what the business is and what the MD likes to keep an eye on. One CEO I worked with always kept the hard copy we had written up lying on the corner of his desk.

Fig 30 shows one Snapshot layout that was created with a client. This layout can be created for any company with specific KPIs for their particular business. For instance, orders or sales of different product groups can be important to include. The example I've included is quite comprehensive, but all rows did not need to be completed every month.

FIG 30. Snapshot of KPIs

COMPANY: ZOOM   **SNAPSHOT KEY PERFORMANCE INDICATORS**

No	ITEM	LAST YEAR	J	F	M	>>>	CUM
1	**PERFORMANCE 1**						
2	Order Intake £						
3	Order Book £						
4	**PROFIT&LOSS A/C**						
5	Sales £						
6	**Gross profit £**						
7	**Gross profit %**						
8	Sales Standards £						
9	Sales Specials £						
10	**Net Profit/Loss £**						
11	Depreciation £						
12	Funds Generated £						
13	Cum Sales to Plan %						
14	Cum Sales to L/YR %						
15	**BALANCE SHEET**						
16	Stock £						
17	Debtors £						
18	Debtor days						
19	Debtors days 75+ £						
20	Creditors £						
21	Creditor days, sales						
22	Bank account £						
23	Capital Expend £						
24	Loan repayments £						
25	**PERFORMANCE 2**						
26	Quotes value £						
27	Quotes number						
28	Ave order value £						
29	No of dir ees						
30	Employees total						
31	Sales per person £						

Napoleon said that "An army marches on its stomach". We could say that a company marches on its data. A lot has been covered until now on the provision and use of data. However, as with Napoleon's comment and reference to the fact that food fills the stomachs to help the soldiers fight, good data provides the ammunition (or information and ability) for management and staff to drive the company upwards. It always has to be upwards because if the company is not progressing and is only standing still, then, in reality, it is going backwards against its competitors. But do not overdo the data, or you could get the data disease, 'Paralysis by analysis'...

LESSON

Use a Snapshot to keep up to date with the KPIs and help see any trends that need action.

Balance Sheet Information

Apart from the P&L, the other important document is the balance sheet. It is not intended to give a lot of detail on balance sheets because of the following statement, mainly applicable to smaller companies: if you look after the P&L, the Balance Sheet generally reflects a good P&L – but do keep an eye on balance sheet items too.

The previous statement needs clarifying with some additional comments, so it has some veracity when managing the P&L. In any case, the accountants can provide detailed views on the balance sheet. The above comment applies more to smaller companies than large ones.

1. Look after the debtors and creditors, and keep stocks to a minimum. This means cash can be generated.
2. A good rule is to only borrow money for investment and efficiency generation to get a good payback. However, ensure the gearing is not

too high. Gearing is the ratio of a company's debt to equity and shows how a firm's operations are funded by lenders versus shareholders.

3. Avoid borrowing money to fund losses to keep the company going; this soon means adding loans onto existing loans. If this has to be done, it should be short term while you tackle the fundamentals of pricing, gross profit, production or service efficiency, and cutting overheads. Borrow money to invest in efficiencies. Just a couple of examples of loans to fund losses are involved in the bankruptcies of Thomas Cook and Yardley Cosmetics.

4. If taking loans for expansion, the banks might require around two times the profit to ensure payment of the interest charges.

Important Balance Sheet Figures

1. Debtors and creditors. Debtors should exceed Trade Creditors by 20% and more.

2. Net current assets. If current assets do not exceed current liabilities, the company is in trouble because it will not be able to pay its creditors. Current assets include stocks which are not particularly liquid. If there are old stocks, they may well be worthless. If a company runs out of cash and cannot pay its debts, it will end up in administration.

3. Pay attention to both the short and long term loans to ensure they do not become excessive.

4. Net worth, or Shareholders' Funds, perhaps excluding intangible assets, are important.

And besides a good balance sheet, an outstanding order book is essential. If not a good order book, there should be an increasing order trend.

Business Plans

Business plans sound a bit daunting to some people. However, if the plan is on one page in graphical form, it is easy to prepare and read, especially for smaller companies. Moreover, the plan can be given to department managers for easy viewing as an action list. Our one-page plans with objectives were easy to follow. Ian, at the factory, kept it on his notice board by his desk, and I could see the upticks on the plan as time progressed.

I have included a copy of the Business Plan prepared for a client. I had worked with the MD, John, at his own previous company, which he had amalgamated into this larger company. The plan in **Fig 31** shows plenty to do. The MD worked hard on the gross profit and increased it by about £1 million within a year. The various functions and activities can be colour coded.

FIG 31. Business Plan: One Page Layout

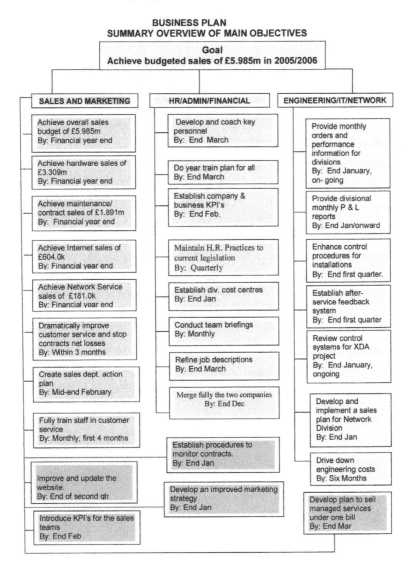

**BUSINESS PLAN
SUMMARY OVERVIEW OF MAIN OBJECTIVES**

**Goal
Achieve budgeted sales of £5.985m in 2005/2006**

SALES AND MARKETING	HR/ADMIN/FINANCIAL	ENGINEERING/IT/NETWORK
Achieve overall sales budget of £5.985m By: Financial year end	Develop and coach key personnel By: End March	Provide monthly orders and performance information for divisions By: End January, on-going
Achieve hardware sales of £3.309m By: Financial year end	Do year train plan for all By: End March	Provide divisional monthly P & L reports By: End Jan/onward
Achieve maintenance/ contract sales of £1.891m By: Financial year end	Establish company & business KPI's By: End Feb.	Enhance control procedures for installations By: End first quarter.
Achieve Internet sales of £604.0k By: Financial year end	Maintain H.R. Practices to current legislation By: Quarterly	Establish after-service feedback system By: End first quarter
Achieve Network Service sales of £181.0k By: Financial year end	Establish div. cost centres By: End Jan	Review control systems for XDA project By: End January, ongoing
Dramatically improve customer service and stop contracts net losses By: Within 3 months	Conduct team briefings By: Monthly	Develop and implement a sales plan for Network Division By: End Jan
Create sales dept. action plan By: Mid-end February	Refine job descriptions By: End March	Drive down engineering costs By: Six Months
Fully train staff in customer service By: Monthly; first 4 months	Merge fully the two companies By: End Dec	Develop plan to sell managed services under one bill By: End Mar
Improve and update the website. By: End of second qtr	Establish procedures to monitor contracts. By: End Jan	
Introduce KPI's for the sales teams By: End Feb	Develop an improved marketing strategy By: End Jan	

Next is an excellent example of a company disaster with regard to an apparent lack of gross profit management, poor P&L management, a poor balance sheet, and the company obfuscated the financial reporting in the Annual Accounts.

The Demise Of Thomas Cook, The UK Tours Company

A perfect example of the need to have clarity in the accounts and manage trends can be seen in the Thomas Cook accounts from Company House.

Reviewing those accounts, Thomas Cook's demise in 2019 demonstrates how a large company needed to use the main KPIs and gross profit management, just as in SMEs or any size of company. I expect that the internal accounts were not clear, and of course, the external ones were 'generalised.'

I have already mentioned Thomas Cook in Chapter Six, with appropriate charts, but now include a further four with additional detail so we can learn from their experience. Thomas Cook's collapse occurred when I started writing this book, so it was interesting to do a bit of investigating! Together with a business friend, Reg, a former auditor and senior partner, and the FD where we worked together, I started looking at the Thomas Cook accounts. Reg had a really careful read of the published annual accounts of 2018, and we looked at the balance sheet and the P&Ls of the group.

I enclose my analysis of the UK Retail operation. Fig 32 has six charts and includes the previous Figs 9 and 10, so the whole set is now included here for continuity of reading. The additional charts provide further analysis. What did Thomas Cook do about the situation? Who knows?

Interestingly I saw Peter Fankhauser, the CEO, being interviewed on the television news after the collapse, and he said, "I've done nothing wrong". I mentioned this comment to another accountant friend; he sighed, rolled his eyes, looked up and said, "He did not do anything wrong because he did not do anything!"

Mr Fankhauser probably did many things, but not necessarily the big thing of managing or overseeing the gross profit and its indications, if only just on the UK Retail side.

A detailed report on the Annual Report and balance sheet with notes on the obfuscations are in **Appendix 2. Fig 32/1** is the overall summary and notes on Thomas Cook's accounts. **Fig 32/2** shows quite clearly the Gross Profit trend and the relationship to sales. This chart and **Fig 32/3** show an evident trend that indicated impending failure years before the collapse. The chart shows that the declining Gross Profit did not cover overheads for at least five consecutive years.

FIG 32/1. Thomas Cook Report & Charts

Thomas Cook Report   **29/10/2019**

The summary is below and with additional five charts including notes.

SUMMARY

> The Thomas Cook Group P&L shows sales grew by £578 million to £9.584 billion in 2018 over 2017. However the cost of sales increased by £635 million and the loss increased by £57m with those extra sales. To be simplistic one could say if they had not made the extra Group sales they would have reduced the losses by £57m. However, looking at the Retail figures, the loss on Retail in 2018 was £51.0m out of the group loss of £57.0m

> Group Sales in 2017 were £1196m more than in 2016. Cost of sales was £1026m more. The difference leaves £170m of GP; this is only 14.2 % extra GP and therefore probably not enough contribution to make the additional business profitable.

> On the Retail side only the sales declined by £85m from 2014 with Sales of £317m down to sales of £232m in 2018. Sales

declined £26m in one year from 2017 to 2018. See chart Fig 31/2. That was a 27% sales decline over five years.

> The figures show a large decline in profitability. Who was responsible in the Group and also the UK Retail Operation for costing and pricing, and overhead management?
>> Fig. 31/2 shows the decline in UK Retail sales and the percentages for GP and sales. The GP drops to a miserly 11%.
>> Fig. 31/3 shows the drop in GP revenue compared to overheads. The GP revenue never covered the overheads for the last 5 years, or even further back.

> There may be a weakness in the monthly management accounts. How were the monthly management accounts presented, and which items shown were clear enough to indicate these trends?

> What corrective and successful actions were taken, if any to restore profitability?
>> Fig 31/4 shows pre- tax profits against sales.
>> Fig 31/5 shows Thos Cook's retail sales per employee.
>> Fig31/6 looks at Hays Travel as a benchmark company, which must be a fairly similar operation; there are enormous variances to Thomas Cook. Even if there are a lot of dissimilar activities, the differences are so large as to be eye popping! Thomas Cook's sales per employee declined 23% since 2014.

Sales per head for Hays are £288,000 p.a. For Cook's Retail, the figure is £51,000! Hayes Wages & Salaries are 7% of turnover. Cook's figure is 34% of turnover!

FIG 32/2. Thomas Cook Report & Charts

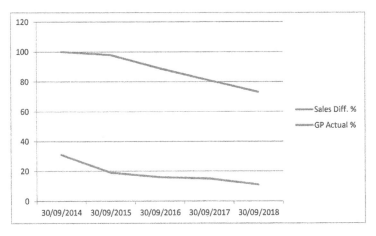

JF
29.10.19

THOMAS COOK UK RETAIL
P & L
INFO.2   **Percentage changes from 2014 for Sales, versus actual GP**

Sales £'000	317,059	310,903	282,311	257,777	232,005
	30/09/2014	30/09/2015	30/09/2016	30/09/2017	30/09/2018
Sales Diff. %	100	98	89	81	73
GP Actual %	31	19	16	15	11

NOTES
1. Sales declined by 27% from 2014.
2. GP percent of 30/31 % should have been maintained.

3.The drop in GP from 31% to 11% over five years is a 20 points difference. This 20% GP
on Sales is a reduction of £46.4m on GP, on sales of £232.005m in 2018, let alone the "
losses" in GP over the previous 4 years.
4. Very few, if any, companies can survive with a GP of 20% and less. And T. Cook retail did not.
5. Corrective action should have been taken years ago. Why was it not? Or not successful?

FIG 32/3. *Thomas Cook Report & Charts*

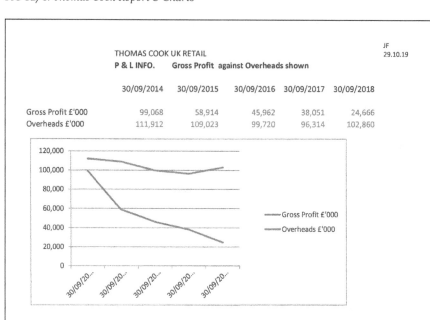

THOMAS COOK UK RETAIL   JF
                                                              29.10.19
P & L INFO.   Gross Profit against Overheads shown

	30/09/2014	30/09/2015	30/09/2016	30/09/2017	30/09/2018
Gross Profit £'000	99,068	58,914	45,962	38,051	24,666
Overheads £'000	111,912	109,023	99,720	96,314	102,860

NOTES

1.Overheads in this case from the P. & L. are- W & S, Dirs Emols,
Depreciation, Interest.

2. The GP is normally calculated after direct wages and so these may or
may not be in these GP figures
or may not have been included before GP. If included before GP then the result is worse.

3. Corrective and successful action should have been taken years before.

FIG 32/4. Thomas Cook Report & Charts

THOMAS COOK UK RETAIL   Jf 29/10/19

P & L INFO.   **Declared pre tax profit against Sales**

	30/09/2014	30/09/2015	30/09/2016	30/09/2017
Sales £'000	317,059	310,903	282,311	257,777
Pre TaxProfit £'000	24,919	-13,179	-202,058	-26,678

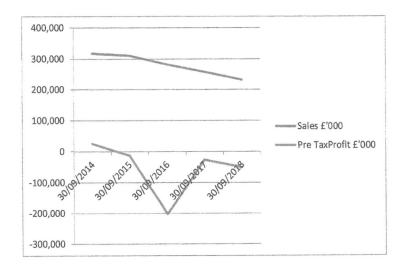

NOTES

1.The big drop in 2016 was owing to the Goodwill write down.

2. Retail had lost money for 4 consecutive years.

3. How much, but not enough, corrective action was taken on the retail operation?

4. Losses according to these figures were £294 million over 4 years.

5. This chart is an indication by using data from the P & L, so the information may not be entirely correct on the pre tax profits,
as not all figures are available.

FIG 32/5. Thomas Cook Report & Charts

THOMAS COOK UK RETAIL   JF 29.10.19

P & L INFO.   Sales (Turnover) per employee

	30/09/2014	30/09/2015	30/09/2016	30/09/2017	30/09/2018
Company Sales £'000	317,059	310,903	282,903	257,777	232,005
Employees	4,824	4,622	4,378	5,147	4,571

	2018/09/30	2017/09/30	2016/09/30	2015/09/30	30/09/2014
Sales per employee £	66,000	67,265	64,528	50,000	51,000

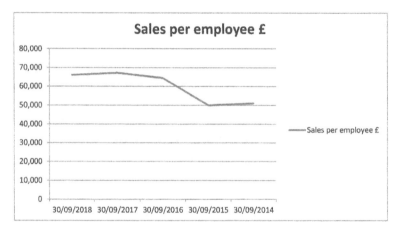

NOTES
1. Sales per employee dropped 23% over 4 years.
2. It would seem prices and efficiency were probably decreasing.
3. Trend continued for years!

FIG 32/6. *Thomas Cook Report & Charts*

THOMAS COOK UK RETAIL   JF 29.10.19

P & L INFO   Sales and Salaries per head versus Hays Travel

	2014	2015	2016	2017	2018
Sales Per Head					
T.Cook Sales £'000	317,059	310,903	282,311	257,777	232,005
T Cook employees number	4824	4622	4375	5147	4571
T.Cook Sales per head £	66,000	67,265	64,528	50,000	**51,000**
Hays Travel Sales £'000	253,055	307,699	333,427	337,785	379,835
Hays employees number	922	977	1080	1201	1315
Hays Travel Sales per head	274,446	341,000	308,000	281,000	**288,000**

W & S per employee

	2014	2015	2016	2017	2018
Cook wages/salaries £'000	99,770	97,244	85,434	82,764	78,974
Percentage to Sales %	31		30		**34**
T Cook employees number	4824	4622	4375	5147	4571
T.Cook ave W/S per head	20,682	21,039	19,527	16,080	17,227
Hays wages/salaries £'000	17,316	16,223	19,679	22,015	25,953
Percentage to Sales %	7		6		**7**
Hays employees number	922	977	1080	1201	1315
Hays ave W/S per head £	18,780	16,604	18,220	18,330	19,736

NOTES

1.Hays Travel may not be an exact Benchmark, but must be fairly similar.

2. The astounding key statistic is that Hays staff are five times productive at £288,000 per head per annum than Thomas

3.Thomas Cooks Retail W & S are 34% of sales compared to Hays at 7%.

4.Hays efficiency cannot all be to do with price, but also better systems.

5. How was Cook's costing and pricing set and conducted?

Further to the notes of Fig 32/6 the table clearly shows from the published annual accounts that Hays Travel is apparently hugely more efficient than Thomas Cook Retail was. Just look at the two measurements of:

1. Hays wages/salaries were only 7% of turnover compared to Cook's 34%.
2. Hays sales per head were £288,000 compared to Cook's £51,000.

Bear in mind these are the figures from the company annual accounts. As has been mentioned, different accountants can show figures differently. However the gap in the figures is so large that the losses for Thomas Cook would indicate key inefficiencies from these two statistics alone.

Hays Travel acquired the Thomas Cook Retail side. I expect Hays looked at these KPI's among others and quickly realised where they could make changes and improvements.

Fig 32/6 looks at KPI's with regards to benchmarking, and shows how useful this can be. An important point in looking to make improvements is, 'If you don't, or can't measure it, you can't improve it.' This means looking at companies both internally and externally.

Further on is this chapter, the aspect of benchmarking is discussed further with regard to the former Yardley cosmetics company.

METHODOLOGY
How To Boost Performance

1. Manage the Gross Profit trend. This is essential in companies of every size.

2. Use graphs to show the trends.

Thomas Cook's Balance Sheet

The problems of Thomas Cook were disguised and obfuscated in the balance sheet, and the analysis makes fascinating reading. My colleague Reg has given an excellent in-depth analysis of the Thomas Cook Annual financial report of 2018, published only a few months before the company collapsed.

His report is enclosed in Appendix 2. Just a few points to mention of insights into Reg's report from correspondence between us. The reason for Reg showing various comments on succeeding dates is because of an email trail between us. We sent our analyses to the Commons Select Committee of the Department of Business, Energy and Industrial Strategy (BEIS), Chaired by Rachel Reeves. We received the minutes of the Select Committee hearing. Reg reviewed them and made further notes which he returned to BEIS with some notes on the Committee Minutes. I have not included further comments on the committee minutes as they mainly confirm the analysis.

Rachel Reeves wrote to the Secretary of State asking for '**a review and improvements of the accountancy standards and regulations**' following the collapse of Carillion and Thomas Cook. Maybe the accountancy regulations will be tightened up in the future?

Some Summary Notes On Thomas Cook From The Balance Sheet Of The Annual Accounts Of 2018:

1. Thomas Cook had current assets of £2 billion and current liabilities of £4.0 billion. It was obviously doomed as it could not meet current liabilities as they fell due.
2. The declared shareholders' funds were less than £300 million, tiny when compared to the liabilities in the billions. The intangible assets were not worth any value, so they should not be included in the shareholders' funds. Therefore the shareholder funds, which is the **company's net worth, were actually a negative £2.7 billion for both 2017 and 2018.**
3. The group made a loss of £163 million in 2018 and had a cash deficit of £345 million.
4. The £1 billion suggested funding asked for from the government, or even £2 billion, would have been money straight down the drain and would have required ongoing support.

The analysis of Thomas Cook's Annual Report in Appendix 2 provides more detailed information...and it is astounding! Yet it is occasionally seen in accounts situations in substantial companies (and smaller companies too) before they collapse. Yardley of London, the cosmetics company, is one example of a smaller company's demise and is covered later in this chapter. As mentioned previously, this book is aimed primarily at helping SMEs. However, it can be seen – most graphically – what can go wrong whatever the size of the company if close monitoring, followed by action, is not undertaken to manage percentage trends and overhead costs.

Smaller Companies' GP Management

Having shown that careful attention to GP is important in large firms *and* smaller ones, there are a few examples I encountered of smaller companies' performance situations that would be beneficial to share. I touched on this example earlier in the book, but it is worth repeating in more detail.

An accountant in our networking group who owned his Accountancy and Auditing company had a customer in difficulties. The company had been losing money for three years, and the overdraft and bank loan had risen to over £150,000. The accountant had started the process of raising a mortgage for £150,000 on the owner's factory to help reduce his debt to the bank. The accountant spoke to the MD owner about me meeting him to help with the situation the business was in.

The MDO told the accountant that he wanted a sales drive. Accordingly, a meeting was arranged for me to visit, primarily to discuss a sales drive for the company to increase sales and profits. On the way to my first visit with the MDO, I stopped by the accountant's office to look at the accounts before I visited the customer. These showed that for the last two years, the GP was 18% and then 24%, so I could immediately see the company was unprofitable. I thought, as was typical in these situations, it was probably due to pricing or production issues.

When I arrived to see Paul, the MD, we discussed his accounts on his computer, and I touched on the gross profit situation. Then, regarding the sales drive, I asked him what percentage margins (gross margin per cent) he made on his various products because, as I said to him, there was no point in doing a sales drive on unprofitable products. He did not know the answer or have the information to hand. He said the production manager might have the figures and I should discuss them with him.

I went downstairs to the shop floor and found David, the production manager. I introduced myself and explained that I was working with Paul and needed to look at the production costs. We sat down, and I explained what I was looking for...hoping he had the information available.

David was young, friendly and helpful, so we made good progress. He had all the required information on his computer – but not necessarily in the right order. I explained to David that it was great to see that he had the information readily available; we just needed to reformat some of it. I asked if he could present the production costs and gross margins for the first six months of the current year, so we could see how the year was progressing.

David first presented a spreadsheet which showed 'sales by customer' in alphabetical order. We looked at the production costs and gross profit for various customers, both large and small. We could see a lot of negative margins for different customers, i.e. the company was selling products at a loss, at negative gross margins. All the material and labour costs were shown, so it was a comprehensive analysis. Sales to nearly every customer showed some low-margin products. There were a lot of pages to see, so the negative margin items did not make much impact. When we looked at the total sales gross margin figure, it was not that bad, but not good enough to cover overheads.

I then asked David to rank the results by gross margin, with the worst at the top. He had not done this before, and the results were startling. As David said a little wryly, "Wow, that really shows up some problems!". It was a revelation for us to see the results when presented by ranking from worst to best. There were a lot of high negative percentage margins against the various products shown down the pages. Because the results had not been ranked in this way before, Paul, the MD, had not realised the poor overall pricing situation. We could clearly see that 50% of sales for the previous six months were either loss-making or making too low a percentage margin.

If you refer to the original reference to this story in Chapter Five and look at Fig 11, the chart shows the first page of the redacted printout for the sales for the first six months, starting with a product with a minus margin of 187%. The list of low-margin products continued down the spreadsheet with sales at increasing volumes with a gross profit per cent below 30% – 50 per cent of the sales value.

Under material analysis, the material cost is marked up by 25% in accordance with the vague accounting rules used (I mentioned these earlier). The sales price should then be arrived at by multiplying up the labour cost by the required factor and adding that to the material cost. The sum should then be the necessary selling price.

I then asked David if he could re-calculate the forward order book and planned shipments for the next 4 -6 months in the same way. He was able to do this, and the result was the same; 50 per cent of products booked for production in the following six months were at an unsustainable low gross margin per cent.

When I looked at the total labour cost in this report, the first six months of labour costs were not the same as the actual direct labour wages paid out for the first six months. Obviously, social costs were part of the difference. What the labour costs probably did not measure very well was the 'lost time' and 'down time' that occurs between jobs. Another variance can be that many products were on out of date 'standard costs.'

I took the two hard copy spreadsheets to Paul, which was certainly a bit of a shock for him. When the table was also presented 'by customer', it highlighted which customers needed to be tackled with price rises as a matter of urgency. However before price increases could be tackled, the target selling prices and margins needed to be established. This did not take long to do (less than an afternoon), and I presented a few scenarios for Paul.

We knew all the overheads for the company after gross profit. There was a 25% mark-up already on the material purchases so that 25% margin value was available towards paying for the overheads. We agreed that the direct labour costs for each product should be increased by a percentage from the difference between the measured direct labour costs and the direct wage costs in the monthly accounts. It was then straightforward to calculate what the mark up on the production wages should be to provide a sum that would help in covering the overheads for profit. This percentage mark up was then applied to the direct labour cost and was added to the material mark up of 25% to reach the sales price for each product. The new sales prices would generate sufficient gross profit to cover the overheads and make a profit. We aimed for a gross profit margin of 40% on most of the products, with a bit less for higher volumes or a known competitive situation.

Those actions took place during my first meeting, and as per the consulting agreement with Paul, I would then visit for one day every two weeks. I suggested we could discuss price rises with the various customers and the tactics we could employ when I came back in two weeks.

Two weeks later, when I returned, Paul told me he had raised all the prices, especially those for the significant amount of business they did with a big oil company. I was a little concerned about his speedy and maybe reckless price rise implementation. One needs to be careful and prepared with a clear understanding of the costs, also perhaps competitive pricing, and to have a clear picture of a 'fall-back position' below which you will not go. (Reference my price situation with Rimmel and others.) I asked him how the price rises were received, especially by the oil company, and he assured me it went well. The oil company had even given him more orders! A great result.

I believe all the price rises went through, and it had taken Paul no more than two or three days of work to implement what would put his company back on the road to profit. In fact, profitability was achieved within a matter of weeks. This negated the need to raise a mortgage of £150,000 on his factory to reduce his bank loans. He could now trade his way out of this debt. He now realised that taking the mortgage route would never have worked while the company continued selling its products with so many low margin and loss-making items.

Paul was soon knowledgeable enough to keep an eye on the quoted prices and to watch the gross profit and trends for material and labour. I asked him how he thought the low margin and loss-making products situation had occurred. He said it must have been mainly because of 'design creep', on product improvements at customer requests on their specials. And, of course, he acknowledged he had not previously checked on and increased the prices for the improvements or inflation when needed.

That was the fastest turnaround of a company that I had helped an MD achieve. Fortunately, the information was all available. The company had special products and customers, and once the MD knew what he had to do, he simply got on and did it. Moreover, I was pleased that the company was saved as a customer for the accountant who had arranged our meeting.

Around the same time, I was also involved with a small group of consultants trying to concentrate on manufacturing. I showed them the redacted spreadsheet (Fig 11) from Paul's company to the leading consultant in the group. The purple column showed all the loss-making products, and I remarked that they had not appreciated the problem and had wanted to do a sales drive to achieve profitability. But the company was selling products at a loss, so a general sales drive might have made matters worse...and could have been fatal.

I was startled when one of the consultants said, "Oh, I thought the more you sold, the more money you made!". I could not believe what I was hearing. I then discovered he was a non-manufacturing MD, so he had a completely different knowledge base because of working with bought-in products with a standard margin on everything.

METHODOLOGY
How To Boost Performance

So far, we have looked at the management of companies with key points as follows:

1. Maintain continuous focus on the two main functions of Sales and Production.

2. Focus on gross profit measurements.

3. Carefully monitor material and direct labour costs in money and percentages to turnover for any cost increases or percentage decreases.

4. Focus on achieving profitable margin percentages for all products.

5. Focus on obtaining accurate and clear data on trends so that action can be speedily taken.

6. Ensure that the IT systems, whether the current one or a future one, really will provide all the clear information required to enable you to save time and to 'rocket the company upwards'.

Cash flow and profitability can also be improved in other areas and are covered next.

Debtors – Accounts Receivable

This and the following sections on creditors and stocks will be familiar areas for qualified accountants. However, in many smaller companies, there is often an unqualified or part qualified or less experienced book keeper. For example, a wife or daughter doing the books. The basic work gets done, but without the knowledge and experience for analysis and interpretation. There were unqualified or insufficiently trained people in some of the company examples mentioned, which of course, led to the unwelcome consequences.

Debtors and creditors are a key area for good management to optimise cash flow. **Fig 30** shows that they are in the Snapshot to keep an eye on.

Trade debtor terms are usually 30 days. If the debtors are managed well, the average days outstanding can be 45 days. If some debtors are not paying after, let's say, 60 days, it is time for the credit controller to start doing a bit more chasing for payment!

My colleagues and I have regularly visited small companies who have debtors on 90 days and even 120 days. Reducing trade debtors from 120 days to just 90 days can bring in a lot of cash. Then reducing from 90 days to 60 days also brings in the same value of cash, halving the sum of the outstanding debtors. As a consultant, you can do debt chasing for a client and get in £30,000 or £50,0000 in two or three weeks!

Let me share a simple example of a company with £1m sales per annum. Its daily sales, excluding holidays, average £3000 per day. So 120 days of debtors due is £360,000 outstanding. If that is reduced to 60 days, that equates to £180,000 cash coming into the company that is otherwise tied up in debtors. So for every extra million of sales, with debtors on 120 days, that £180,000 can be multiplied up.

Here is a typical conversation I have had with a few SME MDs.

Me,   "What about chasing up your debtors??

Reply, "I don't want to upset my customers".

Me,   "How will it upset your customers? You are entitled to be paid".

Mumble, mumble!

Me,   "OK, who do you *actually* sell to? Which person?"

Reply, "The purchasing manager or the MD".

Me, "Fine, and who do you chase for the money?"

Reply, "The accounts department".

Me, "And who is that likely to be in the accounts department?"

Reply, " Probably the accounts clerk or accounts payable clerk."

Me, "OK, and who does the accounts clerk report to?"

Reply, "The accountant or finance director".

Me. "So, who are you upsetting? The accounts clerk, the accountant, or the finance director? How does it upset the purchasing manager or the MD who does not know most of the time that you are chasing, so it won't upset them!".

In true Columbo style, I usually add, "One more thing. The accounts manager or FD perhaps instructs the accounts department and credit controller: 'Don't pay anyone till they chase you.' So it's possible that the people in the accounts department then won't pay you unless you ask.

At the end of these types of conversations, a look of comprehension invariably crosses the MD's face. They realise they can get some money in to relieve the cash flow pressure and that asking for the payments will not upset the customer.

So often, it is necessary to drop the erroneous mindset (if there is one) and chase debtors. Because the company is fully entitled to be paid for what it has supplied. This can save the company from difficulties when cash flow or funds for investment are needed.

There seems to be a common thread that small suppliers are often not paid. This is just a waste of time in the accounts department juggling payments and deciding who to pay when, in total, the payments usually do not add up to much. Just pay the small suppliers and save time and improve efficiency. That is my view, and I have consistently implemented it.

On the subject of saving cash, I can provide a fairly extreme example. Early in my career, I worked for a computer company, Elliot Automation, part of the UK GEC company, a huge conglomerate run by Arnie Weinstock. The word came through to the accounts department one day with the instruction, "Mr Weinstock says to not pay any creditors (accounts payable) for three months". We were told cash had to be saved as Mr Weinstock wanted to buy another company. Not very nice for the small suppliers or the accounts department holding off all the 'requests' for payment. Those customers who did not chase could have ended up with more than three months outstanding, especially if the embargo had come down on a significantly large payment.

I know this still happens – too often. For example, I worked with a particular MD regularly, and at one meeting, I told him I had an outstanding invoice payment. "Oh", he said, not worried, "just said go and see the FD". I did – and when I asked about payment, he picked the cheque up off his desk (one of several) and said, "Ah, here you are." He was just 'sitting' on it, perhaps until I asked, and no doubt was doing the same with other suppliers' payments as well.

When the redesign and rationalisation of packs for Rimmel/Coty were being worked on, the final meeting to agree on our proposals took place at Coty's factory in Barcelona. The meeting was with Mr Udo Webersinke, the Worldwide Operations Director for Benckiser, which had acquired Rimmel, and with a team of his European purchasing managers. We discussed our proposed redesigns and rationalisation of packs to reduce the number of different packs and save hundreds of thousands of pounds a year in pack prices and tooling costs for Rimmel/Coty/Benckiser

Mr Webersinke said Benckiser were looking for savings to fund their takeover of Rimmel/Coty. Then, in addition to our proposals, he demanded 90 days payment terms if giving us the business. We felt compelled to agree to this to be finally awarded the business.

A few years later, Jonathan, the purchasing director for Rimmel, called me and said Mr Webersinke had retired, and he (Jonathan) thought the 90 days payment was unfair. He added, "Would you like to come in, and we'll agree on reducing the payment terms?". That was great news. Getting down to 60 days alone was an immediate cash flow boost to us of about £250,000.

Mind you, even on the 90 days, Roswitha, our FD, came to me once and said Rimmel was late paying and 'could I help?'. I phoned Jonathan, he chased the FD, and we got the payments up to date within a few days. Incidentally, as far as I'm aware, we did not find that anybody was upset...

Creditors – Accounts Payable

Apart from managing the debtors (accounts receivable) sensibly, it is also essential to manage the creditors (accounts payable). Suppliers will generally have the same payment terms of 30 days. The monthly debtor days outstanding should always be more than the monthly creditor days outstanding to ensure the money is coming in to pay the creditors. So, for example, sales might typically be twice the creditors' amount. Then if a company's total debtor days outstanding are 70 days and the creditor days are 25 days because the accounts supervisor is paying too quickly, that means cash is being used that is not coming in from the debtors. So using the £1m company to demonstrate, 30 days of debtors at £3000 per day of sales is £90,000 due from customers. If the company can get the overall debtors/customers' payments in on 40 to 45 days, that is great. The creditors will consist mainly of materials suppliers at say 30 per cent of sales value, then added to that will be overhead variable costs and some fixed costs. Let's say those creditor payments due are approximately 50% of sales, so £45,000 per month. If that £45,000 is paid in 40 days, and it takes 80 days to get in the debtors of £90,000, that means there is not a surplus cash situation available, so money to make payments is tight.

If the debtor's payments due of £90,000 are collected in 40 days on average, and the company pays the creditors the £45,000 due in 40 days, then the company should have a surplus cash situation of £90,000 minus £45,000 = £45,000. Of course, that is the simple version, but it demonstrates the management control needed on debtors and creditors if a positive cash situation is to be maintained.

LESSON

1. Ensure the accounts department chases the debtors for prompt payment.

2. Pay small creditors promptly to save wasting time and to retain goodwill.

Stocks And Stock Control (and A Bit More On Creditors)

Another critical area for cash control is to ensure money is not tied up in stock in the warehouse. Good stock control is essential to conserve cash. Stocks are shown on the balance sheet, and they need to be viewed with the same importance as the debtors and creditors.

A good measurement for stocks is called 'the stock turn.' Stock turn is often measured against sales when looking at a company's balance sheet in the Annual Return (to Companies House) because material usage is not shown. However, a more accurate and useful figure is 'stock turn when measured against the materials purchased.'

At Geka, initially, the stock turn was just four times a year; that is, there were three months of stock on average. I gave Ian at the factory the objective to increase the stock turn to 10 times a year. Some months later, Ian and his team were achieving 12 times a year.

From Fig 25, it can be seen the production material usage at Geka is 31% of sales. So as an example, when the company was turning over £4 million with material usage of £1.240m at 31% with a stock turn of 12, the money tied up in stocks would be one-twelfth of £1.240m, which is £103,333 of stock in the company. If the stock turn was only four times a year, the money tied up would be £310,000. So the cash saving on faster stock turnover would be nearly £207,000. A substantial amount that could be spent on valuable things such as investments in the company for more efficiencies.

> When visiting companies as a Business Advisor, it was interesting to ask the MDs how much stock they had over six months old. One MD told me he had 18 months of stock in total. I asked why so much, and he said because he could get a discount buying in bulk from China. However, he was then renting another building to store it all! The money he had tied up in stocks, and the cost of rent, was greater than the savings he had made to buy in bulk. And, of course, the cash tied up prevented him from using it to improve his business.

Regarding debtors, creditors and stock, when working with Dave, the telecoms MDO, over a few years on various areas of his business, these three areas became crucial. Especially on one occasion when getting the company out of a major cash flow problem. I have included two copied emails from him – the first more to demonstrate the time separation and the build-up to the second email, which resulted in a good learning situation. Also, I think his second email is rather amusing, as was his style.

Email 1:

> Hi John,
>
> As you know you are with me on Thursday, and I have been offered a very interesting proposition from my accountants who have a fellow company keen to sell their company for a low value.
>
> I have now been sent the last three years of their accounts and the business is going backwards, and I feel an opportunity to acquire this business very cheaply which is quite cash rich. Although there is some serious cash burn going on, there are some benefits involved which interest me.
>
> Therefore I have signed an NDA on our behalf and we are going to them on Thursday after you arrive here. I will send you their accounts and their web address is...
>
> Speak to you soon.
>
> DC."

That was interesting, but it leads to an amusing email from Dave after various intervals between projects, with an interesting follow on job.

Email 2.

> Hi John,
>
> Long time no speak, however due to my kind and thoughtful nature, I have a project that someone like you would be excellent in dealing with for me........ now I know you are probably resting in the Sunrise home looking over the small lake whilst sipping on your coco, waiting for another episode of East Enders.
>
> Kick off that dust, brush down your de-mob suit and come and have a chat as there are a few things I would not mind discussing with you. I hope the care home are looking after you, and that meals on wheels turn up on time!
>
> Week commencing 8th avoiding 9th and 10th would be good for me, I look forward to your reply.
>
> Dave."

A good joke, as I was far from retired! It was fun to receive, which is why I have included it – business doesn't have to be serious all the time! I went down to see Dave on the 'various matters' he mentioned in his email. One was that he now urgently required £100,000 as the company was short of cash as a major order had not materialised, and Dave was somewhat worried.

I told Dave that before we did anything else, we should look at the debtors, creditors and stocks. There were a few debtors he could chase up; then, we looked at creditors. He had a couple of big creditor suppliers on 30 days, one was for payment at £30,000 per month, and another was similar. I suggested he contact them and ask for 45 days payment terms for a period of time.

Next, we went down to the stores and found six months of stock on some items. Then we found a box full of printed circuit boards (PCBs) as spares. I asked their worth, estimating they might be about £500 each. I was wrong; they were worth £1200 each...and there were a lot of them! We discussed that he might be able to 'do some deals' on some upcoming orders to shift some of them.

When I returned a couple of weeks later, Dave was a happy man. He had seen two big suppliers and got payment extensions for 60 days. By delaying payments for two months, Dave raised around £60,000. He had also made a couple of sales at nearly £20,000 each from discounted deals using the PCBs.

Consequently, Dave had raised all the money he needed at no cost and within two to three weeks. Dave then said to me, and I remember it well because of the emphasis on his relief, "Thank you SO much; I was rather worried". Then he paused and added with feeling, "How do you know all this?" We had covered quite a few areas of his business over the years, mainly on the sales and the accounts side and P&L information. I reminded him of my experiences 'actually running companies' – experiences his bank manager and the auditor did not have. As Dave had discovered, many accountants and bank managers are not able to give practical advice about running companies.

LESSON
To Save Cash...

1. **It is essential to manage debtors and creditors closely.**

2. **Maximise the stock turn to save cash.**

Dave's story, the lessons he learned and the positive outcome lead to one company with a less than happy ending:

Yardley Cosmetics

Valuable lessons can be learned from the collapse of this company: the management of the company and how critical information can be gained from benchmarking. This is also about managing the overheads efficiently... or, in this case, inefficiently.

We were supplying Yardley with colour cosmetics packs for face make-up and were then awarded the redesign of the packs. We spent time working with their development people, and finally, a design was fixed for the mascara range of packs which would also cover the range of mascaras, compacts and lipsticks. (We used the word 'packs' because the word 'packaging' usually refers to the distribution cartons and the retail packaging.)

> Yardley had changed their mind a few times during the development stages. When they eventually said they would order the injection moulding tooling, we were understandably concerned they might change their mind yet again after we had started to 'cut metal' for the injection moulding tools. When we checked that the design was to be signed off at a high level, we were informed that the marketing director from South Africa was to become the new MD. We checked that he had signed off the design. He had, and that that satisfied us it should not change again. We then received the order to proceed to tool making, cutting metal and spending money.

Not long into the toolmaking, Yardley told us they were changing the design and wanted to eliminate the 'sliding core' in the tooling, eliminating the embossing on their pack designs to save some money. We sent an invoice for (several) thousands of pounds to change the tooling. It could probably have cost Yardley tens of thousands by changing the design and tooling across the range at this late stage. Finally, however, Yardley did launch the new range with packs and products from the combined range of suppliers.

A couple of years or so later, Adrian, our sales manager and I went to a meeting at Yardley. In the reception area, they had up the usual 'welcome board'. On it was shown, 'Welcome to Barclays Bank' and under that, 'Welcome to Lloyds Bank'.

I remarked to Adrian that I had never seen a welcome board welcoming two banks on the same day – it looked bad. I also noticed the welcome board gave us no mention, and we were supposed to be important suppliers to Yardley.

Some weeks later, I was informed that Yardley was extending their payment terms to 90 days. We concluded Yardley seemed to be in a poor financial position, and could they survive? I started checking what we knew and comparing Yardley's information against our other customers.

In **Fig 33,** the Benchmarking table gives some statistics on the information we had heard during visits to customers.

FIG 33. Benchmarking Yardley departments

Benchmarking

Purchasing Departmment Buyers, Planners, Development

COMPANY	Sales per year	Purchasing & Developm't No of People	Comments	Suppliers No of
Yardley	£40.0m	30-35		607
Rimmel	£50.0m	16 & 2 soon		?
Avon	£190.0m	24		89
P&G (H&B)	£236.0m	15	Not Develm'	?

Notes:

1. Basically, whether the numbers are correct or only approximate:

- Yardley has far too many suppliers and nearly twice as many people in purchasing and development for their sales turnover compared to their more efficient competitors.
- Yardley appears to have too many suppliers to be able to manage efficiently. Even 250 suppliers might still have been too many for efficiency.

2. Rimmel is the nearest competitor. Avon is different as it 'sells direct', but even so, the purchasing manager told me he only had 89 suppliers, whereas the buyer at Yardley told me they had 607 suppliers. P&G may be a reasonable company for comparison in some aspects because of their streamlined purchasing and planning.

Although the companies are slightly different, comparisons are possible. When this information is added to other data, a more accurate picture of competitiveness can be achieved.

Fig 34 shows financial information on Yardley compared to its competitors.

FIG 34. *Yardley Financial Benchmarking*

YARDLEY FINANCIAL BENCHMARK COMPARISONS

COMPANY	SALES £ Million	PROFIT £ Million	LIABILITIES £ Million	ASSETS £ Million	LONG TERM LIABILITIES £ Million	FIXED ASSETS £ M.	STOCKS £ M	NO OF EMPLOYS	PROFIT MARGIN %	SALES PER EMPLOYEE £'000
YARDLEY1995	40.07	-1.61	28.15	36.89	40.54	3.88	7.89	725	-4	55.3
YARDLEY1994	36.85	-3.38	46.03	34.07	21.81	3.58	7.92	770	-9.1	47.85
YARDLEY 1993	42.24	-13.07	47.13	31.01		3.28	12.65	909	-30.9	46.5
RIMMEL1994	43.26	4.21	7.11	13.76		8.24	8.3	535	9.7	82
RIMMEL 1993	36.00	2.16	7.53	12.06		8.45	6.03	469	6.1	77
RIMMEL 1992	32.7	0.459	3.7	11.23		9.06	6	481	1.4	68
AVON 1993	187.37	3.89	47.13	36.07		27.83	12.9	2076	2.1	90.26
P&G(H&B)1994	236.29	16.64	76.76	86.71		46.23	20.6	1304	7.1	181.2
REVLON Mnf.1993	32.8	-6.7	23.64	24.5		8.83	12.5	569	-20	57

NOTE: H&B denotes Health and Beauty Division.

In Fig 34, it can be seen:

- In 1995 compared to 1994, Yardley increased sales by £3.2 million, an 8.7 per cent increase.
- In 1995, Yardley showed a good improvement by reducing losses by £1.8 million down to a £1.6 million loss, down from 9% to 4% loss on sales.
- Yardley moved £19 million of short-term debt to long-term. Otherwise, their Current Assets did not cover their Current Liabilities. However, their long-term loans then doubled from £20m to £40m. So £40m long-term loan liabilities on sales of £40m meant the long-term loans were then 100 per cent of sales turnover. The short-term Creditors were reduced, which improved the current assets ratio.
- With the size of these loans compared to sales, one could easily think they were already 'moving deckchairs on the Titanic'.
- For 1995, Yardley had reduced the employee numbers by 45, which was a 6% labour reduction. A good cut, but still far from enough.
- Yardley had increased fixed assets by nearly £300,000, which, if spent on more efficient production machines, then a move in the right direction.
- However, although improvements have been made, it was obviously not enough. The sales per employee are too low at £55,300 per employee. It can be seen in Fig 33 that there were too many overhead people in planning, purchasing and development, and no doubt too many suppliers were a contributing factor to inefficiencies and higher costs.
- In 1994, Yardley employed 235 more people for £6 million fewer sales than Rimmel.

To catch up in efficiency and sales per head to Yardley's benchmark competitors, significant strides needed to be made. For example, Rimmel was 50 per cent more efficient than Yardley in sales per employee, as shown in Fig 34.

Further Comments on Yardley from Fig 34 are as follows:

1. From 1993 to 1994, current liabilities exceeded current assets, so there was no positive liquidity. Many stocks were probably worthless, so the situation would be worse than even these bad figures.
2. Stocks were excessive with very poor stock turn per year. The figure for 1994 is 11 weeks on sales, so approximately three months of

stock, or four times stock turn a year. If the measurement had been on material usage, then the stock turn can be estimated to be approximately just under a year!

3. Sales per employee in 1995 were £55,000 per person. Even after improvements, this was still too low.

4. No liquidity nor profit for years had meant increasing the loans to keep the company afloat. At least there was some investment in fixed assets.

Yardley was like Thomas Cook, a bad situation going on for years, and it was never improved fast enough.

I decided to speak with the manufacturing manager at Yardley, John C., who I knew from when he had been at a couple of other cosmetics companies. I wanted to find out what was going on and what Geka should be prepared for. I also thought that maybe I could help with a few facts and suggestions.

I arranged a meeting with him and did a bit more preparation. I also had a look at financial data on other cosmetics companies. All cosmetics industry data were available at this time on various information sites. For instance, for four years (1990 to 1994), Avon showed improved sales per head at around 5 or 6 per cent per annum.

When I went to see John, I took the benchmark evidence with me and a leaflet on high output filling machines. The figures for Yardley were a year old, but I hoped John would have some better news for the recent year. The discussion revolved around the situation that Yardley was now asking us for 90 days payment terms – up from the previous increase to 60 days. This had caused alarm bells with us, so I had gathered up the benchmark evidence to compare with Yardley. I shared with him the information of numbers for suppliers and the number of people in purchasing in the competitor companies. Needless to say, he found it very interesting...and of concern. I asked him what his gross profit was, and he said he did not know. He said he had just arranged a pay increase for the factory but did not know the resultant gross profit figures yet.

I had also prepared a 'visual aid' to show John (**Fig 35**). I explained what the chart showed:

- Company 1 is Avon, or Rimmel, for example.
- Company 2 is Yardley.
- The graph shows that 'Company 1' is 60 per cent more efficient in sales per head than Yardley.
- Yardley, to catch up to peer performance, needs to increase people efficiency by 40 or 50 % and then keep improving.
- The same peers are improving at 5% p.a, so in another three years, they will have gained another 15% efficiency.
- Yardley had made improvements over the previous year with a 15% improvement in sales per person. But they needed to do that every year for the next 3 to 5 years to make good improvements, narrow the gap and get into profitability. It should have been possible if some overhead departments were made more efficient and people numbers were cut.

FIG 35. *Measurement of Yardley Efficiency Gap*

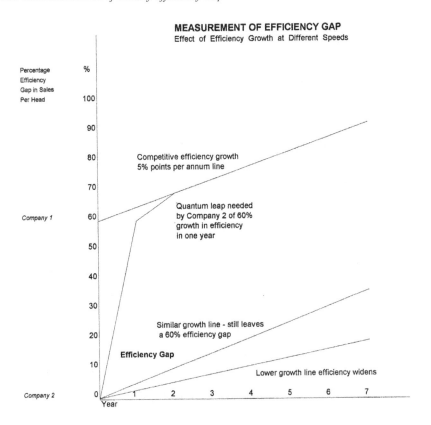

We had a good discussion, and John was very interested in this benchmark information. Towards the end of the meeting, he said he would like me to have a meeting with the Financial Director and tell him this information. Accordingly, a meeting was arranged to happen a few weeks later. However, the FD cancelled a few days before!

Some weeks after that, I wondered how John might be getting on. I called the Yardley switchboard, and they told me he had left the company. He had a new job as a general manager outside the cosmetics industry. I still wonder if that was the result of my visit to him!

METHODOLOGY
How To Boost Performance

1. Benchmark your company against competitors or similar companies.

2. Investigate areas for comparison to indicate areas for improvement.

It is possible to check a company's efficiency by looking at sales per head and doing a bit of financial benchmarking. On this occasion with Yardley, because of our contacts with similar companies, circumstances enabled us to compare overhead manning differences in different departments and the suppliers' numbers in Yardley compared to similar companies.

Overheads Management

A major focus in this book has been on the importance of the gross profit to show how much money is being made to cover the overheads.

Yardley is a good example of checking information and the need to manage the overhead costs expertly with the gross profit achieved. The overhead departments must be run within the limits of the money made from the income at the gross profit line.

This means running all overhead departments efficiently with good people, systems and processes.

Whatever the gross profit made at Yardley, for years, it did not cover the overheads. Perhaps the gross profit was of a 'normal' sufficiently high percentage and income, but I doubt it. It seems the overheads had just been too top-heavy with people and departments for the money from the gross profit to cover the overheads.

However, it also seems unlikely that there was good production efficiency to achieve a good gross profit when the other figures are seen in relation to the running of the company.

The Yardley demise is an excellent example of a company not properly managing its overheads. In this case, it was a situation of over-manning with too many people in Purchasing, planning and development. Perhaps they also had too many people in the accounts department managing the payments to the many suppliers?

The Yardley story leads me to an elementary diagram of an overview I refer to as The Revenue and Costs Sandwich **Fig 36.** This chart is a simple graphic reminder of managing overhead costs in conjunction with the gross profit generated. The percentages are very general. Sales department costs are, in reality, included in the overhead costs – this would make the percentage for overheads of 25%/35% up to 30%/40% in this instance.

FIG 36. *The Revenue and Costs Sandwich*

THE REVENUE AND COSTS SANDWICH
Approx. Costs as % to Sales

SALES Maximise Income / Maximise Margins	**2-7%**
OVERHEAD COSTS Squeeze the Overheads	**20-27%**
PRODUCTION Minimise Costs / Maximise Gross Profit	**55-65%**

Yardley's Stock Management And Administration

There is another part to the Yardley story and lessons to be learned from the information in Fig 34. Yardley's stocks for 1995 are indicated to have a stock turn against sales of five times per year against the sales value; this is worth looking at in a bit more detail.

Sales in 1995 increased over the previous year; the stock turn in 1994 was 4.6, so there was *some* improvement with the five stock turns over the prior year. Of course, year-end stock figures can be up or down on the average for the year, as a stock take happens at a point in time, i.e. just after a large delivery has just been received, or when stocks are low.

If Yardley's material usage for 1995 was, for example, 30% of the £40 million sales, the material usage would be about £12 million per year. With the stocks being shown as £7.8m that would be a stock turn of only 1.5 times a year. If Yardley had improved stock turn to, for example, five times a year on materials, that would be ten weeks of materials instead of 34 weeks. That would have saved £4m or £5m in cash. An enormous amount of money to be tied up in stocks!

However, we could be sure that a lot of the stocks would be old and worthless and should have been written off in the P& L over previous years.

Ongoing With Yardley

After the meeting with John and the cancelled meeting with the Financial Director, we continued supplying Yardley. However, we were now fully aware of Yardley's precarious financial situation and the reason for their payment terms of 90 days to other suppliers and us.

In 1998 Yardley was put into administration. The Financial Times article said they had debts of £120 million on sales of £69.0 million. That's quite horrendous!

Yardley's Administrative Receivership And Stock Situation

I've explained Yardley's poor stock control, but I should also say that some of their old stock was actually still of value. When the company went into administration, we went down to Yardley to meet KPMG, the Administrative Receiver. Our sales administrator accompanied me and brought a detailed list of our orders, deliveries, and what had not been paid for. We saw that our latest shipment was standing on the factory floor being used for the last production run, which had stopped. That shipment was due for payment. The Yardley storeman checked his records against ours, then drove the forklift truck down the warehouse and came back with a pallet load of our products that had been shipped to Yardley one year earlier! These had been paid for but not used...the stores and stock management had not been run efficiently either!

We received a £45,000 cheque from KPMG for the shipment on the shop floor. The pallet in the stores was also worth about £45,000 as it was the same products and quantity and should have been used a year ago. So that was £45,000 tied up in stocks for a year, which was unnecessary. How much of that multi-million pounds sterling of stock was tied up in unused deliveries because of poor FIFO management. FIFO means stocks should be managed 'First In, First Out', not LIFO, 'Last In First Out'.

Dealing With Banks

One of the things about running a company is the necessity to deal with the banks. Geka UK was, shall we say, 'supported' by Barclays in its early days. In addition, there were another three or four long term loans from, for example, the European Coal and Steel Fund (ECSC), 3i, and Hypo Bank, all loans we had gradually paid off. Geka UK had been with Barclays from the beginning, which was 20 years by this time. As we moved into profit with a positive cash flow and started expanding, we were considered a good customer of Barclays by paying back loans, running an overdraft, and using invoice discounting.

We had an excellent relationship with the Senior Corporate Manager, Ian K, who was based at the Corporate Banking offices in Guildford, Surrey. Then one day, Ian informed us he had been promoted and was moving to the London offices. His assistant Mark would take over managing our account. Ian told us that he hoped the new relationship would work out all right, and if we have any problems, to let him know.

Only a few months after the people changes at Barclays, I received a letter from Mark, our new Barclays manager, asking Roswitha and me to visit him 'next week' and he specified a date. I was not available for about ten days and suggested a date which Mark accepted.

Roswitha and I went to see Mark in Guildford. He told us that he thought we were now supporting the German company, and he wanted to reduce our overdraft by £100,000 with immediate effect.

He showed us a cheque Roswitha had raised, paying BP Chemicals £30,000 for moulding powders. He said if we did not pay the requested sum from our overdraft immediately, he would not authorise payment to BP. I told him we could not 'find' £100,000 overnight – if he didn't authorise the payment to BP, it would bring the factory to a standstill with dire consequences. Our contract with BP, and with many customers, was 'Just- in-Time' deliveries, and BP would stop supplying if we didn't pay.

When asked why he was being unreasonable, he huffily replied, "I asked you to come last week"…that was his good reason.

Under no circumstances would I jump through hoops trying to find £100,000 for him 'immediately'. In any case, it would have been impossible. I told him that amount of money we would have to go to the investors in Germany, and I believed them to be on holiday in the Bahamas or somewhere. Mark said he did not care, and he wanted the money paid immediately. I was not going to give in; we argued some more and dealt with threats and counter-threats but to no avail.

I was perplexed. Did he want to be responsible for causing a loss of business and, potentially, redundancies at the factory? He did not understand or care about any of this. Finally, I could only think of using an emotional argument with which to confront him. I said, "There is nothing I can do to get £100,000 in three days, but maybe two weeks was possible. If you insist on the three days, it could lead to suicides." He was a bit shocked at this, and after thinking for a minute or so, while Roswitha and I stared at him, he eventually said, "I'll give you two weeks." Roswitha and I then stood up and departed without another word.

On the way back to the office, we discussed how unreasonable the demand for the instant reduction of the overdraft was and how badly Mark had handled it. We decided no point in talking to Ian, his old boss, or whoever his new boss was, as Roswitha did not want to work with Mark anymore. And, what if Ian and other bosses knew what Mark was going to do? Did they actually condone that he would start bouncing cheques 'the next day!' It was unthinkable. We agreed that Roswitha would talk to Geka Germany and ask for help to organise the money. Mark had severely annoyed both of us, and we agreed he had picked the wrong people with whom to be unreasonable!

Roswitha and I had a good long chat and decided we would change banks as quickly as we could. When we got back to the office, I heard her talking to the FD in Germany, explaining that we needed £100,000 within two weeks to reduce the overdraft with Barclays...could they help? She told them Barclays was initially only giving us about three days to pay but, in the end, extended that to two weeks. Ingrid, on the other end of the phone, must have asked what did we say to get an extension as I heard Roswitha say, "John asked him if he wanted to cause suicides, so after a longish silence, all the while glaring at each other, he gave in and said, alright I'll give you two weeks".

With collaboration and support from Geka, Germany, we managed to get the money together and pay Barclays two weeks after our meeting. Roswitha then started looking for another bank.

Barclays were in Guildford, Surrey and our opinion was that in the South of England, they were not so conversant with manufacturing, so we looked around in the North-East near our factory. Roswitha found a Bank manager she liked who understood manufacturing and was based at Lloyds Bank in Washington, County Durham – not far from our factory. (Even more useful as Barclays in Guildford required us to pay for their flights to Newcastle to see us!) We transferred our account to Lloyds, and in the process, we saved quite a bit of money. We got a lower interest rate on the overdraft, a lower rate on our loan, and a lower rate on the invoice factoring. So, in the end, a good outcome.

Roswitha worked well with Bryan, the bank manager at Lloyds, and there was no difficulty with him being able to meet up with us at the factory occasionally. Bryan also helped us with the financial arrangements and loans for building the new factory unit. The relationship with Lloyds went well for a couple of years, then one day, Bryan called Roswitha to say he was leaving Lloyds to join another bank. He told her that his assistant would be taking over. That was not good news, and we had a feeling of Déjà vu – could this be another situation where the relationship with the assistant did not work out?

After a few months, Bryan phoned Roswitha to say he was working at RBS Bank and would we like to change banks and work with him again? Despite the work involved when switching banks, Roswitha had no hesitation. The move to RBS was another success pushed through by Roswitha. We got even better rates than when we had changed to Lloyds, so this was our second reduction in banking costs.

The feeling we got at that time from those two 'assistant' banking people was they thought they were doing us a favour rather than treating us like customers that they wanted to keep. I hope the situation has improved since then. Like we did with any supplier who was not up to scratch, we changed the bank. Three banks and two reductions in payment rates were a good result in the end.

The reason for sharing this anecdote is it highlights the importance of interpersonal skills in business. If Ian K. of Barclays had still been managing our account, no doubt he would have handled it ten times better, and we would have continued with Barclays.

So now I have written about our experiences with several accountants, lawyers, and bankers. Some care is needed to pick good people and suppliers with whom to work. Unfortunately, we don't always know what people and their organisations are like until we work with them. Recommendations from others can often be helpful in advance of deciding who to work with.

METHODOLOGY
How To Boost Performance

1. Measure the statistics, values and percentage trends to identify improvement areas.

2. Control the 'balance sheet' items to maximise cash generation.

3. Control the annual overheads with a target percentage.

CHAPTER SUMMARY

This chapter has covered quite a bit of ground:

1. Treatment of GP figures in the accounts.

2. The importance of measuring the trends of GP percentages.

3. Easy to read account layouts with percentages.

4. Consider the analysis and demise of Thomas Cook Retail.

5. Simple and useful business plan layout.

6. Monitoring, managing and squeezing overheads.

7. Benchmarking of Thos Cook against Hays Travel and demise of Yardley Cosmetics.

8. Importance of stock management.

Chapter Thirteen
Leadership, Motivating And Training

Key Function 6: how to easily boost morale and output. This chapter discusses some basic leadership requirements for increasing productivity: delegation skills and the motivators and demotivators for staff. Some tips for improving communications and problem solving are included.

The first five Key Functions and methodologies have been covered. The question to be answered now is: how can company management expertly integrate the key functions and the interdependent departments and drive the company forward?

At the base of the Rocketship diagram (Fig 1), two areas propel the Rocketship: Management and Leadership.

MANAGEMENT is to Plan, Organise, Control, Staff and Motivate (the acronym is POCSM.) **LEADERSHIP** is needed to propel the rocket upwards.

When I originally used the acronym, POCS, and the phrase 'Doing the POCS', it was alright. But POCS does not sound like the best or most polite acronym (it led to some amusing incidents, though!). Also, it did only cover basic management 'stuff'. As Geka grew rapidly and recruited continually, there was a requirement to improve delegation. I realised a key aspect that brings it all together is Leadership and Motivating, so I added 'M' to the acronym... POCSM.

Delegating To Improve Performance

When visiting Ian at the factory, I was aware that some of the managers, particularly the production manager, would frequently come into his office while we worked.

They would often use statements like, "You'll never guess what's happened now". The problem would then be described, and Ian would provide the solution. I regularly told Ian that he should encourage them to provide solutions, not problems. They should tell you what's happened, by all means – but end by telling you what they've done about it!

Ian would invariably reply that it was usually quicker for him to give them the solution. My reply was that "You can't keep doing that as the company continues to grow. You haven't got time to micromanage, and you'll find yourself getting stressed out if you do".

This conversation, or ones very similar, occurred a few times. Quite often, when I was speaking to Ian on the phone, he would finish by saying, "I need to go now; people are waiting outside my door". (Which meant peering through his office door window!)

We had initially started working together with about 35 people in the company, but by this time, we had over 100 people ...and were still expanding. Later, the company employed over 140 people plus some homeworkers. The larger company needed to have broader leadership skills and further empowerment down the management line. I remember calling Ian once to ask if he "had the POCS sorted yet". (You can see why the acronym amused us!) He immediately replied, "Yes, I plan to organise and control my staff better!" We had a good laugh, but it was reassuring that Ian was making good strides in training the subordinates and asking for solutions, not problems.

In my experience, maximising the power of the management team and empowering and motivating subordinates to drive the company forward requires using four rules (or situations) to help foster delegation.

These situations arise for feeding information or problems back to the manager. In other words, the rules and outcomes for delegation to subordinates.

Four General Rules For Delegation:

1. **A problem affecting a customer**, so the boss needs to know about it. Especially if it is reasonably serious and involves an important customer as the customer might call, and the manager should be prepared. Maybe the customer should be advised, for example, if there is a delay in delivery. Sometimes a customer calls and speaks to someone further down the line with an innocuous question? The fact that these contact calls have been received and information exchanged should ideally be passed to the relevant people in customer service, which can help handle the customer relationship.

2. **If it is a serious supplier problem** like an equipment or vehicle breakdown, which will affect deliveries, output, or efficiencies, especially planned shipments for the day or the week. Perhaps a customer needs to be quickly called by the account executive or relevant person. Another serious problem is if equipment repair will cost money, as well as delays. The manager does not want to go around the 'shop floor' and discover a big problem they knew nothing about. However, the subordinate manager or person should not only inform the manager or relevant person of the problem but, where possible, provide the actions taken so far to solve the problem – and the timescales. If the problem is serious, then potential solutions can be discussed with the manager.

3. **If it is a problem requiring advice and help** on how to progress. Help in discussing alternatives and implications may be needed.

4. **If the problem could be political** or a situation involving a supplier or customer, it is necessary to keep senior management informed.

An interesting experience I had whilst working at Metal Box (29,000 employees worldwide) related to points one and four, and, initially, I did not report the incident higher up because all senior managers were out.

> I was at my desk at Head Office in Reading, Berkshire, when I had a call from a Unilever buyer. I was not the usual contact person as I believe they were also unavailable. The Unilever buyer wanted urgent delivery of Birds Eye Frozen Peas plastic bags packaging from our factory in Liverpool. I called the factory, and they told me there was no way they could change the schedule. So I relayed the information back to Unilever. A couple of hours later, I had a call from the secretary of Sir Alex Page, our Managing Director, to say that Sir Alex had received a call from the Chairman of Unilever. I was told to call the factory and get the Unilever order started immediately! Which I did...and they did. Great fun!

However, perhaps my call to the factory should have gone to someone more senior such as the factory manager, not the factory production planning department?

Another point to note about receiving a call like that: the recipient should ask a few questions and find out more. Questions such as 'Why is there an urgency?' or 'What has caused the delay?'. This would help in understanding where the difficulty arose and what can be done about it in future. Was it a Unilever planning and production problem or a Metal Box problem to be solved?

Fig 37 shows a method for delegating to subordinates.

FIG 37. Delegation Three Ways

DELEGATION

THREE WAYS OF DOING IT

BUY IT BACK

Let **ME** think about it.......
I'll let you know........
Leave it with **ME**........
Let **ME** just check a few things......

Delegation is negated. It's still YOUR problem!

PUT IT IN LIMBO

See **ME** later about......
Drop **ME** a memo about it.......
Let **ME** know if you need some help.......
I may need to talk to you about this.....

Delegation is only partly completed. Progress may be slow.

ESTABLISH ACCOUNTABILITY

What are **YOU** going to do now......
I am confident that **YOU** can do this......
What is **YOUR** plan for completion.......
I've given **YOU** this responsibility because.......
Let me have **YOUR**summary and recommendations.......

Accountability established. Delegation completed

To reiterate, delegating helps a manager save time and become more effective, and it helps to train up and motivate the subordinates, which then allows the company to prosper.

Yet many managers struggle with delegating and communicating.

The Fig 37 Guide Sheet is an aide-mémoire to establish what kind of delegator you are. Once you have found that, it's critical to develop your expertise in delegating and establishing accountability. To put delegation methodology into a successful habit does take practice and reflection.

Fig 38 is a coaching guide showing a methodology to assist in practising and improving delegation skills. It is detailed by the necessity of larger companies and is 'high level', but key aspects are there for all company sizes.

FIG 38. *Delegation: Approach to and tips*

APPROACH TO DELEGATING – SOME TIPS

1. Make a plan for the meeting well in advance.
2. Talk to them about their objectives, as well as your own. Focus on the benefits to the other person, not to you.
3. Tell them about the task, how it contributes to corporate goals, and how it fits into the broader scheme of things.
4. Make clear why you have selected them, build their confidence.
5. Give them recognition for past achievements relevant to the task you are about to delegate.
6. Talk to them about the task in a positive way.
7. Ask for their opinions, and show respect even if you do not agree. Explore them.
8. Let them save face if they misunderstand you or if they say something inappropriate. Get feedback.
9. Let them take ownership of any ideas that you initiate.
10. Be open to suggestions on changing methods.
11. Agree on support, monitoring, standards and controls.
12. If they really do not want to do it, accept their decision.

Successful delegation is when the person given the task can report back efficiently. This saves everyone's time. **Fig 39** provides a clear process to train delegated staff in reporting back.

FIG 39. Six 'S's of Reporting

THE SIX 'S's OF (VERBAL) REPORTING TO MANAGEMENT

Excellent verbal reporting to colleagues and management is a key skill to be acquired. The correct, succinct method improves efficiency for the individual and the company. Moreover it improves the manager's respect for the colleague, and much time can be saved.

1. State subject	Use a one sentence signpost where possible.
2. State Situation	One or two sentence summary. Usually should include, if appropriate, a time and cost statement.
3. State solution	If reporting a problem, and when it will be solved. State key risk areas and actions if requested or appear necessary. (costs/time/difficulty/risks).
4. State key risk areas	If reporting a project and if appropriate.
5. Specify/clarify key risk areas	If requested or if guidance required. Clarify action and timing.
6. Summarise and conclude	If still necessary. Get approval if required

ACTION

Signal the solution or the situation at the beginning. Avoid unasked for and unnecessary details and repetition, unless more information is requested.

Quick summary of above is: Subject, Situation, Solution.

Motivators And Demotivators

Professor Herzberg of the University of Utah, USA, conducted research into the 'motivators and demotivators' for employees, as well as the basic aspects of employment, which he calls 'hygiene factors'.

Fig 40/1 shows Professor Herzberg's research. The big three motivators are **achievement**, **recognition** and **responsibility**. The next three crucial factors after 'the big 3' motivators are the **enjoyment of the work**, **advancement**, and **growth**.

To help see the information in a quick graphical format for the Rocketship organisation, this can be summarised by what I have termed 'The Pyramid of Importance' showing how the growth and achievement of individuals help a company to prosper, Fig **40/2.**

FIG 40/1. Herzberg Charts

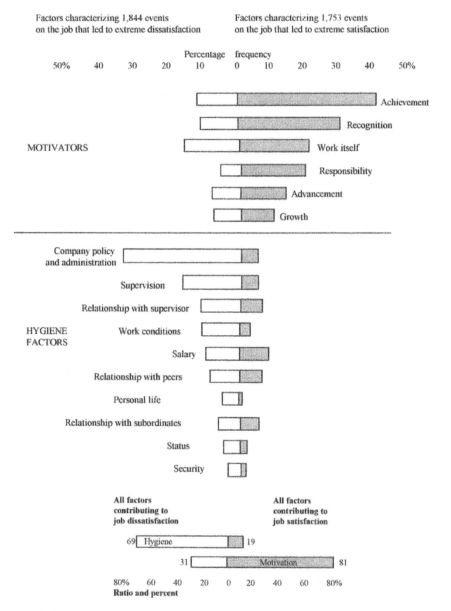

FACTORS AFFECTING JOB ATTITUDES - as reported in 12 investigations

Factors characterizing 1,844 events on the job that led to extreme dissatisfaction

Factors characterizing 1,753 events on the job that led to extreme satisfaction

Source: Prof. Herzberg

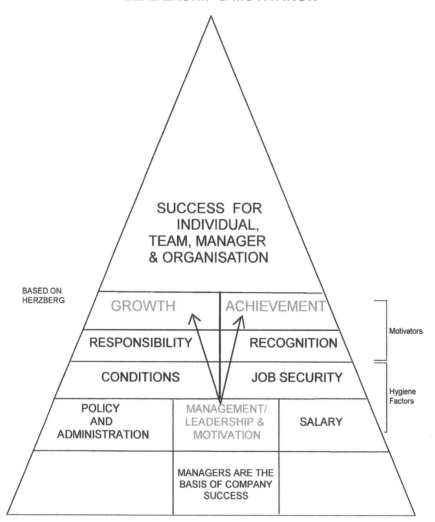

**PYRAMID OF IMPORTANCE
FOR
LEADERSHIP & MOTIVATION**

Both charts need to be read in conjunction with each other, and the greater detail of Demotivators in Fig 40/1 needs to be recognised. The top few Motivators and Hygiene Demotivators need to have an initial focus on them to improve performance.

The results in the Proudfoot Report (in the Introduction to the book) show that 'Inadequate Management' and 'Poor Morale' are significant contributors to causes of low productivity.

From Herzberg's research, poor 'company policy and administration' is a big demotivator and is no doubt a contributor to the findings in the Proudfoot Report.

The Herzberg report points to the need for better training on these basic Hygiene aspects, which will, of course, lead to improving the Motivators and company morale. The Motivators must also be worked on for improvement.

Training sessions and courses are very good for motivating and improving the performance of staff. Training is common in large companies but is sadly lacking in many smaller companies. I have heard the comment, "If you train people, they will leave," and nothing is done. I have replied, "If you don't train them, they will leave anyway".

One of the key points about good delegation is that it involves the staff, trains and motivates them by developing their skills and confidence and making their day more interesting. It gives them growth and achievement. Further, because decision making is passed down the line, the lower levels of employees feel more encouraged to discuss situations for company improvements with their supervisors and managers, which can lead more quickly to improvements.

Many companies set an annual training budget. Our company training budget was generally 1.0 to 2.0 per cent of turnover per year. Not a lot but a useful amount which achieved good results in improving morale, efficiency and output.

Communications

One of the essential motivators to maintain good morale in a company is keeping people informed. A good expression is:

"Communication- is information- is motivation."

It is demotivating if people are not communicated with, and the buzz goes out of the growth drive. At Autotype, we used to have a monthly sales and marketing managers' meeting. We were growing the company fast, and all the managers were generally 'nose to the grindstone'. The marketing director had left to be managing director of another group company, and we had a new Sales and Marketing Director who came back from running the smaller USA sales distribution operation. There was a drop in the team working because of a decrease in the communication to the teams. This had caused a drop in the previously passed information to subordinates, who started asking, "why are there no more briefings. What's happening in the company?"

One of our team managers was Brenda, who ran the Shipping and Public Relations Departments. One day Brenda said to the new director, "We have not had a marketing managers' team meeting for a while. When are we having one?" The new director replied, "Everything is going well. We don't need one". Brenda replied in her no-nonsense way, "That's what you think!"

When Brenda told me this, I said, "Oh, that was fairly blunt. What did he reply?"

Brenda replied, " Nothing, he just went on his way." So not a helpful response. Eventually, we did start the meetings again.

Have you ever encountered the following statement? "We don't know what's going on here. Nobody tells us anything." Sensibly structured meetings, and briefings, should eliminate the issue of people not feeling involved and therefore becoming demotivated and less productive. To achieve a good level of communication, the following can be done.

After each monthly Management meeting, a briefing note is prepared to cover some key points like sales, order intake, outstanding orders, customer information such as forthcoming visits to the company, upcoming investments, etc. The briefings need only be for 10 or 15 minutes and just once a month. People are asked if they have any questions, and the briefings are a good motivator. Briefings can be to the whole company if a small company. If the company is larger, the briefing notes are passed down the management line, and briefing meetings are held within departments, led by the departmental manager, preferably all at the same time around the company.

We always informed the shop floor personnel when customer visitors were coming and who they were. If operators were working on that customer's product, they would know who was speaking to them or peering over their shoulder. We also involved supervisors or department managers and asked them to give a small briefing to the visitors. This involved them more than if the manager or director conducting the tour did all the talking. This was very effective in involving and motivating supervisors and departmental managers.

Politeness And Consideration

A major part of motivation is simply being polite. Also, talk to people and listen to them.

The following is a personal experience which was a bit demotivating but subsequently helped me in my management roles and also in executive coaching.

The Metal Box Company had a new Head office built at Reading, Berkshire, relocated from London's West End. The new office building was mainly open plan except for the Divisional and Group managers who had individual offices. I was a Product Manager, and my desk was just outside the office of the Group Manager of the Paper and Plastics Division. He had to walk past me to get to his office but never once spoke to me in a whole year. I said good morning as he walked past, but he never answered me or anyone else.

At the time, I was reporting to the Marketing Manager, who sat further along the floor, also in open plan. He reported to the Flexible Packaging Division Manager not far from him, who then reported to this Paper and Plastics Group manager. One day after a couple of months of this aloof attitude to nearby colleagues and me, I asked my marketing manager whether I should say good morning or not. He was not sure either but thought it perhaps best to. However, it did not feel worthwhile or motivating to do it.

In the future, I always made a point of acknowledging or being polite to employees. When at Geka, if I flew to the Newcastle factory for a day, I could be in the office at 9 am, and I always opened the general office door and said good morning to the staff and everyone on my way to Ian's office. One particular day, when I went to the factory and got to Ian's office, he just had to finish a few things before we could get down to business. He asked if I could give him some more time to finish. I usually went around the factory with Ian, but not always, so I said, "That's fine, I'll just go round the factory and see what's going on". Ian replied, "That's great, when you do that, it makes my job a lot easier".

That was really nice to hear, and also useful to know, so I was happy to do more of it and go and chat with employees. There was certainly a very good spirit which existed.

In his book 'In Search of Excellence', Thomas Peters called it 'Managing by Wandering About'. It is an essential part of learning about what is happening and achieving progress and success with the employees. And also it keeps up morale.

Coaching And Building Relationships

A few years later, when I was doing some executive coaching, I was coaching a Group Finance Director of a very large European manufacturing group owned by an American company. The FD, Sam, had his office on the second floor of the building, and his finance team was in an office on the ground floor. Sam was having difficulty with some staff; he had started having intermittent accounts department meetings, and one chap was rather disruptive. (Perhaps demotivated and not appreciated, and lacking in receiving communication?) So in one of the coaching sessions, especially thinking of my own experience sitting outside the Group Manager's office at Metal Box, I asked some good probing questions about behaviour.

Sam used to get into the office at 7.30 a.m. and work till 6.30 p.m. or more when he was then on the phone with colleagues in America.

I asked Sam to tell me exactly about his day's activities. We got to the point after he had come into the office, read correspondence and sent email replies. Then he said,

"About 10.00 am, I go down to the accounts office and go and see David, my accounts department manager."

I knew where the office was because it was a room off the reception area, and the door was always shut. I had not been in there. I said to Sam, "Tell me exactly what you do in detail. You go down to reception, then what?"

He said, "I open the door and go in; then I walk down through the office to the end where David's desk is and speak to him".

I asked about the office layout. There were about twenty people in the office, with desks on either side of the walkway down the office to David's desk. I asked, "Do you walk straight down there without saying anything to anyone on either side?" "Yes," said Sam

I said, "How do you think you would feel if the big boss, you, comes into the accounts office every day and you are sitting there as he walks past, but he does not even say good morning to you?" Sam sat back in his chair at this, thought about it, then he sucked in his breath and said, "Oh...I would not like it".

When I returned after two weeks for our next session, he said he had mended his behaviour by going into the accounts office and had been saying 'good morning' to his staff. Sam reported that the staff had responded with smiles and that the attitude and morale in the department had already improved.

LESSON

Simple politeness makes a big difference to morale, team working and motivation.

It later happened that the disruptive person had settled down. In addition, Sam had held an accounts department team meeting which he said had gone well and a lot more smoothly than on previous occasions.

My other main coaching objective with the Group FD was to save him time. He worked from an early start to later in the evening and answered about 180 emails every Sunday. A major problem was helping him delegate and empower his subordinates.

After only three coaching sessions, Sam said to me he realised a few things about his leadership. This is what he said:

"I thought I was a good delegator, and I realise I am not."

"I thought I was a good team leader, and I realise I am not."

Those were his own conclusions arising from the questioning techniques. I did not tell him these things, and it surprised me how quickly he had realised.

Before getting the assignment from the MD and HR directors to coach Sam, he had asked me, "Am I going to be criticised?". I replied, "No, we will only work together on areas for improvement."

Coaching uses questioning techniques to help the coachees reach their own conclusions and ways to improve. We also provided guide sheets to help along the way and set objectives and tasks to be carried out between coaching sessions.

Mentoring, on the other hand, is telling people what you know and what they should have done. It does not embed change and full understanding in a mentee.

We used a good acronym. We worked to RULE. This meant–

- **R** Recollect and reflect
- **U** Understand
- **L** learn
- **E** Embed

I mentioned Sam's self awareness on delegation. Below is a copy of the satisfying letter I received from Sam at the end of the coaching showing in his own words the benefits that can be obtained from coaching business leaders at all levels and sizes of business.

Dear John,

May I take this opportunity to thank you personally for your guidance and support in the last few months. I have found the coaching an extremely challenging and rewarding experience. I now have the basic building blocks to move forward for the benefit of me, my family, the team and the company.

I enclose a token of my appreciation. I hope it is something which you will enjoy.

Thanks for all your help.

Sam

Group Finance Director.

METHODOLOGY
How To Boost Performance

1. This letter shows that there is always room for improvement, even at the highest levels.

2. Good training, coaching and mentoring are great motivators for the person and a great benefit in all sizes of companies.

3. Productivity is increased, morale is raised, and labour turnover is reduced.

I also coached other people in the same company at their head office and at a factory. Tim, one of the managers, when at the end of his coaching project, said to me,

"Apart from the coaching, which was a great benefit to me, a strange thing has happened – my batting averages at cricket have improved".

That was really interesting for me to hear from him how improved job confidence and satisfaction improve inner belief, boost morale, and improve other aspects of personal life.

One of the most remarkable leadership events in delegation and motivating that happened to the teams and me at Autotype International was when our boss Graham, the Marketing and Sales Director, went away on a six-week residential General Management Course.

Graham called the four of us managers who reported to him into his office. He said,

"I am going away for six weeks on a General Managers Course. I don't want any telephone calls, any correspondence or copies of stuff, and I don't want anything on my desk when I get back. You guys carry on and run the sales and marketing as usual". That was amazing, so we carried on with our individual and teamwork without our Director for the next six weeks.

Also, with our rapid growth, we had just had the offices extended and a new office building completed. The marketing and sales department expanded into the new offices a few weeks before. Three of us had been out in a Portakabin for two years, so my colleagues and I were pleased to be back indoors, especially as we had just had a freezing winter. One morning the temperature outside our 'hut' at 10 am was minus 12 degrees Celsius in Oxfordshire! As you can imagine, our secretary needed Eskimo boots for work!

While Graham was away, we found the offices were again not big enough as we were once more a bit cramped with extra staff coming on board. One of my colleagues assessed that we needed more office space again and should get the Portakabin back.

When Graham arrived back for his first day in the office after six weeks away, he had the clean desk he asked for with nothing in the in-tray. The four of us sat in front of Graham at his desk, ready for the off! The first item on our verbal reporting agenda at 9 am on Monday morning was for another Portakabin. We were feeling a bit tense about this as Graham had not been in the offices to see how cramped they were getting and maybe would think he did not want this problem after being back for only 15 minutes.

Fortunately, he quickly and calmly saw the reasoning. He said, "Ok," and immediately picked up the phone and called our Works Manager to get the Portakabin offices back outside. One of our other team managers volunteered this time to work in the Portacabin. Then Graham said, "Anything else serious?" and we settled down to a more relaxing update on sales, the markets, publicity, customers and new products. Graham had enjoyed his General Management course, and we had all enjoyed our learning experience, managing ourselves as a team, and the opportunity to learn. Those were amazing, motivating and exciting times at Autotype and the growth enabled us to apply for and be awarded the Queen's Award for Export.

METHODOLOGY
How To Boost Performance

1. **Delegation improves communication, which can improve morale and motivation around the company.**

2. **Regular team meetings and monthly briefings are necessary and greatly benefit company efficiency and productivity growth.**

There is a key point regarding motivation and morale, and that is how problems are dealt with and how disciplinary or major errors are dealt with. The rule is **praise in public and rebuke in private.**

The outcome of a major telling off in public is that it demotivates the person who made the error and can affect the team and the feelings towards the boss. In public, it can be a situation of saying, "Okay, so how do we overcome this problem and what do we learn".

Then in private, if needed, a tough conversation can take place and probably a learning experience discussed as well. Managing by fear and shouting does not lead to success and often leads to increased labour turnover, especially among the better people who can more easily obtain another job.

Investors In People Award

In the early 1990s, a government-sponsored business initiative started: the Investors in People Award (IIP) for UK companies and organisations. The IIP Award is an excellent process for motivating, training staff and promoting company success.

It was relatively easy for Geka to obtain the award as many of the requirements had already been implemented from what I had learned in previous companies or which we had developed. The consultant we had hired in Buckinghamshire audited the Newcastle factory too. On his return from Newcastle, the IIP consultant told me, "If your factory was down south, I think you would have consultants wanting to crawl all over it." That was good to hear.

After obtaining the IIP award, I was later invited to join the Thames Valley Training and Enterprise Council (TEC) on the IIP Recognition Panel. There was a lot of training for that. I sat on either a two or three-person panel for the recognition of organisations, and there were quite a lot of interesting situations.

One recognition panel meeting that was really noteworthy and of most interest was the awarding of the IIP recognition to the Royal Air Force (RAF) Strike Command at High Wycombe, in Buckinghamshire.

When the assessor came to the panel meeting, one of the first questions I asked was to say, "I am a little surprised at the RAF applying for IIP, I would have thought that the RAF would have their personnel systems and procedures well sorted out, so I am wondering what is the IIP going to do for RAF Strike Command?"

The assessor replied with the following:

1. The RAF base was now building its planning more from the bottom up rather than just top-down. This was revealing training needs.
2. The result of this partly bottom-up review and consultation is that they recognised that having RAF personnel looking after housing and accommodation was a waste of their RAF personnel's skills, so they are now going to outsource that.
3. The accountants and finance personnel were going to get more training and qualifications.
4. RAF Northolt is only used for Government and Royal Personnel flights, so it is obviously expensive. The IIP review has made 'the powers that be' do some further evaluations. Now the RAF will allow other organisations with suitable vetting to use the airport and pay accordingly.

Subsequently, on point 4, this was implemented with apparent savings to the UK taxpayer.

The panel judged those key points to be a great result. Again, communication, listening, training and motivation all played a part in that IIP award. It was very interesting to hear of the benefits it was already bringing to RAF Strike Command to achieve accreditation.

METHODOLOGY
How To Boost Performance

Many organisations, whether large or small, can benefit from the Investors In People programme and the morale and productivity improvement. If you now add another 1% or 2% improvement to other 1% improvements, the business will start to show further big improvements.

Personal Training And Development

A final mention of leadership and training. This is about Dale Carnegie's training. Dale Carnegie, an American, wrote a book called 'How to Win Friends and Influence People'.

The book is a great read, and the content is very impressive. Today that same book could easily be called 'How to Succeed in Business and in Personal Relationships'.

The Dale Carnegie organisation runs personal development courses for business people around the UK and no doubt in the USA and other countries, and I enrolled myself and the company managers on the courses, bringing many great benefits. Dale Carnegie wrote:

'You can't change peoples' character and personality, but you can change their attitude and behaviour'.

I have found that if people can change their attitude or behaviour just a bit, it affects their personality beneficially. They can become friendlier people and nicer to be around, their work improves, and they feel more confident. I have mentioned this to a few Human Resources people who have also agreed with Mr Carnegie's viewpoint.

I touched on behaviour and self-awareness in the example of coaching the Group Finance Director. One of the critical points of Dale Carnegie in becoming a nicer person is never 'Criticise, Condemn or Complain'. This is a good way to start with mistakes in a company. Successful managers achieve good results with a 'no blame' culture. Just work on, 'what went wrong, what do we learn, and how do we improve?'

At Geka, I employed a consultant Public Relations lady called Debbie, who also helped with recruitment.

She happened to be quite attractive. I mention she was attractive because she had apparently put up barriers in the past which had affected her acceptance at work, so it has some bearing on this Dale Carnegie training example. We found we both had an interest in the Dale Carnegie principles and the courses.

Debbie became HR director at a big international company's factory. I asked her, "How did you get to such a high position at a relatively young age?" She replied, "I went on a Dale Carnegie Training Course. I found out (as part of the homework in the office) that the people in the company thought I was a bit stuck up, and I did not have much interpersonal contact with people, especially on the shop floor. After the Dale Carnegie course, I learned to be a friendlier person. When I walked around the company, I smiled at people, and they responded. Basically, that changed my life, and so I progressed on to HR director." A great story of attitude change leading to personal success.

I highly recommend you read Carnegie's book and learn some basics. The Dale Carnegie courses are structured specifically for business use and are powerful. You hear some executives talk about repeating the same old mistakes in their business career and what went wrong yet again. The course teaches them to become more self-aware and finally to know what they need to do to put their careers back on track. The benefits of the course extend from business life to personal life, as I heard from our own people who went on a Carnegie course or had personal coaching.

METHODOLOGY
How To Boost Performance

1. Team briefings, good communication, delegating skills and listening skills are essential.

2. Politeness, training and personal development are essential.

3. Understanding and working with Herzberg's findings.

4. Managing by 'walking about' is an essential ingredient for Rocketship Management.

Written Communications

I have mentioned the importance of good communication with staff. But of course, good communication with customers is of paramount importance too.

To ensure improved communication, we developed the 'Six C's' checklist. There is nothing like an acronym or mental list to help cover what one needs to do!

Fig 41 shows the Six 'C's and how to use them. It is self-explanatory. The main thing is that staff should learn them off by heart and use them.

FIG 41. *Six 'C's of Communication*

THE SIX 'C'S OF (WRITTEN) COMMUNICATION

Communication is one of the most important parts of our lives at work. For success both personally and as a company we must learn how to do it as well as possible. This is a simple aide memoir to ensure good communication.

1. COMMUNICATE   We must inform people. It is part of the teamwork needed for success. People are demotivated if they feel they are not kept in the picture whether in general or specifically.

2. CLEAR   Be clear. People should be able to easily understand what you mean. No hidden messages, don't let people assume what is meant.

3. CONCISE   Make the point quickly – don't waffle.

4. CORRECT   When you make the communication check that it is right and that you are sure of your facts.

5. COMPLETE   Don't leave anything out that requires an answer, or which is needed to keep people informed.
Include the answer to the next question!
Have you used any evaluation and opinion with balance and political awareness regarding colleagues and the company.

6. CONCLUSION   Let people know what you are going to do, or what you want from them, and by when, e.g. I look forward to hearing from you.

ACTION

Learn the six 'C' words by heart viz:

"**Communicate** – and make it – **clear, concise, correct, complete, and with a conclusion**".

Use the six 'C's as a regular checklist to improve performance when communicating and writing to people.

LESSON

1. Learn the six 'C' words by heart: "Communicate and make it clear, concise, correct, complete, and with a conclusion".

2. Use the six 'C's like a checklist to improve performance when communicating and writing to people.

Here is one simple in-house example of the application of the Six 'C's.

One day our sales manager was writing to a customer and asked my view on what she was writing. I said, "just say the Six 'C's'". So she said, "clear- yes; concise-yes; correct- I'd better check that; complete- ah yes, I had overlooked something." It was a great self-check.

Here is an important external example. In 2015 my FD Reg and I had a meeting with the large accounting firm Grant Thornton (GT) concerning advice on corporate tax and VAT issues. The GT accountant said he would write the letter on our behalf to the tax authorities, HMRC. During a phone call with him the next day, I asked to see the letter before he sent it. He asked why? I said, "Well, I am your customer, I am paying for it, and I want to know what you are saying". He sent the draft letter to me, and I found inaccuracies in his notes about our company. Also, a paragraph was completely unclear. I passed the letter to Reg and asked, "Do you know what that paragraph means?" Reg did not understand it either. We sent the letter back with our corrections and asked for clarification of the paragraph. We approved the rewrite for sending off, and no doubt, that cost us a lot more! If top, highly paid people are writing badly, you can imagine what may be happening in so many companies: confusing customers and others and giving a bad impression of your company.

It was easier in pre-email times to see what was being written. It is now harder to check in the files and folders about an individual's communication skills. Nevertheless, it is a good idea to do so occasionally. There is now software available that enables the emails of groups to be viewed. It is like keeping an eye on margins, prices and such things to ensure that either you struggle to survive or rocket along. One vital thing is that staff do not copy the email trail of internal emails to customers by mistake. On one recent occasion for me, a senior manager did this to a top customer, who wrote back to say, 'Why are you washing your dirty linen in public?' I had to call the customer and ensure the problem and solutions were quickly sorted.

Problem Solving

An excellent type of training course which I found very useful was on problem-solving. **Fig 42** is my updated version, based on several variations around. The first three points below are particularly important:

1. **To carefully define the problem**. Too often, there can be a tendency to solve the incorrect or first perceived problem, not the real problem.
2. **Ask what happens if we do nothing**. We have, over many years, only decided on two occasions to do nothing. Mostly something always needs to be done to solve the problem. If it is not solved as quickly as possible, you get overtaken by events and lose control. Or, to put it another way...it comes back to bite you.
3. **Consult everyone involved**. If you don't, something often gets overlooked and causes further problems.

The remaining points in the procedure are straightforward.

FIG 42. *How to Problem Solve*

HOW TO PROBLEM SOLVE (OR FIND A SOLUTION)

THE 10 POINT ACTION PROCEDURE
(Six key points)

Problem solving and solution oriented thinking is one of the key performance factors for success in a company.   Good problem solving capabilities improve personal performance, build teams, provide customer and colleague satisfaction, create a positive attitude and drive a company to success.

1. DEFINE THE PROBLEM

2. Ask, "What happens if I do nothing?"

3. CONSULT EVERYONE INVOLVED

4. Collect all the facts and analyse the problem.

5. FULLY EVALUATE THE FACTS AND ALTERNATIVES, SELECT BEST SOLUTION

6. MAKE AN ACTION PLAN

7. Communicate the Plan.

8. IMPLEMENT THE PLAN (TEAM BRIEFINGS)
   Review actions and successes while ongoing. Loop back and review as required.

9. Follow up the Plan (progress it)

10. ENSURE THE PLAN AND ACTIONS ARE COMPLETED

ACTION
Learn and practise the logical steps. There are the 6 key points in bold. Use for both a short-term (immediate) problem, or when working on a solution for a major or important project, or situation.

NOTE: Separately, if applicable, find out what went wrong, or what caused the problem and correct the root cause using this method. This procedure can help develop a no-blame culture and one of problem solving and customer service.
Many plans fail simply because of F.T.I. (failure to implement) properly.

LESSON

There are six key points in bold. Use for both short-term (immediate) problems or when working on a solution for a significant project or situation.

If applicable, find out what went wrong or what caused the problem and correct the root cause using this method. This procedure can help develop a no-blame culture of problem-solving and customer service.

Many plans fail simply because of F.T.I. (failure to implement properly).

METHODOLOGY
How To Boost Performance

Key items are:

1. Improving and helping with self-awareness.

2. Self and business awareness on some general skills.

3. Understanding and working with Herzberg's findings.

4. The importance and necessity of delegating.

CHAPTER SUMMARY

We covered delegation skills and their necessity and explained
there are generally four rules for delegation.

Also included in this chapter were:

1. Herzberg's motivators and demotivators

2. The importance of politeness, consideration, and
   listening skills.

3. Communication skills.

4. Personal training and development.

5. How to improve written communications.

6. How to improve problem-solving.

Chapter Fourteen

What Happened To The Geka Parent Company?

This chapter contains some points that are essentially a repetition of what has already been covered. Such points are unclear accounts, poor costing and pricing, and loss-making customers.

Several people have asked me about this. The simple answer is that it had the same fate as similar companies that folded or were sold because of the reasons covered in relevant chapters. The summary story is as follows.

In the early 1990s, Geka (Germany) kept asking us to pay more quickly and send money. In October 1993, I decided to go to Germany and try and find out what the situation was over there. I made the cover excuse of another meeting to hide my real reason for the visit.

My first action was to ask the sales office manager for a printout of sales to the customers by sales value and gross margin if they had it. Angie went to a filing cabinet and retrieved a printout. I asked if they were analysed but was told, "Er... no, we don't have the time".

I spent a day or two in the offices and time in my hotel room analysing the data. This is what I found:

1. There were ten major loss-making customers with total sales of over DM 1.0m per year.

   The sales prices to these customers had excessive material content of 60 % to 90% of material.

2. There were 20 other customers with very low margins with sales at DM 500,000 p.a. that were also very unprofitable.

3. In summary, the company could drop those customers or product sales of about DM1.5 million p.a. and improve gross profit by approx. DM 1.0m p.a. (Approx £375,000 at the then prevailing exchange rates).

4. After reviewing the profit and loss accounts, and after working out the true position to obtain 'clean cost of goods' figures, the figures revealed a forecast loss was coming up for the year-end of minus 15% on sales.

5. The presentation to the directors provided this summary:

   "There is a choice here, either raise prices substantially to a sensible and competitive profit level or stop supplying those loss-making customers and make more money.

6. The presentation covered an analysis of the P&L and a 'clear cost of goods' layout down to the gross profit line, prepared by the production director. At last, we could all see the percentage cost of direct labour and materials. The production director promised he could work on reducing the direct labour cost by about 1% or 2%, which was a considerable amount to boost the gross profit.

7. The result. Prices were raised substantially, and I was told that no customers were lost. By March, five months later, at the financial year-end, the company was back into profit. A turnaround to profit within just months. In 1994 Walter S., the production director, increased output by 15 % and reduced the direct labour personnel, which was a significant contributor to the much-improved profit performance.

   We also worked on how they should lay out the P&L accounts and keep their eyes on the 'clean gross profit per cent' to ensure it did not drop again. About four months later, the group MD called me to say the P&L format we had agreed for Germany 'was too much extra work', and they would stop doing it. My intention had been for the

'Anglo Saxon accounts format' to be used instead of how they were doing it until then. Then I was told, "We will look at the gross margin per cent and profitability data on the computer per customer every month instead. I promise I'll keep an eye on it".

I informed Roswitha about the call I had just had, and she said, "Oh no, they will take their eye off the ball again, and the problems will come back." And so that forecast proved to be correct.

Actually, if they carried on with their own accounts format, it should have been easy enough to prepare a separate page showing the 'clean gross profit' with direct wages and materials costs and percentages because the figures would already be prepared as a basis for their normal accounts preparation. Perhaps their accountancy systems were more confusing than I thought?

The German method of doing the accounts is confusing to British accountants. I can summarise this as follows from the 'European Accounting Guide, 5th edition' concerning GAAP (General Accepted Accountancy Practice) and the differences; these are described as:

'There are disparate regulations, customs and accounting practices in Europe which provide industry professionals with constant challenges.' A nice understatement.

One other thing is that Roswitha spoke to the FD in Germany to get more information on loans and the balance sheet. Geka Germany's loans in 1992 were about DM 23.0 million on sales of DM 33.0m. This made loans to sales at 70% of sales, so a bad situation.

Four years later, Germany was asking Roswitha to quickly send more money again even though we were now already sending a lot of money in what was now called Head Office charges. Then according to the accounts for 1998, the German loans were up to DM30.4m from DM 25.9m in 1997. The 1998 loans were now DM6.0m (£2.2m) more than in 1992 and were 51% of sales.

8. Finally, in 1999, the group MD called me and said they wanted to sell the group, and could I help find a buyer? I think the key shareholders had got fed up by then!

I contacted Ron Marsh, the CEO of the RPC group (about £350 m sales at that time), who was making a lot of acquisitions. When he looked at the UK accounts, he said he would pay £7.5 million for the UK company and, accordingly, was interested in purchasing the group.

We flew to Germany together for him to see the German operation and discuss their accounts. When we were on the plane flying back, Ron said he did not want to take over the loss-making parent company and the group, as he did not want to get involved in taking on a 'turnaround' project. Therefore he was backing out.

I also approached Rexam, another large packaging group with a Health and Beauty division, and they were interested.

Finally the group was bought by Halder, a Dutch investment company, which offered DM 23 m. When I called Rexam, they said they did not want to pay that much to match the current offer. Interestingly the CEO of Rexam's Health and Beauty division, some years later, became chairman of the Advisory Board under the tenure of the 3i investment company, which had then bought the Geka group.

The payment for the Geka group at DM 23 m was about £8.4 million. If the UK operation was worth £7.5m, the difference was a payment of only £900,000 for the rest of the Geka group, including the assets and probably the loans.

In summary, the ongoing losses and large loans finally saw the company having to be sold. One could say they were lucky to sell the group because many other companies in that situation go into administration. The saving points for the company were the good customer base, product expertise, and the 'contracted' sales to large customers.

9. Halder, the purchaser, owned and improved the group for a few years through a new supervisory board and chairman, then it was sold to

3i, the large investing group. 3i further invested in the Geka group, closed the UK operation and set up manufacturing in Brazil and Singapore. Then in 2016, a Press Release from 3i stated they had sold the group to Sulzer of Switzerland for Eu 102 million.

CHAPTER SUMMARY

Sadly, a few points on the causes for the sale of the group are; unclear accounts for managing the business, poor costing and pricing, poor sales skills, loss-making customers, and excessive loans taken on instead of sorting out the fundamental problems.

Chapter Fifteen
General Summary For Productivity Improvements

This chapter will now show the suggestions for solving the **productivity problems found in the Proudfoot Report of 2002 and ONS Report of 2017 with summary suggestions for methods for improvement.**

The problems can occur in any company and can be improved with a few 1% improvements and incremental steps as discussed throughout this book.

In the Introduction was the summary of the Proudfoot Report on the causes of low productivity in the UK. The key functions and methodologies discussed in this book demonstrate how to improve the productivity weaknesses identified in the report.

Some important things should have been learnt for running a successful business. Even if just one or two tips are implemented, those could make big improvements to a company and to personal life and wellbeing.

The Proudfoot Report was followed up by the report of the Office for National Statistics, which is shown in Appendix 1. This later report has a different emphasis on the UK's poor productivity; however, both reports show the common findings of:

-> inadequate and poor management,
-> poor leadership;
-> and that most of the remaining problems derive from those two reasons.

Companies fail for several broad reasons. However, the principles and methodologies covered in this book are fundamental, and improvements should be undertaken diligently to improve the business. When there are any weaknesses in sales/selling skills, costings, pricing, production efficiencies, IT, gross profit management and leadership skills, then the weaknesses build into more significant problems. If not corrected, the company can eventually collapse, or perhaps with luck, may get sold on – (but at a knockdown price). The reasons for failure are generally well documented and with various emphases on different aspects. Apart from the reasons for PEST in Appendix 3, other less common reasons for a company's collapse are fire, flooding, and environmental disaster. Also, sabotage and government actions; such action can be suddenly cancelling an order for reasons of government cutbacks on an order for a project already given to a supplier. (This is from personal experience.)

The report findings on low productivity shown in the introduction are now shown again, and included is a suggested summary of some methods to overcome the common business problems.

Problems and summary of the methods for improvement. These are shown against the problems and the percentages shown in the Proudfoot Report:

1. Insufficient Planning and control: 43%

   Suggestion:

   Measure the clean gross profit and trend.

   Monitor outstanding order book and trend.

   Continually look to invest in cost effective greater production speed and output.

   Carefully plan investment and payback periods. Consider the 'Opportunity Revenue' against other investments under consideration.

2. Inadequate Management: 23%

Suggestion:

Regularly check margins on individual products. Measure output in sales per head and drive the trend upward.

Undertake thorough costings and pricings for quotations.

Fully manage the sales function. Invest in sales training.

Adopt Kaizen and continuous improvement.

Invest in management training.

Manage debtors, creditors and stock control for cash maximisation.

Control and manage the overhead percentages.

Benchmark your company.

Keep the overhead departments lean where possible.

3. Poor working morale: 12%

Suggestion:

Improve communications with company and team briefings.

Manage by walking about: chat, listen and learn, and it boosts morale.

Review and consider regularly Herzberg's findings, Fig40.

4. IT related problems: 8%

Suggestion:

Invest in good IT and ensure it does what you want it to do.

Consider taking professional external advice and support.

5. Ineffective communication: 7%

Suggestion:

Improve communications with company and team briefings.

Also use the notice board and emails to keep staff informed.

6. Inappropriately qualified workforce: 7%

Suggestion:

Establish training programmes.

Train in-house and send people on courses.

Bring in professional trainers for team training, e.g. for sales, and Japanese production techniques.

Employ better qualified or experienced people.

Getting out to events, meeting people you know, attending local business group meetings and chatting to competitors and peers can also be extremely useful. The skill is also to obtain some information from competitors without giving away your own useful information by showing how knowledgeable you are. Only give away obvious points. I was given two huge but simple tips to improve profitability.

One was a chat with a competitor in the USA. I asked him about the speed he was achieving on his assembly machines. He told me 4000 per hour. (That may not have been true, but I thought it useful.) When I got back to the factory and chatted with Ian, I asked if he could find an automation engineering company that could build us a machine to assemble 4000 mascara/cap/rod brushes an hour. After some research, Ian found a company he liked, whose credentials and experience looked good. They said they could not do 4000 per hour but could do 3000 per hour. So we proceeded with that company and cooperated with the design.

After installation, during trials, and later in production, the 3000 an hour speed was not achieved. However, it was significantly better than we were achieving on current machines. The improvement saved one operator per shift, three operators a day over three shifts, which was a big improvement.

A second big tip obtained was in a chat with an MD who had turned a loss-making plastics company around. I asked him how he achieved that result, and he replied, "By 'light-weighting' the products". I thought that was a good idea, so we set out to do likewise.

Every improvement made a difference. For example, on light-weighting, if you look around today at milk bottle caps, you can see the cap skirt which screws onto the bottle is much shorter than it used to be some years ago, so saving weight and cost.

Finally, a squeezed summary for Rocketship Management is shown in **Fig 43**.

FIG 43. Wheel for Success

WHEEL OF SUCCESS
Six Spoke Wheel of Focus Areas

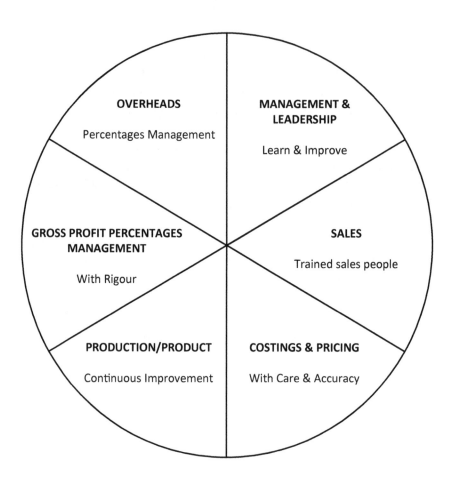

OVERHEADS

Percentages Management

MANAGEMENT & LEADERSHIP

Learn & Improve

GROSS PROFIT PERCENTAGES MANAGEMENT

With Rigour

SALES

Trained sales people

PRODUCTION/PRODUCT

Continuous Improvement

COSTINGS & PRICING

With Care & Accuracy

Chapter Sixteen
Conclusion

The Rocketship Management key principle should now be clear. The two top functions of Sales and Production, or Product, or Service, are the primary drivers of a business. The four other top functions must also be optimised to obtain improved productivity.

Most growth and profitability can be achieved by focusing on the **Six Key Functions.** Additional focus on the supporting departments by the continuous improvement of people, processes and systems is also essential to enhance company performance. The real-life examples given should assist in providing ideas and areas for improvement.

Gross profit in value and percentages is probably the most influential new area of focus because it seems to have been generally overlooked. Yet, it can help indicate the fastest improvements for most underperforming companies.

There is a Chinese saying I have found helpful for trying and adopting new things, whether in business, sport, or hobbies.

> - I hear, and I learn
> - I see, and I understand
> - **I do, and I can**

As a final reminder, making just 1% improvements is the road to success. It is crucial to adopt a mentality of continuous improvement. The first steps in making just a 1% positive change here and there can start the improvement trend, gradually improve the workforce's motivation, and soon lead to a massive increase in company performance. Those who do it succeed.

Appendices

List of Illustrations

Appendix 1
ONS Report: Reasons for Poor UK Productivity 2017

According to the Office for National Statistics (ONS) UK productivity has fallen to levels it held in 2007. Productivity in the UK has consistently lagged well behind Germany and France and has now been overtaken by many other countries. This is the key reason why wages, growth and competitive performance are all held back. Why is this and what can be done about it?

Let's start with some likely causes:

1. **Low Capital Investment.** British firms have been reluctant to invest in the capital equipment and processes necessary to improve productivity. Why invest large sums now when the future is so unclear – especially with all the uncertainty surrounding Brexit?

2. **Cheap Labour.** Why invest in an expensive strawberry picking machine when you get plenty of East European Labourers to pick fruit and pay them the mini mum wage. Ironically we may need labour shortages and higher wages to provide incentives to find smarter and more productive ways to do things.

3. **Creaking Infrastructure.** Much of the UK basic infrastructure is strained and overloaded. Look at the roads and railways. As traffic congestion increases care workers, salesmen and delivery drivers all take longer to make their journeys. They make fewer calls in a day – reducing their productivity.

4. **Slow decisions or no decisions.** Consider the desperate need for increased airport capacity in the south-east of England. While China builds more airports we cannot make a decision on where one extra runway should be placed. Weak political leadership, lobby groups, regulation and enquiries lead to a paralysis of decision making and action.

5. **Low skills.** Low educational standards particularly in scientific and technical fields are holding back the economy. We have critical skill shortages in engineering, software, data analysis and IT. Who is going to design and programme the robots?

6. **Resistance to change.** Many organisations in the private and public sectors are operating in their comfort zones busily doing what they are doing. Managers and staff are often risk averse and reluctant to change. Look at the opposition to driver operated trains on Southern Rail. Most attempts to reform the NHS are met by a chorus of criticism but we need more experimentation and bold reforms if we are to find better ways to meet the needs of a growing and aging population.

7. **Lack of innovation.** Small firms in the UK are leaders in innovation but many large firms are sluggish. Local government has had to introduce many innovations in order to cope with cuts, but central government, the NHS and major state bodies are just not innovating fast enough (or at all). Consider Parliament as a metaphor – it seems to revel in its archaic practices.

8. **Low investment in Research and Development.** The UK spends less than 0.5% of GDP on publicly funded research putting it at the bottom of the G8 nations on this key indicator.

9. **Employees who are not engaged.** The UK ranked 18th out of 20 leading countries in a survey of employee engagement involving 7,000 respondents by research firm ORC International. Only 37 per cent of UK workers surveyed felt they were encouraged to be innovative and fewer than half felt valued at work, according to HR magazine. This reflects the next point.

10. **Poor management.** If employees lack motivation, feel unvalued and lack engagement then it is the fault of managers. Poorly trained or incompetent managers are the major cause of employee dissatisfaction at work.

11. **Poor leadership.** It is the job of the leaders at all levels to set the strategy and vision, to inspire and motivate their teams and to create a culture of progress and innovation. This plainly is not happening in many sectors.

Improving productivity in the UK is not a matter of getting people to work harder. It involves training, investment, innovation and finding smarter ways to do things. Above all we need to improve the quality of management and leadership across the board.

Appendix 2
Thomas Cook: Analysis of 2018 Company Annual Report

Thomas Cook: Notes to the House Of Commons BEIS Select Committee

Some extracts from report to BEIS

This summary prepared by
Retired Senior Partner of UK top 4 Accountants.
(Summarised from emails exchanged between us.)
30 October 2019

Observations based upon my reading of the Annual Accounts filed with the Registrar of Companies for the year ended 30 September 2018

Initial observations dated 23 September 2019

Observations based upon the latest filed accounts for Thomas Cook. These cover its years ended 30th September 2018 and 2017. They were approved by Richard Wilson of Ernst & Young on 28th November 2018 (bizarrely, a day before the financial statements were approved by the Board: this should never happen).

The auditors' report contains a welter of information – about eight pages of small print. In earlier years, the audit report contained about five lines and could usually be relied upon. The approach now seems to be to explain everything in detail – presumably a legal device designed to defend the auditors if they got it wrong.

Salient features noted:

a) On a turnover of £9 billion, the Group made a profit of £9 million in its 2017 financial year (i.e. wafer thin.).

b) On a turnover of £9.6 billion, the Group made a loss of £163 million in its 2018 financial year.

c) The Group generated a cash surplus of £122 million in its 2017 financial year.

d) The Group generated a cash deficit of £345 million in its 2018 financial year.

e) The Group had debtors and cash of approx £2 billion but current liabilities of approx £4 billion – i e net current liabilities of £2 billion – in addition to long-term liabilities of approx £2 billion in each of its latest two completed financial years. In my opinion, by any sane assessment, the company was doomed as it could not meet its current liabilities as they fell due.

f) The Group reported net Shareholders' Funds of less than £300 million: small compared with liabilities in the billions – but after deeming assets purchased over the years to have valuations which were greater than the actual assets acquired by more than £3 billion. These assets are called "intangible assets" and should have no value in the balance sheet of any company unless justified by "super profits" from the acquired businesses.

g) Given that there were no "super profits" and that the business was making significant trading losses, was chewing up substantial amounts of cash and was totally illiquid, clearly these fake assets should have been written off, which would have shown **Shareholders' Equity to be negative to the tune of £2.7 billion for each of the two previous years.**

h) Richard Wilson of Ernst & Young effectively says in his report that he has considered the value of the intangible assets and concluded that they are fairly stated. As a result he considers the "going concern" assumption on which the accounts have been prepared to be appropriate.

In my opinion, both of these conclusions are clearly irrational in the light of the company's negative trading results, negative cash flow, illiquid current asset position (with net current liabilities of £2 billion each year), and its long-term liabilities of £2 billion against a real shareholders' equity of minus £2.7 billion: one can't even talk of a "highly geared" position when shareholders' equity is negative.

In the light of the above, in my opinion it was clearly only a matter of time until the whole house of cards collapsed. How the Audit Report ever got written by the Audit Partner and his team – and presumably (as normally required for listed company audits) – passed by the firm's quality control procedures is astonishing.

It is a sad situation that such financial statements can be filed (they have been on public record for about ten months) without Companies House or any financial regulator challenging them and placing them under special urgent review.

Additional Observations dated 30 September 2019

An injection of £200 million or even £900 million would not have saved Thomas Cook. As expected, the Government has been blamed for not rescuing Thomas Cook: a rescue would have cost billions – and vast additional sums every year for ever – unless there was proper management, taking the sort of steps needed to turn around the business.

In my opinion it is clear from just a superficial reading in comparison with the accounts at 30 September 2018 that the audit report and conclusions reached were completely inappropriate.

EBITDA: Thomas Cook did not use EBITDA, but their own invention: "Underlying EBIT". A tiny footnote says that this means "trading results that are adjusted for separately disclosed items". In other words, it means whatever they want it to mean! As a result, their Annual Report – which ran to 194 pages in 2018 – contained a <u>completely distorted and misleading message</u>.

Of course, the legally required disclosures are given – but after **109 pages** of distorted information and then 8 pages by Richard Wilson saying basically that he's thought about this and everything is fine. The average shareholder (other than those trained in these things) would look at the cover and flip through the 109 pages (if they even did that) and say something like "That's good – everything's fine".

For example: (Just a couple of the key 9 points from the original report to BEIS)

> Then there are shown 12 "KPI's" which again are mostly meaningless: things such as "Differentiated Hotel Gross Profit"; "Group Airline Own Distribution"; "Ancillary Gross Profit per Customer". *What does any of this mean? The constant repetition of the word "Profit" is clearly intended to convey the impression that the business is profitable when it is not.*

> There are then an additional 13 pages of marketing jingo in what is headed "Financial Review". Despite saying "Our financial performance in 2018 was disappointing", this section mostly focuses on "Underlying EBIT" (again!), "Number of Customers" (makes the business sound very successful!), "Exceptional Items" – which are without legal definition, and are really selected to say that the outcome was affected by unusual items which do not normally occur – despite a not very much better result the previous year and

a chronic financial position which has obviously existed for at least several years.

It all sounds very good, despite a few small disappointments! How the Board – including independent directors – approved all this nonsense beggars belief! When Richard Wilson of EY saw it, he should have objected in the strongest terms. His report should have commenced with the professional equivalent of "Despite all the distorted information and out-right lies in the previous one hundred pages, this business is on life support and not expected to last much longer". (i e – effectively an Adverse Audit Opinion)

According to their Cash Flow Statement, net finance costs for the 2018 financial year were £150 million – so it really helped to exclude these costs in their repeated references to EBIT. Also I see that Depreciation was £264 million – but, rather than adding this back to give an EBITDA, they preferred their own invention of EBIT because they were then able to deduct all sorts of other costs which they wanted to pretend were "Exceptional". This is open to abuse and is precisely why they can't do this in their Annual Accounts – so they found a way to obscure what was really happening by over 100 pages of distorted information.

Frankly, I am astonished at EY letting this Annual Report and their own opinion out of the door............

Further Observations dated 23 October 2019

The primary culprits for the Thomas Cook collapse are of course the directors; they were running an unprofitable business for several years, and – judging by the fact that they did not take effective action to change their failing business model – must have been incompetent. Clearly they could not bring themselves to restructure the business so that it made profits; and if they just could not turn it around, they should have closed it years ago. I do not understand why shareholders or loan creditors did not make wholesale changes in the leadership of the company.

The key facts to me are:

a) The Thomas Cook Group was making losses;

b) It was chewing up cash;

c) It had net current liabilities of £2 billion;

d) Excluding its clearly valueless intangible assets, it had negative shareholders' equity in the billions.

This was an impending disaster staring everyone in the face, but the directors did nothing until they finally ran out of cash – and the auditors persuaded themselves that despite overwhelming evidence to the contrary, everything was fine.

In fact, the directors actively sought to conceal the facts, judging by over 100 pages of distorted facts and misleading information in their 2018 Annual Report – in particular, repeated references to "profits" when there were none. <u>This ought to be a criminal offence (perhaps it is!).</u>

If this is all auditors now do, then the value of their opinion is debased indeed.

Prepared 30 October 2019

Appendix 3
PEST Analysis Template

The table below shows a PEST Analysis Template that consists of some typical kinds of factors people would consider in developing a PEST Analysis model.

Political
- Tax policy
- Employment laws
- Environmental regulations
- Trade restrictions and tariffs
- Political stability
- Political purchasing decisions

Economic
- Economic growth
- Interest rates
- Exchange rates
- Inflation rate

Social
- Health consciousness
- Population growth rate
- Age distribution
- Career attitudes
- Emphasis on safety
- Dangerous or deprived locations

Technological
- R&d activity
- Automation
- Technology incentives
- Rate of technological change
- Step change in business models

Consider also:
- Superior competitors
- Effect of acquisition of customers and other suppliers (M&A's)
- Cyber and IT security
- Infrastructure (Local and National)

Ingram Content Group UK Ltd.
Milton Keynes UK
UKHW010742130423
420098UK00009B/829

9 781739 606800